GENDER DYNAMICS IN CONGRESSIONAL ELECTIONS

Contemporary American Politics

The **Contemporary American Politics** series is intended to assist students and faculty in the field of American politics by bridging the gap between advanced but oft-times impenetrable research on the one hand, but oversimplified presentations on the other. The volumes in this series represent the most exciting work in political science—cutting-edge research that focuses on major unresolved questions, contradicts conventional wisdom, or initiates new areas of investigation. Ideal as supplemental texts for undergraduate courses, these volumes will examine the institutions, processes, and policy questions that make up the American political landscape.

Books in This Series

DO CAMPAIGNS MATTER?
Thomas M. Holbrook

GENDER DYNAMICS IN CONGRESSIONAL ELECTIONS
Richard Logan Fox

GENDER DYNAMICS IN CONGRESSIONAL ELECTIONS

Richard Logan Fox

SAGE Publications
International Educational and Professional Publisher
Thousand Oaks   London   New Delhi

For information address:

SAGE Publications, Inc.
2455 Teller Road
Thousand Oaks, California 91320
E-mail: order@sagepub.com

SAGE Publications Ltd.
6 Bonhill Street
London EC2A 4PU
United Kingdom

SAGE Publications India Pvt. Ltd.
M-32 Market
Greater Kailash I
New Delhi 110 048 India

Printed in the United States of America

Library of Congress Cataloging-in-Publication Data

Fox, Richard Logan.
     Gender dynamics in congressional elections / Richard Logan Fox.
        p. cm. — (Contemporary American politics)
     Includes bibiliographical references and index.
     ISBN 0-7619-0238-4 (acid-free paper). — ISBN 0-7619-0239-2 (pbk.:
acid-free paper)
     1. Women in politics—California. 2. Elections—California.
3. United States. Congress—Elections, 1992. 4. United States.
Congress—Elections, 1994. I. Title. II. Series.
HQ1236.5.U6F7   1997
320'.082—dc20   96-25313

This book is printed on acid-free paper.

97 98 99 00 01 02 03 10 9 8 7 6 5 4 3 2 1

Acquiring Editor:	Peter Labella
Editorial Assistant:	Frances Borghi
Production Editor:	Astrid Virding
Typesetter/Design:	Janelle LeMaster
Indexer:	Juniee Oneida
Cover Designer:	Candice Harman

For my parents

Contents

List of Tables

Acknowledgments

The origin of this book was my inability to come to terms with the fact that at the beginning of this decade there were so few women serving in positions of high elective office. The seeming unfairness of this predicament led me to investigate what was truly happening to women when they entered the electoral arena as candidates. This book explores the role of gender in the political process by examining how the dynamics of elections change with the inclusion of female candidates. My sincere hope is to broaden our understanding of the challenges that face women seeking public office. In exploring this topic and writing this book, there have been a number of people whose input and support have been essential and I would like to thank them individually. From the very beginning of this undertaking Eric R.A.N. Smith and Kent Jennings helped guide the project and have stayed with me until its completion. Both of them have helped me on short notice and with great insight. The study would have been impossible without their support. Eric even funded the first wave of interviews out of some money from one of his own grants. The baton was then handed to the two editors of this series, Barbara Sinclair and Richard Niemi. I am eternally grateful to them. They recognized a kernel of potential in what was originally a poorly presented proposal. They demonstrated great patience and gave me the opportunity and guidance to significantly improve the manuscript. I must also recognize the thoughtful, careful, and insightful review of Sue Thomas, whose comments dramatically improved the finished product.

A number of other friends and colleagues played vital roles in the development of this project. All of the following read and commented on portions of the manuscript: Tess Marchant-Shapiro, Byron Nichols, Jim King, Gayle Binion, Robert Schuhmann, and Ken Ardon. In addition, Ken Ardon and David Moriarty helped code and analyze the data. I am grateful to Union College and Dean Christina Sorum, who funded the 1994 interviews with a grant from the Faculty Research Fund. I must also thank Teresa Ortega, whose fine editorial assistance improved both the substance and quality of presentation. Also, my dear friend Kira Poplowski tirelessly and repeatedly proofread many of the chapters. I would be remiss if I did not mention the helpful staff at the Center for the American Woman and Politics (CAWP), who graciously helped me track down numerous arcane facts. Finally, I would like to thank the candidates and campaign managers who took the time to speak with me, often right in the middle of a heated campaign. There would have been no book without their cooperation.

200 words

Introduction:
Women on the Rise in
California Electoral Politics

In 1992 there was a dramatic change in the face of California politics.
Female candidates were running for top elective offices across the state
in far greater numbers than ever before. The 1992 "year of the woman"
elections were in high gear in California. Due to an unusual set of circumstances, both U.S. Senate seats were being contested simultaneously in 1992
and in both races the Democratic Party nominated women—former San
Francisco Mayor Dianne Feinstein and Congresswoman Barbara Boxer.
These were the first female candidates to receive a major party's nomination
for the U.S. Senate in California since 1950, when Helen Gahagan Douglas
lost a dramatic showdown with Richard Nixon. Again in 1994, female
candidates were running in the most important statewide contests in California. Dianne Feinstein, who had been victorious in her 1992 Senate campaign,
was up for reelection to a full term in the U.S. Senate. The Democrats also
nominated Kathleen Brown to run against incumbent governor Pete Wilson.
In addition to competing in the marquee electoral contests, female candidates
were also waging battles in lower-level elections. In each of the 1992 and
1994 elections, nineteen female candidates won major party nominations to

run in California's fifty-two congressional districts, easily surpassing the previous record of thirteen major party nominees in 1984, and more than doubling the 1990 total of nine. The sudden emergence of female candidates running for federal legislative office from California presents the opportunity to examine what happens to an electoral environment when female candidates become an important presence in an area where they have never before had a presence.[1] This book tells the story of the women running for election to the U.S. House of Representatives in California in 1992 and 1994. The experiences of female House candidates are compared with those of male House candidates to fully understand the different challenges women face in the electoral process.

With the broader inclusion of women in the election process in 1992 and 1994 it is important that we further consider how gender dynamics alter the conventional norms of electoral politics. Are women campaigning differently? Are women feeling more or less resistance than men from the media, the parties, and the voters? How are men in the electoral system responding to women? In answering these questions throughout this book, considerable evidence arises to show that the presence of female candidates is having a profound effect on the electoral process. In addition, this study reveals that the electoral arena is still not a level playing field. The influx of female congressional candidates in the California elections highlighted many of the additional hurdles female candidates still must confront in waging campaigns. For instance, in a hard-fought congressional race in central California that pitted a three-term male incumbent against an experienced female challenger in 1992, the female candidate's campaign focused on making sure that no one could question her authority and expertise on what have typically been viewed as "men's issues." Her campaign director explained,

> Our polls showed that the voters had more confidence in our opponent to handle the economy and the immigration problem. We regarded this as a man/woman thing. He was no more qualified to deal with these issues than we were—unless of course you consider immigrant bashing a qualification. . . . To offset our weak image on these issues we spent a lot of time in the early summer, many months before the election really heated up, devising detailed policy positions on the economy and military and immigration. She [the candidate] wanted to completely dispel any notion in the minds of the voters that because she was a woman she was less qualified to deal with these issues.

Similarly, a female challenger running in a congressional district in southern California in 1992 commented that she was under constant pressure to prove to the media and voters that she had the qualifications to hold national office and address the country's economic woes:

> Every time I spoke to groups out in the community, I started by talking about my career as a CPA. I needed people to take me seriously as someone who could help improve the economy. The economy was the big issue around here, and I don't think people thought that I had the strength to carry on the tough fight. . . . The people were very skeptical of me. I don't know what the reason was. I guess it was because I am an older woman, although I hate to think that.

Both of these female candidates made important decisions about campaign strategy because they perceived a bias or stereotyping of women by voters. In both of these instances female candidates believed their credibility was challenged. In the case of the more experienced woman, she made her decision to emphasize "men's issues" because internal campaign polls revealed that her opponent was regarded more favorably on immigration and economic issues. The second woman, who was operating a much less sophisticated campaign, altered her strategy based on the impressions she received from discussions with voters.

As women were facing certain challenges, their presence was causing male candidates to reevaluate their own campaign strategies. Several of the entrenched male incumbents in California, who had only known a male-dominated congressional election process and who had never before run against women, employed campaign strategies that they had never previously considered. As the manager for one incumbent asserted,

> You can't go after them [women] in the campaign. In our case we didn't want to look like we were attacking an elderly woman. You have to do some things differently when you run against a woman.

This sentiment, expressed by a veteran campaign official working for a California congressman, typified the feelings of many men who found themselves running against women for the first time. When the campaign official was asked why "you can't go after them," he responded,

> We would not want the public to see our youthful candidate with a distinguished military history tearing apart the positions of a nice older woman. The voters don't

like to see their congressman bullying a woman. . . . Our opponent was a raving liberal and we really wanted to go after her record, but we were very careful in how we addressed her. Nobody likes to see an old lady roughed up.

An aide to another long-time male member of the California House delegation also running against a woman noted that "1992 was the first time the Congressman formed a special group of women supporters as part of his campaign." Reporting his reasons for creating the group, the aide commented,

The women in our district needed to know we cared about them as much as she [the woman opponent] did. We wanted them to know that just because the Congressman is a man doesn't mean he does not care about the concerns of women in the district.

Although the strategic changes of these male incumbents was seemingly minor, behavioral changes such as these show that the presence of female candidates may have important consequences. For instance, when a male candidate feels he cannot criticize his female opponent's issue positions, then the agenda of issues that are debated in the election changes. If a male candidate pays more attention to women's concerns because he faces a woman opponent, then that also changes the substance of debate in the election. Also, the strategic changes made by male candidates reveal that they do not necessarily view women as their equals. Studying how the presence of female candidates affects the behavior of male candidates provides us an opportunity to more fully understand the broader effect and importance of female candidates. These four examples of candidate behavior from the California congressional elections demonstrate that gender considerations can play an important role in a campaign. In each instance the candidate made significant strategic decisions based on the sex of the opponent and the perceived gender stereotyping of voters.

The Central Thesis

In the course of exploring the gender dynamics of congressional elections, this book advances a three-part thesis. The first part asserts that there are many important differences in the challenges that women and men face in the electoral process. Also, there are many important differences in how women and men behave as candidates. Throughout this analysis it will be shown that in almost every facet of the electoral process, from the candidate's decision to run for office to the votes cast on election day, men and women have different experiences. This is not to suggest that there are extraordinary differences between men and women in all aspects of the electoral process. Most of the differences are very subtle but pervasive.

 The second part of the thesis asserts that most of these differences are the result of traditional sex-role stereotyping. Understanding the prevailing attitudes about sex roles is fundamental to assessing the effect of gender on the electoral process. The prevailing attitudes being referred to are derived from the traditional conception of the family. As Conover and Gray (1983) note,

> When the role of a woman is defined by her reproductive, sexual, and childrearing functions within the family, then there is a . . . division of activities into the public extrafamilial jobs done by the male and the private intrafamilial ones performed by the female. (2-3)

Historically, these attitudes have implied that only men are suited to public/political life and women to private/familial life. Substantial vestiges of these antiquated stereotypes still play an important role in how men and women compete in the electoral process. For instance, as recently as 1993, 26 percent of the respondents in the General Social Survey (GSS) admitted that they agreed with the statement: "Most men are better suited emotionally for politics than are most women" (Davis and Smith 1993). For a quarter of the population to openly agree with this statement suggests that the traditional constructions of public and private life, and the sex-roles prescribed within those constructions, can be important factors in electoral politics. Consequently, as we move through the various components of the electoral process in this analysis, we will see how traditional attitudes about women and men often cause women and men to have different experiences in and perceptions about the electoral process.

The third part of the thesis suggests that for most circumstances within an election, traditional sex-role stereotyping makes the electoral process more difficult for women to compete in effectively. Female candidates have to address numerous challenges and obstacles that men do not encounter. As the comments from the two female candidates mentioned previously indicate, women often have to consider the substance and credibility of their campaign message in ways that that male candidates never have to be concerned with. Thus, although most overt discrimination against women has disappeared, there are still many stereotypes about gender roles that work against women.

In the course of advancing this thesis, it is important to define several terms, some of which have already been used. Following is a list of these terms and how they are used in this analysis. Whenever these terms are used in this analysis, unless otherwise specified, they are defined as follows:

sex and *gender*—In most feminist writings the word *sex* is used to refer specifically to the biological sex of an individual and *gender* is used to refer to the social construction of separate roles for men and women. Because of the close connection of these terms, and because the use of the word *gender* usually includes considerations of biological sex, these words are used interchangeably in this analysis. For instance, when the term *candidate gender* is used, it usually refers to both sex differences and social role differences.

gender dynamics—This term refers to the interaction of gender (social role construction) with other factors, depending on the context. For instance, the phrase, "gender dynamics in the electoral system" refers to how gender considerations interact with the components of the electoral process.

gender stereotyping—This term refers to instances where there is reliance on the traditional notions of male and female sex roles, for example, that women are more suited for domestic responsibilities and men more suited for professional responsibilities.

women's issues and *men's issues* (referred to previously)—These classifications refer to those groups of policy issues that female and male policymakers are more likely to prioritize or for which voters have shown a tendency to favor women's or men's leadership (the literature that distinguishes these classifications is discussed later in this analysis).

female traits and *male traits*—These terms refer to the stereotypes about personal qualities that are usually associated with women and men. As these terms are used in this analysis, they indicate traits that are the result of traditional sex-role socialization, not any innate qualities of being a woman or man (the literature that distinguishes these classifications is discussed later in this analysis).

Database

The methods employed in this study focus on "getting inside" of the electoral process and fully understanding the dynamics occurring during the campaigns. This information is often elusive because of the ephemeral quality of elections. The decisions and events of elections are usually not systematically chronicled, and within days or sometimes hours after an election, campaign offices are disassembled and campaign workers have left the area to seek their next battleground. In trying to study the internal dynamics of campaigns, the data set for this study is drawn almost entirely from the state of California during the 1992 and 1994 elections. Several factors make California an outstanding case study. The large number of women who ran for office in California in both elections makes it unique. In each of the past two election cycles, two women received major-party nominations for the highest statewide offices on the ballot (Dianne Feinstein [U.S. Senate] and Barbara Boxer [U.S. Senate] in 1992, and Feinstein [U.S. Senate] and Kathleen Brown [Governor] in 1994). This uncommon selection makes California an important testing ground for the effect of candidate gender on the campaign. In addition to the top-level nominations, almost twenty percent of all the major-party female candidates running for the U.S. House of Representatives in 1992 and 1994 were from California. Further, California is often considered a pathbreaking state. Political changes in California, such as tax reform and the use of the initiative process, often precede similar movements elsewhere. Also, California presents a diverse sample of different types of congressional districts—urban, rural, wealthy, poor, ethnically mixed, and so forth. Thus, although we must be cautious in drawing general conclusions from this examination, California's diversity makes it an extremely important case study. The findings that emerge from this analysis have implications for women running for the U.S. House of Representatives across the nation. Finally, the California elections allow important comparisons between 1992 and 1994. With almost the same number of female candidates running in the state in both of these elections, we are able to see how candidate gender affects the election process in two very different political climates (the different political climates are discussed in greater detail in Chapter 1).[2]

To examine the effect of female candidates on the electoral process in California, I chose to focus on the congressional elections in 1992 and 1994. Although the larger statewide races featuring women intensified gender awareness in the California electoral environment, the larger sample of House candidates created a big enough pool of candidates to permit systematic and quantitative compilations. The data set is composed of thirty-two general election congressional races in 1992 and twenty-nine general election races in 1994, for a total of sixty-one races and 122 major-party candidacies. There are fifty-two congressional districts in California, which means there were a total of 104 elections across the two election cycles. My objective was to study a group of races with a female candidate in each election and to compare those with a group of races with only male candidates in each election. In selecting the two samples of races, the first group consisted of all races featuring a female candidate. Of the 104 congressional elections that took place in 1992 and 1994, there were a total of thirty-four races with female candidates. I excluded five of these races from the sample because they involved extremely "safe" incumbents who engaged in almost no general election campaign activity (see Appendix A). This left a total of twenty-nine races (fifteen in 1992 and fourteen in 1994) with a female candidate. In three of these races both major-party candidates were women. The final sample of thirty-two female candidates was composed of twenty-five Democrats and seven Republicans. Thus, as we examine the role of candidate gender in the election process, we must be exceedingly careful to distinguish between partisan and gender effects.

The comparison group of races with only male candidates was selected from the remaining seventy races. In four of these races the male incumbent was running unopposed, leaving sixty-six races from which to select comparison sets. Two characteristics were employed in selecting the sample of male-only races. The first characteristic was the type of race, which refers to whether the contest was over an open seat, a seat held by an incumbent, or a newly created seat.[3] Based on the types of seats that women were running for, a corresponding pool of male candidates was chosen to match. For instance, whenever possible, an open-seat race with a woman running would be matched with an open-seat race with only men running. The second characteristic employed in selecting the male-only sample was the party registration of the district. Again, a system of sample matching was performed so that party registration in the races with women and in the races with only men would be as close as possible. The goal was to have two pools of races of roughly equally competitive elections. In the end seventeen male-only races were selected in 1992 and fifteen were selected in 1994. Appendix A presents a complete listing of the House candidates and elections chosen for this analysis.

The primary data source for this project consisted of interviews with the campaign managers of each candidate. In 1992, pre- and postelection interviews were conducted and in 1994 only postelection interviews were conducted. For the 1992 races, the majority of interviews were conducted in person. In addition, several hours were spent observing campaign operations. For the 1994 elections, most interviews were conducted over the phone. Campaign managers were selected because they were considered the most knowledgeable campaign official with regard to a campaign's message and overall strategy. In addition, campaign managers were more accessible than candidates and had more time to take part in the survey. Fifteen candidates had no campaign manager, and in these cases either the press secretary or the candidate was interviewed. Over 200 interviews were conducted for this project. Of the 122 candidates in the sample, the campaign manager, the candidate, or a campaign official from 109 of the campaigns participated in the interview process. The survey instruments are reproduced in Appendix C.

Throughout this analysis, specific quotes and references to the campaign activities of particular candidates are kept anonymous. About a quarter of the managers interviewed preferred to remain anonymous, and thus to protect their identities it was necessary not to attribute any quotes (see Appendix B). Assuring the campaign officials of confidentiality led to more candid and revealing interviews. For instance, several of the experienced campaign managers harshly criticized the performance of their own candidates. Others revealed campaign strategies that could provide useful information to future opponents. To feel safe divulging these types of details about their campaigns, the managers had to be certain that this information would not become public. Although confidentiality was promised for the interview data, when discussing public information, such as FEC reports (Chapter 4) or the performance of the candidates with the voters (Chapter 5), the candidates and districts are mentioned by name. To supplement the interviews, campaign literature, direct mail, and newspaper coverage were collected for as many campaigns as possible. Campaign literature and direct mail were collected from eighty-nine of the 122 campaigns in the study.

Meeting with the campaign managers and speaking with them directly allowed me to build trust, and, in many cases, to get an inside view of the campaign that is usually not available to academics or journalists. Ultimately, however, this study relies heavily on perceptual data. The advantages of this kind of data are that the investigator can pick up nuances and inside accounts of an election that are not available in examinations of objective data or even from systematic reviews of journalistic campaign coverage. Thus, the primary contribution of this study is its interpretation and analysis of interview data. The number of interviews and races covered brings to the literature on female candidates a richness and depth that is often missing.

Much of the recent literature relies on only aggregate data (Darcy, Welch, and Clark 1994; Burrell 1994) or on single-race case studies (Cook, Thomas, and Wilcox 1994). This work combines both in-depth analysis and some degree of systematization. The recent literature on female candidates is discussed in the following section.

Admittedly though, there are certain drawbacks to relying on perceptual or interview data. First, the quality of the interviews varies tremendously. Some campaign managers were extremely evasive and secretive, and in at least three preelection interviews in 1992 the manager seriously asked if I was a spy working for the opposing campaign. Alternatively, some managers were so open they detailed their entire campaign strategy, including the contents of upcoming mailers and commercials. The secretiveness and distance of some managers may have obscured some of the gender-based campaign decisions. Some managers, as discussed more fully in Chapter 3, were reluctant to discuss how they used or strategized about issues of candidate gender. The subject of candidate gender and how the campaign dealt with this issue was often a delicate topic in the interviews. However, these limitations were not overly detrimental to the interviews. Many of the questions asked of campaign managers were only attempting to determine the public message that was being put forward by the campaign—questions about which managers would have little reason to be deceptive (see Appendix C).

The Recent Literature on Female Candidates

The questions explored and the data employed in this book make it an excellent complement to the growing body of literature on female candidates. Since the "year of the woman" elections in 1992, there has been an increasing interest in the subject of female candidates. This work hopes to build on much of this recent research and add to our understanding of the different challenges facing female candidates. From the mid-1980s to the early 1990s, there were only two extensive academic treatments of female candidates: Susan Carroll's pioneering work, *Women as Candidates in American Politics* (1985) and Darcy, Welch, and Clark's *Women, Elections, and Representation* (1987).[5] Both of these books have been updated and expanded as second editions in 1994. Carroll's book has been the foundation for many examinations of female candidates. In her second edition she added an analysis of the 1992 elections. However, one of the drawbacks of the updated version is that it is almost entirely based on her 1976 survey of female candidates. My study updates and extends Carroll's work by offering in-depth assessments of candidate behavior during the elections of 1992 and 1994. My work also has a male comparison group that helps to more clearly illustrate the experiences of female candidates. Carroll acknowledges that a male comparison group would have been a useful addition to her study, but that the size and extent of her survey made that impossible (1994, 196, n27). By studying and observing the behavior of men who competed against women, we have a clearer conception of how women are treated in the electoral process.

Both editions of Darcy, Welch, and Clark's (1994) work systematically to analyze election data from myriad sources with the goal of further explaining the disparities in the number of women serving in elected positions. In trying to determine the cause for the low proportions of female officeholders, they explore three potential explanations: differences in the vote for men and women, differences in how political elites treat men and women, and differences in the ability of men and women to effectively wage campaigns (1994, 28). Although Darcy, Welch, and Clark do an excellent job compiling aggregate data to explore these explanations, their work suffers from the limitations of aggregate data. My study complements their work because it goes beyond quantitative analysis and explores the perceptions and experiences of female and male candidates. In studying elections, quantitative analysis can sometimes obscure the important nuances that exist beyond numeric representations. For instance, comparisons of fund raising totals or vote totals do not reveal the candidates' experiences in these areas. As this analysis shows, despite the similar successes of women and men in raising money and getting votes, they often had different perceptions and employed different strategies in these areas.

In addition to the works by Carroll and Darcy, Welch, and Clark, two other recent studies have come out that have specifically examined the 1992 "year of the woman" elections. Cook, Thomas, and Wilcox (1994) edited *The Year of the Woman: Myths and Realities,* which chronicled the important developments in the 1992 elections. This anthology added greatly to our understanding of the pivotal 1992 elections with case studies of some of the most important U.S. Senate races involving women. Other articles in the anthology used aggregate data to examine the interactions between gender and party support, PAC contributions, political advertising, and voter behavior. My study picks up where Cook, Thomas, and Wilcox's examination leaves off by studying the role of gender in the electoral process in the first electoral cycle after the 1992 election. The role of gender in the electoral process after the 1992 elections provides the first assessment of how important the 1992 elections were in breaking down barriers to the continued progression of women into elective office.

In a work more directly related to the focus of this examination, Barbara Burrell's (1994) *A Woman's Place Is in the House* thoroughly examines the professional backgrounds and electoral experiences of female House candidates from 1968 to 1992. Her work pays particular attention to the 1992 elections. Burrell's study is useful in that it lays the foundation for historically situating the 1992 elections. This is an important source for supporting and confirming many of the findings presented in this investigation. However, Burrell relies primarily on quantitative compilations to explain the experiences of female candidates in relation to the experiences of men. Although she does include some anecdotes from personal interviews, they are only presented to supplement the quantitative nature of her study (1994, 10). The interview findings presented in my account are an excellent complement to Burrell's work because they often are able to clarify some of the conclusions that she draws. For instance, Burrell contends that most of the negative preconceptions about women's campaigns, such as funding shortfalls and voter bias, are not true. The findings in this study confirm her general conclusions but go beyond her analysis and often disagree with her contentions about the overall fairness of the electoral process for women.

Ultimately this study hopes to sit alongside recent examinations of female candidates, combining some of the strengths of these works and adding to the depth of the literature on female candidates. This study is the only examination among those discussed that relies on the results of extensive interviews with campaign officials during and shortly after the elections.[6] The interviews offer a much richer sense of the gender dynamics transpiring within an election.

Overview of the Following Chapters

The findings of this study are presented in Chapters 2 through 5. However, before moving to the analysis of the findings, it is necessary to further lay out the foundations for this examination. Chapter 1 explores the two primary theoretical issues motivating this study of female candidates: the fundamental importance of electoral politics to the American governing process and the need for greater representation of women in the political process. In addition, Chapter 1 also places the elections of 1992 and 1994 in historical context by examining the unique characteristics of each election. Due to the limited time period studied in this book, two election cycles, it is important to understand the particular qualities of these elections and how they affect the gender dynamics of an election.

The rest of the book is organized as follows. Chapters 2 and 3 focus on the behavior and campaign practices of female and male candidates. Chapters 4 and 5 compare how male and female candidates are treated by the various components of the election process (e.g., fund-raising networks, party support, the voters, etc.). Each of the data chapters in this book is organized around a set of questions that emerge as a candidate moves through the election process. The experiences of the candidates are traced from their initial motivations for running for office through the vote totals on election day. Each chapter explores the different experiences of male and female candidates to answer the questions laid out earlier and to advance the central thesis of the book: Prevailing attitudes about traditional sex-roles dictate the gender dynamics in an election and most of these attitudes make the electoral process more difficult for female candidates.

One underdeveloped area in the literature on female candidates is the campaigning styles of men and women. Most of our understanding of gender differences in campaigning style come from case studies of individual races (Cook, Thomas, and Wilcox 1994; Tolleson Rinehart and Stanley 1994; Morris 1992). There are great challenges to systematically studying the gender dynamics in larger numbers of campaigns because the decisions and actions of campaigns are not recorded and are often secretive. To broaden our understanding of the gender dynamics during the course of an election, Chapter 2 relies on the interviews with campaign officials in over sixty House races. The in-depth nature of the interviews allows systematic comparisons of the campaign strategies and the styles of male and female candidates. Included in the analysis in Chapter 2 is a comparison between female and male candidates in their motivations for running for office, their use of negative campaigning, their degree of personal interaction with voters, and their media strategy. The findings suggest that in many subtle but potentially important ways, women and men campaign and compete for office in different ways.

The analysis in Chapter 2 moves beyond comparing the campaign styles of male and female candidates to assess whether male candidates change their behavior based on the sex of their opponent. This topic has been largely ignored by previous studies of female candidates (see Renner 1993). The reason for this underexplored area is that examinations and surveys of female candidates have seldom studied the behavior of their male opponents (Carroll 1994). The question of whether men change their behavior in reaction to female opponents is an important area of investigation because if it is revealed that male candidates are modifying their behavior, then this may suggest a much broader effect of female candidates on the electoral process. The findings presented in this chapter confirm that some male candidates make strategic alterations in their campaign styles when running against a woman. What we learn from these changes is that male and female candidates are often responding to sex-role stereotypes in themselves and in the voters.

Chapter 3 compares the substantive campaign agendas of male and female candidates. To assess the campaign messages of the candidates, Chapter 3 relies not only on interviews with campaign officials but also on campaign literature collected from each campaign. This chapter examines the campaign message of male and female candidates in three distinct areas: 1) the presentation of personal characteristics and images; 2) the use of general campaign themes; and 3) the use of specific policy issues. Each of these areas offers insight into the gender dynamics in an election. In terms of personal characteristics, we know that candidate image is playing an ever-increasing role in voter decision making (Niemi and Weisberg 1993; Lodge, McGraw, and Stroh 1989). Yet as Tolleson Rinehart points out, most of this literature fails to include a consideration of candidate gender (1994, 27-28). In addition, the different decisions by male and female candidates about how to present themselves to voters reveal that female candidates still feel they must combat sex-role stereotyping.

The second half of Chapter 3 focuses on the substantive policy differences in the campaigns of female and male candidates. This is an important area of investigation because if female candidates raise and emphasize different issues in the campaign, then they may change the policy debate within an election. Previous investigations have shown that women present different policy agendas once they are in policy-making positions (e.g., Thomas 1994; Dodson and Carroll 1991). The conclusions of Chapter 3 reveal that there are important differences between men and women in all three areas (personal traits, central themes, and policy issues) of the campaign messages. However, these differences are often not the result of fundamentally different beliefs or attitudes between female and male candidates, but of strategic decisions made by candidates to counter the gender-role stereotyping of voters.

In Chapters 4 and 5 the focus of the study moves from the behavior of the candidates, both male and female, to the role gender plays in determining how candidates are treated by the electoral process. The fairness of the electoral process is of fundamental importance to questions of equal representation for women. Chapters 4 and 5 assess whether the electoral process is truly open to female candidates. The subject of representation is discussed further in Chapter 1, and it is the guiding theme of these chapters.

Chapter 4 examines the structural aspects of the election to determine if there are any significant differences in the challenges that confront male and female candidates. The experiences of men and women are compared in terms of fund-raising, party support, and media coverage. What we know about each of these areas is still quite limited. Comparisons of raw fund-raising totals between female and male candidates have shown that there is little or no gender bias (Burrell 1994; Uhlaner and Schlozman 1986). However, these analyses do not fully examine the sources of the money or the perceptions that female and male candidates have about the challenges of fund-raising. The interviews with the campaign managers employed in this analysis allow an in-depth comparison of the fund-raising experiences of male and female candidates. The campaign managers were also asked about their experiences with party support and media coverage. In terms of party support, Baer (1993) suggests that research on women's roles in party organizations has not been sufficiently examined. Regarding the research of media coverage, only recently has Kahn (1993, 1992) shown the persistence of stereotyping in media coverage of male and female candidates. Overall, the analysis in Chapter 4 reveals that in the 1992 and 1994 elections women were by most objective indicators not at a disadvantage with regard to these electoral factors, and in several areas appeared to have a clear advantage. However, despite the seemingly equal or advantageous playing field for female candidates in 1992 and 1994, a number of female candidates perceived that they were at a disadvantage in all of these areas: fund-raising, party support, and media coverage. Their perceptions of unfairness, whether grounded or not, may have important ramifications for the future willingness of women to enter electoral politics or government positions (Naff 1995). Chapter 4 concludes by discussing the importance of differing perceptions between female and male candidates.

Chapter 5 turns to the voters. The current literature on the interaction between candidate gender and vote choice has left many questions unanswered. Huddy and Terkildsen (1993b), in an experimental survey of college students, have shown that voters employ gender stereotypes that work against female candidates running for national office (518-20). Several experimental studies have found significant levels of voter stereotyping, but no actual bias in voting behavior (Leeper 1991; Sapiro 1981-82). However, with the ever-changing dynamics of the election process, especially in the 1992 elections, the full effect of candidate gender on voting behavior is largely unclear. Chapter 5, the final data chapter, attempts to add some additional evidence to this discussion by assessing how voters responded to the sex of the candidates in the California elections. Did voters have different conceptions of male and female candidates? Were there certain issues that affected how voters perceived candidates? In answering these questions, this chapter relies less on interview data and draws instead on analysis of raw vote totals and the California version of the Voter Research and Surveys (VRS) general election exit polls in 1992 and 1994. Without the availability of district-level polling, many of the assessments of voter behavior rely on the polling for statewide offices. The primary goal of this chapter is to determine how candidate gender affects voters' attitudes and the outcome of the election. Chapter 5 tries to assess the importance of political climate, incumbency, and candidate party affiliation in determining the overall effect of candidate gender on voter decision making. This chapter illustrates that voters engage in some degree of gender stereotyping, but the important conclusion is that gender bias and stereotyping can work either for or against a female candidate depending on the political climate of the election.

At the conclusion of the interviews, the campaign managers were for the first time asked directly about what they viewed as the role of candidate gender in electoral politics. Chapter 6 presents the summary assessments of the campaign managers. Also, a brief summary of the major findings of this study is provided. Chapter 6 concludes by suggesting future research directions that need exploration as we continue to examine the fluctuating fortunes of female candidates.

Notes

1. In 1990, Dianne Feinstein's candidacy for governor may have helped pave the way for the success of women in 1992 and 1994 (see Morris 1992).

2. Another reason for examining California is that there is currently only limited academic work on the role of gender in the California election process, see Tolleson Rinehart (1994) and Morris (1992).

3. After the 1990 census, California gained seven new seats in the House of Representatives. These were first contested in the 1992 elections and thus the category of "newly created" seats only existed in 1992.

4. As discussed in Chapter 6, the campaign managers were only asked specifically about the role of candidate gender at the conclusion of the interviews.

5. This is not meant to suggest that there has not been other fine work done on the role of gender in the election process. The Carroll and Darcy, Welch, and Clark works were simply the most recent comprehensive and quantitative examinations. For other good early examinations of women in elections, see Mandel (1981), Diamond (1977), Githens and Prestage (1977), and Kirkpatrick (1974).

6. Another substantial work coming out after the 1992 elections was Witt, Paget, and Matthews' *Running as a Woman* (1994). This is a lively and fascinating assessment of the major issues facing women in the electoral arena. The work combines interview data with some election and campaign fund-raising data. However, this is for the most part a less academic treatment of the subject, almost entirely ignoring the body of academic literature on female candidates.

Gender and Political Representation in the Elections of 1992 and 1994

What is the reason for studying female candidates? And why study female candidates in the 1992 and 1994 elections? Before moving on to present and assess the experiences of the congressional candidates in California, it is important to further discuss the theoretical and contextual underpinnings of this study. The experiences of female candidates have great significance for understanding recent electoral politics and the continued underrepresentation of women in governing institutions. Elections provide the best window into the dynamics of the political process and the clearest opportunity to determine whether women have been accepted into that process. Elections, as discussed below, are the primary medium for political representation in the United States. Further, it is essential that we examine the broader trends and characteristics of the 1992 and 1994 elections. In many cases these were unique elections and any examination of gender dynamics in 1992 and 1994 must be considered in light of the other aspects of the electoral environment. The fact that this only examines female candidates over a two-election cycle mandates that these elections be placed in the proper historical context.

The Importance of Examining the Role of Gender in Electoral Politics

Aside from the timely significance of the 1992 and 1994 elections, studying the role of gender in the election process is important for two broad theoretical reasons. The election process is the primary means of political representation. Elections are the engine of democratic governance in the United States. Regardless of the skepticism or contempt one might hold for the election process, the simple reality remains that elections are the means by which we choose the leadership of the country. Thus, if election dynamics change with the addition of a new political group—in this case, women— then it is of central importance to grapple with the ramifications of how this change affects the selection of top leaders.

In addition to their importance in selecting leaders, congressional elections are vital areas of study because they help shape the policy agenda of the nation. In an examination of decision making by members of Congress, Kingdon (1989) has shown convincingly how the preferences of district voters are taken into consideration by members of Congress, especially on highly salient issues. Within the confines of a reelection campaign, members of Congress are in closest contact with the preferences of voters (Fenno 1978). Issues of high salience to voters are brought out in elections, and these issues may guide the legislative behavior of the election winner. Arnold (1990), building on Kingdon's work, introduces the reelection motive as a predictor of decision-making for members of Congress. Arnold demonstrates that members of Congress behave in accordance with voter preferences on any issue that is salient to the public. The members do this so that they will not offend a large enough share of voters to jeopardize their future reelection efforts. In other words, issues that voters care about are those for which members of Congress are most likely to follow the desires of the voters. Further, because the issues raised during the course of an electoral campaign are those with the highest salience to voters, they are the most likely to become priorities of the election winner. This becomes particularly important in light of the studies discussed below, which identify different policy priorities for male and female legislators.

What we know about the agenda-setting role of the media also supports the contention that elections help shape the policy agendas of elected officials (see for example, Cook et al. 1983). The availability of political information to voters is heightened greatly during an election period. Information comes from the increase in political coverage by the media and from the onslaught of campaign literature, direct mail, and television and radio advertising put out by the candidates. The information and media coverage emanating from an electoral campaign are formative in determining the issues salient to voters. Thus, the substantive issues that are addressed in a campaign, whether raised by the media or the candidate, shape the political agenda of the election winner. Most important to consider in this investigation is whether female candidates are introducing different policies or policy approaches in elections. If women address different agendas, this may alter legislative priorities in Congress. Also, if women change the ways in which campaigns are run, then the effect of this change must be examined to understand more fully the dynamics of electoral politics. Because of the centrality of elections in the political system in the U.S., it is vitally important to get inside the election and uncover the role that gender plays in the actions of candidates. Ultimately, that is what this study proposes to do.

The Representation of Women

The second important theoretical topic examined in this study is the political representation of women. Despite the advances women made in the 1992 elections and sustained in 1994, there remains an enormous inequity in the number of women who currently serve in top leadership positions in this country (see Table 4.1). When the 103rd Congress (1993-94) ended, women held just under 11 percent of the seats in the House, and 7 percent of the seats in the Senate. For the 104th Congress (1995-96), the numbers were unchanged in the House and women gained 1 seat (1%) in the Senate. Heading into the 1996 elections, only one of the fifty states has a female governor (Christine Todd Whitman of New Jersey).

In considering these large numeric disparities, two types of representation must be considered: symbolic and substantive. The desire for symbolic representation suggests that it is important for the governing institutions to reflect the composition of the citizenry. Tolleson Rinehart (1994, 27) notes that we are often interested in the numbers of women serving in legislatures and other governmental institutions because something seems inherently wrong when a group composing over fifty percent of the population holds few important positions of political leadership. Thus, at the very least, as Tolleson Rinehart notes, more women must be included among the political leadership out of a sense of "simple justice." However, beyond considerations of simple justice and symbolic representation, many examinations of female political actors are imbued with the expectation that women are different from men in substantive ways. More specifically, that women bring with them to positions of political power different viewpoints from men, and different leadership styles from men—in essence, a brand of representation different from that of men. For instance, Bachrach (1967, 71) has argued that members of racial or socioeconomic groups receive better representation from members of their own group. Amundsen (1971, 173-74), speaking more specifically about women, asserts that their best chance for receiving adequate representation is by having more women included in the decision-making process. Thus, examining the effect of female candidates and the role of gender in elections is perhaps crucial for addressing questions of representation. This is particularly important in light of the growing evidence that men and women may have different sets of "interests" and different political orientations.

In addressing the issue of representation, the first question that arises is whether men and women have different sets of interests. At a general societal level, women exist in a social realm different from that of men. For the most part, women earn lower incomes, own less property, and serve in fewer positions of public and private leadership.[1] In addition, women's continued responsibilities as the primary caretakers of the family further illustrate that women, as a group, function in a different role than men. However, Sapiro (1981, 707) argues that "women's interests" should not be viewed simply as political issues that address specifically women. In modern political debate it is common to regard "women's interests" as being limited to policy areas such as abortion, day care, and parental leave.[2] Sapiro argues that almost all policies have a differential effect on men and women. An example used by Sapiro involves the seemingly gender-neutral policy decision to reduce the money supply. She argues that this increases the domestic labor burden of women who then have to make food and clothing budgets last longer (704). More generally, Carroll defines "women's issues" as any issues in which policy consequences have a more immediate and direct effect on a larger portion of women than men (1994, 15).

The primary question that emerges is whether a system dominated by men can serve the distinct interests of women. Carroll uses the examples of the Equal Pay Act, the Equal Rights Amendment, and a national day care system to illustrate the deficiencies of the current political system. Despite being favored by a large majority of women, these policy issues were either slow in coming, as in the case of the Equal Pay Act, or were never enacted, as in the case of the Equal Rights Amendment and national day care. Carroll concludes that a system dominated by men cannot effectively represent the interests of women (1994, 17).

Several problems work to prevent rectifying the underrepresentation of women in the political system. Bestowing women with more rights or greater representation involves treating women as a group. Debate over "group rights" raises an ideological furor even when more homogeneous groups are involved. Fiss (1976), in an early analysis of the "group rights principle," argues that it is difficult to propagate group rights under the confines of the 14th amendment and the Bill of Rights. The constitutional framework of the United States mandates the protection of individual rights.[3] To further complicate the situation, women are a unique political group. Claims of political underrepresentation are brought forth within the seeming contradiction that women have achieved full political rights and compose a majority of the voting citizenry. Women are not organized as a single political group, and thus any specific attempts to address "women's interests" cause conflict among women.

Another problem in dealing with the representation of women is the historical separation between public and private concerns (Siltanen and Stanworth 1984). Many of the "women's interests" that Sapiro (1981) and others refer to exist in the private domain of the home. Politics and the debate over policy issues transpire in the public realm. Thus, "private issues" concerning domestic life have had trouble receiving attention in the public domain. For years feminist scholars and the leaders of the women's movement have tried to tear down the barrier between what is considered private and public. Okin (1989, 124-33), in her analysis of the public/private split, notes that the perpetuation of this dichotomy stems from a traditional patriarchal view of society that assumes different roles for men and women. Much recent feminist analysis, such as Okin's, attempts to transform this perspective through the widespread claim that the "personal is the political." Okin and others argue that issues such as domestic violence, child custody law, and marital rape all require public debate. Yet these issues have often remained outside public debate because they have traditionally been regarded as private matters. The public/private split remains an important factor in shaping policy debates and altering the potential representation of certain "women's interests." This barrier has undoubtedly reduced the amount of attention some "women's interests" receive in the political process.[4] Significantly, though, Thomas (1994) has shown that female state legislators have been able to bring many formerly private-sphere issues into the public domain for political debate (see also Dodson and Carroll 1991).

Further evidence that women's interests are not fully represented is found in the expanding body of social psychological and political science literature that suggests that women have political attitudes and societal orientations that differ in important ways from men. These perceptions of differing approaches to politics by men and women are based on the premise that men and women have different life experiences. One conception of differences between men and women is encompassed in the work of Carol Gilligan. Gilligan (1982), in her landmark book *In a Different Voice*, argued that men and women "construe social reality differently" (171). What emerges, argues Gilligan, are distinctly female and male perspectives. Gilligan asserts that the female voice embraces the ideals of responsibility, caring, and interconnectedness (172-73). Conversely, the male voice embraces the notions of adherence to rules and individualism. The existence of these different modes of conceptualization for men and women has been further explored by Belenky et al. (1986). They assessed how women are influenced by the two most powerful socializing agents, family and school, and determined that women are confronted with hurdles of emotional, psychological, and intellectual development that do not parallel the experiences of men.

Emerging from these social psychological studies are composites of men's and women's behavior that potentially have great import for politics. Although applications of these social psychological studies to questions of political behavior need to be handled carefully, there are some constructs for male and female behavior that may be useful when examining the performance of male and female candidates. Kathlene (1995), in assessing the attitudes of male and female legislators in the policy area of crime, has shown how Gilligan's identification of distinctly male and female voices can be useful in trying to understand and explain differences between how male and female state legislators understand and explain the crime problem (697-99). Kathlene derives two constructs from Gilligan's work that she believes are useful in examining attitudes of legislators: instrumentalism (male voice attribute) and contextualism (female voice attribute) (698).[5] The summary of these points, especially in political terms, is that women are more con-

cerned with context, community, and relationships, and men are more concerned with rules and individual rights. In this analysis of congressional
candidates, we will find that these constructs of male and female behavior
can help explain some of the differences in the campaigning styles of men
and women.

In thinking about gender differences that are more directly political, a
growing number of investigators report important differences in the behavior
of men and women in the political process. Male and female legislators have
been found to have different legislative and policy priorities. Thomas (1991)
found that under certain circumstances, female officeholders adopt and
pursue different policy goals than men (967-970). Women prioritize legislation concerning women, family, and children, whereas men prioritize business and economic legislation. Thomas further asserts that the women's
perspective or priorities are more fully exhibited when women are able to
attain a minimum threshold of seats within the legislative chamber. Her
estimates range from 15 to 20 percent (1991, 964, 973-74). Similarly, in a
study of city council members, Boles (1991) uncovers a more specific set of
issue differences (39-41). Boles selected six stereotypical "women's issues"
and surveyed both male and female council members on the importance that
issue played within their legislative agenda. Boles found that on the issues
of day care, domestic violence, sexual assault, displaced homemakers, children's library services, and childbirth in public hospitals, women were far
more likely to place them on their legislative agenda (41). In a final example,
Schumaker and Burns (1988) studied thirty randomly selected issues that
were before the city council of Lawrence, Kansas. They found a gender
cleavage between members of the city council on twenty of the thirty issues.
For example, issues surrounding economic development consistently received more attention from male council members. Female council members
were more supportive of neighborhood preservation and social welfare
(1075). Studies such as these have led to the classifications of "men's" and
"women's" issues, defined in the introduction.[6]

The conclusion that must be drawn from this analysis of women's interests
and representation is that success in electoral politics is the clearest avenue
to greater political representation for women (Burrell 1994, 6-7; Carroll
1994, 20-21). The growing body of literature previously touched on suggests
that substantive representation would be significantly altered by the greater
inclusion of women in the political process. In addition, even if claims of
differences in substantive representation between men and women are over-

stated, "simple justice" remains a compelling reason to elect more women. Further, the controversy over group rights and the strength of the public/ private dichotomy pose practical political limitations to the representation of women's interests that can best be offset by dramatic increases in the number of female officeholders.

Studying the Role of Gender in the 1992 and 1994 Elections

With the focus of this study on the 1992 and 1994 elections, it is important to understand the unusual circumstances and qualities of each of these elections. They were both unique. In considering gender dynamics we must also consider the other dynamics that were transpiring in these elections, particularly at the congressional level. For instance, in 1992 the patterns and norms of congressional elections were disrupted. Nelson (1993) describes the usual trends in congressional elections:

> Historically, congressional elections have been marked by great regularities. Overwhelmingly, the winning candidates are "white men in blue suits." Incumbent members of Congress, especially in the House of Representatives, almost always are reelected. The victorious party in the presidential election usually gains seats in Congress. (152)

However, in 1992 all of these "regularities" were disrupted. In some ways the 1994 congressional elections were even more historic. The Republicans regained control of the House of Representatives for the first time in forty years. Michael Beschloss, a presidential historian, posited that the Republican takeover of Congress and the Republican seizure of the political agenda with *The Contract With America*, may have severely limited the power of the presidency for the foreseeable future (1995, 45). Although this assessment may be a bit overstated, as we consider the gender dynamics for these two elections, it is important to remember that they were not ordinary elections.

"The Year of the Woman" and the 1992 Elections

The historic breakthroughs made by female candidates in the elections of 1992 provide an important starting point for studying gender dynamics in campaign politics. The forces that came together to propel in the participation and success of female candidates in 1992 were multifaceted. Public awareness and the media sensation began in 1991 with the televised Senate Judiciary Committee's hearings on Supreme Court nominee Clarence Thomas. The spectacle of the hearings, which for many women showed a believable woman being derided by a panel of older white men, helped mobilize professional women to become active in the 1992 elections (Wilcox 1994, 7). In addition, when female candidates achieved unexpected electoral successes in early state primaries in Illinois and Pennsylvania, there was a great deal of momentum surrounding all female candidates. These developments resulted in both the Democratic party and media commentators labeling 1992 the "year of the woman." One might cynically note that 1974, 1984, and 1990 were also called the "year of the woman" and seemed to result in only minor electoral gains for female candidates.

The other side of the "year of the woman" elections, the side the media and public was not focusing on, was the fact that the 1992 elections presented a window of opportunity for a large number of female candidates who had been steadily climbing the rungs of the political ladder. The increase in the number of female candidates in 1992 did not emerge out of nowhere. Women had been increasing their numbers in state legislatures and local government offices since 1970. For instance, in 1970, women held 4.5 percent of state legislative seats; by 1992 the number had grown to 18.4 percent (CAWP Fact Sheets, 1992). This group of women was strategically primed to run for higher office in 1992. With media momentum, mobilized support, and a pool of women ready to run, all that was needed were the electoral opportunities. The opportunities became available in 1992 because there were more open seats in the House of Representatives than there had been in over forty years. In total, 75 of the 435 elections for seats in the House of Representatives had no incumbent running. Congressional redistricting and the large number of retirements created many of the open seats. In California alone there were a total of sixteen open seats in 1992. In addition to these developments, congressional disclosures such as the House Banking and post office scandals led to the vulnerability of many incumbents and also partially explains the high retirement rate (Burrell 1994, 37-38).

Thus, the "year of the woman" elections had two general components, the public and media frenzy that developed suddenly, and the institutional developments of increasing numbers of women in lower-level offices and a high rate of open seats and vulnerable incumbents. Both of these phenomena came together in 1992, and nowhere more fully than in California. However, some commentators (mostly political conservatives) derided the notion of the "year of the woman," suggesting that it was the creation of the liberal media and should be called the "year of the Democratic woman." Burrell (1994, 47) asserts that this was not true and that Democratic women were simply more likely than Republican women to take advantage of the window of opportunity in 1992. However, several indicators of the electoral environment showed that the 1992 elections differed from previous elections in terms of the role of female candidates.

For one, more women than ever before received major-party nominations to run for federal legislative office. In the House of Representatives, 107 women were nominated, compared to the previous record of seventy set in 1990. In the Senate, eleven women received major-party nominations, just above the old mark of ten set in 1984. The record number of candidates, although more striking in the House, clearly demonstrates that women were competing more successfully for major party nominations.[7] One official from the Democratic Congressional Campaign Committee (DCCC) asserted that their polling and research found that the ideal congressional candidates, in terms of appeal to voters, were women with local electoral experience. This would include women who had served on city councils and school boards.[8] The Democratic Party operated under this premise and sought to recruit female candidates. The Democratic Party's support for women was illustrated during the first two days of the Democratic National Convention. Female candidates and officeholders were showcased before prime-time viewing audiences. Speakers such as California State Treasurer Kathleen Brown, Washington D.C. Mayor Sharon Pratt Dixon, and Senatorial candidates Carol Moseley Braun and Barbara Boxer put forth the message that women would bring change to Washington. The substance of their message was that women, seemingly because they were women, would offer a different approach to government. In response to the Democrats, the Republicans trotted out their own array of female political leaders to show they too were in touch with the representational needs of women. However, despite their efforts, the Republicans were less successful at recruiting women to run for high elective office (Biersack and Herrnson 1994, 168).

In addition to party support for women, political action committees and interest groups that promote female candidates were more active than ever. Political action committees, such as EMILY's List and the Women's Campaign Fund, far exceeded any previous year with regard to the amount of money they were able to raise and contribute to the campaigns of women. EMILY's List contributed over $6 million to female candidates in 1992; four times greater than their previous record of $1.5 million in 1990. The Women's Campaign Fund almost doubled its previous record level of contributions.[9] Women's interest groups, such as the National Organization for Women and "pro-choice" abortion groups such as NARAL, also mobilized on behalf of female candidates, usually through financial contributions (Nelson 1994).

Another indicator of the unique environment for female candidates was the media's role in promoting the "year of the woman." Some of the notable advances made by women in the elections helped to create a media sensation around all female candidates. Carol Moseley Braun's historic candidacy in Illinois and her election to office as the first black female senator garnered tremendous media coverage (Jelen 1994). The possibility of California becoming the first state to elect two female senators was also the focus of much media attention. During the course of the election and because of the sensation over female candidates, CNN developed the program "Crier and Company," hosted by Catherine Crier (later changed to "CNN and Company"). The program featured political analysis on a wide range of issues but interviewed only female commentators. Other news stations spent considerable time focusing on the role of female candidates. With programming such as this, the media helped to promote the "year of the woman" and the notion that women offered a different perspective on political issues.

Combining with these factors to propel women forward was the high level of discontent expressed by voters. A CBS News/*New York Times* poll taken in March of 1992 showed that only 18 percent of Americans approved of Congress's job performance. The same poll found that 81 percent of Americans were dissatisfied with President Bush's handling of the economy. These levels of voter dissatisfaction represented some of the highest levels recorded since the inception of public opinion polls (Jacobson 1993, 162-164). In addition, in exit polls on election day, almost 80 percent of voters rated the economy as "poor" or "not so good." In the same exit poll, when voters were asked to compare their financial situation with 1988, over 75 percent said their situation was the "same" or "worse." When voters were asked which candidate qualities mattered in their vote for President, the most frequent response was "[The candidate that] will bring about needed change" (Quirk and Dalager 1993, 81). These markers of dissatisfaction help explain the success of the independent presidential candidacy of Ross Perot.[10] Perot, despite a series of campaign blunders, including his controversial and self-damaging withdrawal and reentry into the presidential race, received 19 percent of the presidential vote. Although there is no correlation between Perot voters and supporters of female candidates, Perot's support in 1992 indicates that voters, to a greater extent than in other recent elections, wanted something different.

All of these developments suggest that the conditions surrounding female candidates in 1992 were different from any of the other "year of the woman" elections. The host of congressional scandals, the dissatisfaction with the economy, and the negative job performance of the Republican standard-bearer, President Bush, made voters hungry for change. Female candidates, who were strategically well situated because of all the open seats, were able to capitalize on voters' desire for change. The widespread inclusion of women in the election process and the ensuing coverage of and concentration on female candidates was unlike that of any other time in recent history. Again, nowhere were these trends more apparent than in the California elections. With such a large number of female candidates running for office, California became the center of much of the frenzy over the "year of the woman."

Although women made substantial gains in the 1992 elections in California and across the nation, one of the most important and persistent questions is whether the 1992 elections created a lasting change in the political environment for women, or whether what occurred in 1992 was simply an aberration. Analysis of the 1994 elections offers the first opportunity to assess whether 1992 transformed the electoral environment for female candidates.

The Atmosphere for Female Candidates in 1994

A paradox emerged regarding female candidates in the 1994 elections. Once again, as in 1992, near-record numbers of female candidates received major party nominations for the Senate and House. There were nine female Senate candidates and 112 female House candidates. However, female candidates as a group in 1994 did not receive any of the overt special attention from the media or the parties that they received in 1992. Candidate gender did not arouse any great interest in the 1994 elections, a mere two years after the excitement generated in 1992. *New York Times* reporter Richard Berke (1994) surveyed the 1994 political landscape for female candidates and noted that across the country female candidates were in conflict over whether to use their sex as an issue in the campaign. This dilemma stood in stark contrast to the 1992 elections, when many female candidates across the nation overtly spoke of the need to elect more women. Many of the female candidates with whom Berke spoke believed that appeals to voters based on gender might hurt their candidacies. This dramatic change in the atmosphere for female candidates can be explained by several factors.

First, a clear shift in the partisan preferences of the electorate took place between 1992 and 1994. The partisan shift was coupled with or possibly even partially caused by a tremendous anti-Clinton sentiment that swept the country. Voter surveys showed that more voters were "strongly hostile" to Clinton than viewed him favorably. This translated into about a quarter of the electorate admitting that their vote in the congressional election translated into a vote against Clinton (Greenburg 1994, 3). Democratic congressional candidates' association with Clinton became the subject of Republican attack ads. On election day 1994, Clinton and the Democratic Party experienced their worst performance in congressional elections in over sixty years. Most of the gains in the U.S. House of Representatives by women in 1992 were by Democratic women. Thus the anti-Democratic tide hurt women because thirty-five of the forty-seven women in the House were Democrats. Many of the female House candidates in 1994 were vulnerable first-term incumbents. In the end, eight first-term Democratic women were defeated in the 1994 House elections.

Another shift occurred with regard to how the media and political environment addressed female candidates. By 1994, female candidates were no longer viewed as something new and different. Whereas female voters and activists were spurred on by the Thomas/Hill Hearings in the 1992 election, there were no events of similar magnitude to electrify women in 1994. An advisor to Dawn Clark Netsch, the 1994 Democratic gubernatorial nominee from Illinois, noted, "Women are demoralized for some reason. They aren't coming out with the support that they did two years ago" (Berke 1994, A1). Netsch herself noted: "Nobody is really paying much attention [to candidate gender]. Maybe it's our fault for not having made more of it" (Berke 1994, A1). Candidate gender was not used by candidates or the parties as a means of attracting voters in the 1994 elections.

The final major change in the political atmosphere between 1992 and 1994 concerned issue agendas. The issue agenda that was dominant in most congressional elections in 1994 may have been one of the prevailing reasons for the lack of enthusiasm for female candidates. The 1992 election saw "woman-friendly" issues dominate the political discourse (Burrell 1994). Job creation and health care were among the most important issues in the minds of voters. Abortion was also an important political issue, ranking as one of the most pressing concerns for voters in California (see Table 5.7). However, by the 1994 election season, after a year and a half of highly publicized acts of random violence, crime had become the most important issue for voters (see Chapter 5). Celinda Lake, who has conducted extensive surveys on issue priorities in relation to candidate gender dynamics, found that voters have more confidence in men to address issues such as crime (Berke 1994, B10). Another issue on which voters may prefer to have male leadership is immigration. Immigration fits in with crime, because voters believe that its policies require "cracking down," which they feel that, stereotypically, men are more suited to carry out (see Burrell 1994, 24-25). This issue was especially important in California in 1994, where voters were also voting on Proposition 187, the ballot initiative that sought to deny government services to illegal aliens.

All of these developments helped create an environment that may have stifled the candidacies of women or, at the very least, Democratic women. After the large national electoral gains in 1992, women gained only one Senate seat and no House seats in the 1994 elections. The national patterns discussed previously were indicative of the environment for female candidates in California. In 1992, the support for female candidates and the enthusiasm surrounding their campaigns in California was electrifying. Dianne Feinstein and Barbara Boxer captured both U.S. Senate seats and women increased their representation in the House delegation from three to seven. In 1994, despite almost the same number of female candidates running for the same types of offices, Dianne Feinstein barely won reelection to the Senate—an election she had won by seventeen points two years earlier. Also, gubernatorial candidate Kathleen Brown was squarely defeated and the California House delegation added only one additional female member.

Despite the preceding description of the political climate in 1994, a number of analyses have argued that 1994 was a good year for female candidates (Matthews 1995; Mandel, Kleeman, and Baruch 1995; Mott 1995). These commentators suggest that in light of the high number of defeats for first-term Democratic female incumbents, female candidates did very well to maintain their 1992 levels in the U.S. Congress. Mandel, Kleeman, and Baruch note that what occurred in 1994 was a partisan balancing, which means that different women's voices will be heard (1995, 10). Before the 1994 elections there were thirty-five Democrats and twelve Republicans; after the election the gap narrowed to thirty Democrats and seventeen Republicans. Matthews even goes as far as to suggest that "one might propose [1994 as] the year of the Republican woman" (1995, 6). The 1994 election did mark the first substantial infusion of conservative women into Congress.[11] If women are going to ever become fully included into the governing institutions of the United States, they are going to have to become influential in both parties, not just among the Democrats.

Notes

1. For a recent assessment of women's economic status in American society, see McGlen and O'Connor (1995, chapters 3 and 4).

2. In their platforms and public positions during the 1992 general campaign, both parties discussed family issues as "women's issues." For a description of how the parties treated family issues, see *Los Angeles Times*, "Bush vs. Clinton: The 'Year of the Woman'—and of Families," 5 October 1992.

3. The debate over the treatment of groups by the Constitution has many sides. Fiss (1976) offers only one perspective, but most analyses at least acknowledge that the language of the Constitution is individualistic in nature. For other viewpoints see Brest (1976), Perry (1979), Ely (1980), and Lawrence (1987).

4. For a summary of the role of the public/private dichotomy in political debate, see Pateman (1989, chapter 6).

5. Kathlene rightly points out that we must remember that Gilligan has created ideal types that are a "gross simplification" of the complex nature of gendered behavior. (Kathlene 1995, 698). In two later works, Gilligan has more thoroughly added context and explanation for the different voices that she first wrote about in 1982. See *Mapping the Moral Domain: A Contribution of Women's Thinking to Psychological Theory and Education*, 1988; and *Making Connections: The Relational Worlds of Adolescent Girls at Emma Willard School*, 1990. Although Gilligan modifies her original ideas in these works, the general constructs remain intact.

6. There is now a large body of literature that has found gender differences in policy interests, leadership styles, and priorities of male and female political figures. Other examples include Thomas (1994), Berkman and O'Connor (1993), Reingold (1992), Dodson and Carroll (1991), Tolleson Rinehart (1991), Kathlene (1989), Saint-Germain (1989), and Mezey (1978).

7. The performance of female candidates in California will be discussed fully in Chapter 5. For a complete summary of how female candidates fared in House elections throughout the United States in 1992, see Jacobson (1993, 170-74).

8. Based on an interview with the California director of the Democratic Congressional Campaign Committee, September 7, 1992, anonymous.

9. Campaign financing will be discussed further in Chapter 4. For a summary of the increased involvement of women's PACs in 1992, see Carpini and Fuchs (1993, 29-36) or Burrell (1994, 129).

10. Success here has to be measured in relative terms: Ross Perot was the most successful (in terms of popular vote) presidential candidate not nominated by one of the two major parties since Theodore Roosevelt ran in 1912.

11. For instance, Republican Representatives Helen Chenoweth of Idaho, Barbara Cubin of Wyoming, Sue Myrick of North Carolina, and Andrea Seastrand of California are all considered ardent conservatives within the "freshman class" of 1994 House members.

Women and Men
on the Campaign Trail

summary p 55

In California and across the country in 1992, pundits and media commentators expected the infusion of female candidates to provide an alternative to status-quo politics. Many questions arose about how women would differ as candidates. Would women have different campaign styles? Would female candidates attack their opponents in different ways? Would women employ different campaign strategies? Harriet Woods, president of the National Women's Political Caucus, listed several of the stereotypical expectations about female candidates in an editorial a few months before the 1992 election (Woods 1992). One, female candidates would refrain from negative campaigning. Two, women would set a higher standard of behavior within a campaign by offering a more honest and less manipulative presentation to voters. Three, female candidates would engage in a more conciliatory style of politics in which women would be less combative and more willing to compromise than men. In sum, women entering the political arena would not be deceitful and uncompromising politicians, but would be principled and candid participants (Woods 1992). These stereotypes suggest that women are fundamentally different in nature from men. However, many gender politics scholars have argued that any differences in the campaign styles of men

17

and women are driven not by fundamental differences in the personal qualities of the candidates but by the candidates' reactions to the political environment.

In one recent analysis, Kathleen Hall Jamieson (1995) has argued that women in the public eye are caught in a double bind. The *double bind* in this sense refers to the idea that women who choose to enter public life must successfully fill two roles, one as mother and caretaker of her family, and two, as an extra-competent public servant. Women must be extra competent because when they step out into the public eye they will be more heavily scrutinized. The problem or "bind" arises because these two roles, as they have historically been constructed, are often incompatible. Women must maintain their stereotypically feminine qualities while also competing in a forum that does not embrace the traditional conception of women's roles. A woman must be perceived as a good mother or wife while at the same time showing the toughness and tenacity to be an effective campaigner and legislator. Voters still possess many traditional notions about "female" and "male" traits, which make it difficult for women to break out of their roles and be accepted by the various components of the political process. The consequence of the double bind is twofold. First, women have to be perceived as successful in more social roles than their male counterparts, which makes it more difficult for women to compete effectively. In essence, as several campaign managers for female candidates in this study noted, women have to be better at more of the qualities necessary for running for office (these managers' comments are explored in Chapter 6). Second, the increased challenges facing women may have the effect of turning away many well-qualified female candidates who choose not to be encumbered by the unfair burden that women must endure when they enter public life. This is certainly a problem faced by women in many different realms of public life, but it is undoubtedly heightened in politics where scrutiny is much more intense.

The next two chapters assess these gender dynamics and the role of traditional stereotyping by examining behavioral differences in female and male candidates in the California election process. By focusing on the experiences of the candidates, it becomes clear that traditional socialization is the cause of many of the different experiences of women and men. This chapter compares the motivation, strategies, and behavior of female and male candidates. The analysis is broken down into six sections: first, a discussion of the factors that motivate candidates to enter a race for elective office;

second, a description of the campaign organizations formed by women and men; third, an analysis and comparison of the strategic objectives of female and male candidates; fourth, a comparison of the specific campaigning styles of female and male candidates; fifth, an analysis of the voter targeting strategies of the candidates; and sixth, an examination of how male candidates respond to having a female opponent.

Motivations for Entering the Campaign diff

Why did these women and men choose to run for office? In this study there were sixty-six candidates (25 women and 41 men) who made the decision to challenge an incumbent or run for an open seat in the U.S. Congress. Understanding why they chose to enter a campaign is important for a number of reasons. For instance, some analyses suggest (Darcy, Welch, and Clark 1994) that the election process is a level playing field for men and women, and that increasing the number of female candidates is the best solution for remedying women's underrepresentation in positions of political power. Thus, examining candidates' motivations may increase our understanding of the continuing disparity in the number of women and men serving in elected positions. In addition, studying candidate motivation provides insights into the political socialization of men and women. Candidates' reasons for running for office may expose how they conceive of political activism. The existence of gender differences in socialization toward politics may also help us to understand the continued underrepresentation of women in elective office.

The campaign managers for the congressional candidates were first asked to describe what they believed was their candidate's primary motivation for entering the race. The maagers cited three types of motivation. First, many managers offered the ambiguous and generic response that the candidate was "committed to public service" or wanted to "make government better." About one-third of the sixty-six challengers' campaign managers gave this type of response. This often came across as the stock answer pulled from the bag of political clichés. For instance, when one seasoned campaign manager was asked about his candidate's motivation for entering the race, he responded with sarcasm: "Commitment to public service, of course." The public service response had a superficial quality for some candidates, but many of the managers were sincere in explaining their candidate's desire to improve the general welfare of the country. Nonetheless, the "public service"

Table 2.1   Primary Motivation of Challengers Running for Office

	Female Challengers (25)	*Male Challengers* (41)
Primary Motivation:		
"Commitment to public service"	16%**	43%
Political ambition	20*	37
Specific issue or ideological concerns	52**	17

NOTE: Columns do not add up to 100% because of other miscellaneous responses left out of the table.
*$p < .10$; **$p < .01$ (one-tailed t-test).

answer had two common aspects: the candidate expressed a desire to "do good" and the candidate provided no specific explanation of the meaning of "doing good."

The second type of motivation offered by campaign managers was the candidates' desire to acquire political power. Candidates coded into this category said they were motivated to run for office because they had always wanted to be in Congress. Other candidates in this category said they ran because the election presented a good opportunity for winning. A little less than a third of the managers for challengers gave this "political ambition" response. None of the candidates who were motivated by political ambition stated any particular reason for running other than the desire to hold office or win the election.

The final type of response attributed candidates' motivations to a specific policy issue or ideological concern. These candidates entered the race to fight for issues that were important to them. Again, about a third of the challengers' managers offered issue concerns as the prime motivating factor. When the challengers' responses are broken down by candidate gender, some important differences emerge. Table 2.1 offers a comparison of the motivations of female and male challengers in this study. Table 2.1 is only broken down by sex and not party affiliation because comparisons between Democrats and Republicans revealed no differences in the types of motivations they acknowledged.

Male challengers were significantly more likely to give the public service or political ambition response. Female challengers were significantly more likely to identify specific issues or ideological concerns as reasons for entering the election. The broad differences exhibited in Table 2.1 are examined further in the following pages.

Issue Concerns and Ideological Considerations

Female and male candidates in this study offered very different reasons for deciding to become candidates for public office. Many women identified specific reasons for entering the race for public office, whereas men were more likely to rely on general statements of wanting to "do good." Over half of the women in this study offered specific ideological or policy concerns as the motivating force for their decision to enter the race. Less than a fifth of male candidates did the same. Furthermore, several of the issues that motivated women were not mentioned as motivating factors by any male candidates, Republican or Democrat. For instance, one female candidate running in an inner-city district entered the race to promote education. Her campaign manager described her candidate's passion about this issue:

> This is a very poor district. . . . [The candidate] believes that improving the educational system is the only way to change the lives of the people here. She got in the race to change the way people think about the public education system. This issue has been the basis for her life-long interest in politics.

The campaign manager for a female candidate running in central California explained how his candidate came to run for Congress:

> Several years ago she went to Africa to help on a hunger relief effort. What she saw completely changed her life and pushed her towards public life. The politics of hunger caused her to get involved and run for Congress. I think her dream is to someday, as a government official, go back and help those people. She really wants to end human suffering.

A female candidate from northern California explained why she decided to run for Congress:

> The environment was being destroyed. I could not stand by and watch our valley and the coasts continue to deteriorate under current policy. When I see the environmental devastation that our congressman presided over, I just can't take it anymore.

All three of these candidates were motivated by specific issues that they felt strongly about. The issue concerns for these women are distinctly "liberal" causes. However, none of the male challengers in the study, including the liberal Democrats, expressed focused passion over issues such as these. The few male challengers who were motivated by issues to enter their race were concerned with economic- or business-related issues such as NAFTA, taxes, and government regulation. The notion that male and female politicians have different motivations for running for office has been found in previous research. Darcy, Welch, and Clark (1994), calculating data compiled by Welch and Bledsoe (1988), found that women running for city council positions were significantly more likely than male council candidates to be motivated by an "issue concern" (1994, 39). Darcy, Welch, and Clark attribute this difference to women's greater involvement with and support from single-issue groups (40). This potentially explains the behavior of female candidates in this study, although their level of support from single-issue interest groups was not determined.

In addition to using specific issues as a springboard for their candidacies, women had larger causes motivating their candidacies. For instance, two female candidates were motivated to run because of concerns over the representation of women. The manager for a female candidate running in northern California in 1992 stated,

> The Supreme Court confirmation hearings of Clarence Thomas showed that Congress was completely out of touch with women. It was the trigger to get my candidate into the race. She really feels strongly about breaking up the old boys network in Washington.

This candidate was following the examples of U.S. Senate candidates Carol Moseley Braun in Illinois and Lynn Yeakel in Pennsylvania, who both used the Thomas/Hill confirmation hearings to ride to surprising primary victories prior to the 1992 California primary (Jelen 1994; Hansen 1994). The other female candidate who was motivated by gender concerns entered the race in 1994 because of her opponent's attitude toward women:

> He [the incumbent] comes across as such a backward redneck. He has made so many atrocious statements about women and gays. . . . He once said that we should consider quarantining gays. . . . He has all but defended the Navy's behavior in the Tailhook scandal. . . . Somebody had to get in there and challenge him. The deadline to file [to run] approached and it looked like nobody was going to run. . . . I couldn't stand the thought of him running unopposed.

These two female candidates entered the race because of what they perceived as the lack of representation for "women's issues." Similarly, two other female challengers entered the race because of their opponent's support of the Christian Coalition. The manager for one of these women noted,

She got in the race to stop the Christian Coalition from taking over the politics of the district. To put it nicely she views them as extremist nuts. Well I guess that isn't too nice—she originally became aware of the radical fundamentalists when they took over a majority of positions on the school board. The congressman in the district is fully supportive of the religious extremists. She really fears the extremists taking over our schools and setting women back.

A theme common among all of these statements is that female candidates viewed their candidacies as part of a cause. All of these women entered the race to forward or stop specific concerns or agendas. Along similar lines, some female candidates said they entered the race only to provide an alternative to the incumbent. As one female candidate commented,

My opponent is so detestable, I wanted voters to have another choice. Even though there was little chance of my winning I wanted to get my message out and educate voters abut this guy.

Or as the manager for another candidate stated,

The congressman's voting record is terrible. His extremeness coaxed her into the race. She doesn't understand how anyone who knows anything about [the incumbent] could possibly vote for him.

Another female candidate became very concerned when she found out that the filing date for entrance to the primary had passed and that no Democrats were running against the heavily favored Republican incumbent. She decided to run a write-in campaign for the primary. California law allows write-in candidates to be placed on the general election ballot if they receive over 1,500 votes in the primary (she received over 1,800). Her campaign manager explained why she went to these lengths:

She had wanted to run for the seat in Congress, but she felt she was not ready and assumed someone else would challenge the incumbent . . . when she learned that no one was going to challenge, she felt she had to try to offer an alternative. . . . Can you imagine the lengths we went to trying to run a write-in campaign in a primary? It was difficult to find any interested voters. She worked tirelessly just to make sure that she got the 1,500 votes necessary to qualify to be placed on the general election ballot. She wanted voters to have another option in the general election.

Several of these female candidates ran campaigns knowing they could not win but feeling that it was important to give voters a choice. Overall, five out of twenty-five female challengers (20%), but only one out of forty-one male challengers (2%) said they got into the race simply to provide an alternative for voters. Although these candidates were acting as "sacrificial lambs," it was not because they were recruited by the party but because they saw some value in running despite the prospect of almost certain defeat.

Early studies of the electoral opportunities for women argued that women were much more likely to be put forward by their party only in unwinnable elections (Jennings and Thomas 1966; Lamson 1968). More recent examinations of gender differences in elections with a "sacrificial lamb" running have not found bias against women (Darcy, Welch, and Clark 1994). However, there is still some speculation that Republican women are more often slated as "sacrificial lambs" (Berch 1994; Carroll 1994). The elections in California do not in any way suggest that the increase in female candidates led to more women running against safe incumbents. In fact, in California, women were more likely than men to run for the open and new seats—the more desirable electoral opportunities. However, many of the female candidates running for unwinnable seats in the California congressional elections viewed their candidacies as important to the process, not as throw-away efforts with no real importance.

Conversely, whereas many of the women based their candidacies on policy issues and political causes, the male candidates in this study were much more likely to make broad and ambiguous claims about how they were committed to public service. For instance, one manager stated,

> This may sound corny, but he just believes in giving something back to the community. He has been very successful in his life and now he feels it is his duty to try be a force for change in our society.

Or as another manager noted,

> He has dedicated his life to service and helping people. He wants to go to Washington and fix what is broken—he believes he can make a real difference.

The manager for a San Francisco area male candidate stated her candidate's motivation:

> For him it is a matter of honor to serve his country. He has made a lot of money in his life and he is a patriot. He wants to give back to the society that allowed him to succeed.

These male candidates were motivated by ideals such as "duty," "honor," and "service," language not used by the managers for female candidates. Further, the stated motivations of women and men appeared to have nothing to do with their chances of winning the election. One might expect that the chance of winning might alter some peoples' motivations or motivate different types of candidates to enter the race. However, both the female candidates who were likely winners and those who were likely losers expressed similar types of motivations. The same was true of the male candidates' motivations (see Chapter 5 for a recounting of the election results).

The different motivations of women and men are consistent with literature asserting that women and men have different conceptions of politics. The male candidates were more likely to conceive of things in broad or abstract terms and the women were more likely to conceive of problems in contextual or concrete terms. These findings present a good fit with Gilligan's original conception of different social orientations between women and men (1982). In discussing their reasons for running, women were far more likely to be motivated by a particular issue that apparently demonstrated their care and concern for others. Conversely, the male candidates demonstrated a stronger sense of hierarchy in their desire to enter Congress, often seeing the election as an opportunity to seize a better position than they were currently holding. Similarly, Astin and Leland (1991), in a study of female leaders in the field of education, found that female leaders were more likely to embody a passionate commitment to specific problems. Although the Astin and Leland study is narrow and does not include elected officials, the characteristic they identify is consistent with the idea that female candidates are more often driven by commitment to a particular cause (see, also, Dodson and Carroll 1991). This is not to say that women are morally superior to men because their motivations for running for office appear more concretely oriented toward public service and less self-aggrandizing. Such a view has been argued before by noted political scientists in the 1950s (Lane 1959; Riesman 1956). These early examinations suggested that women were more "moralistic" than men and thus tended to shy away from the petty and nasty elements of politics. By today's standards this explanation of moral differences between men and women is very problematic. The early analyses finding that women were more moral were essentialist claims about fundamental differences in the social and political belief systems of women and men. Instead, the differences may lie more clearly in how men and women have been socialized toward political involvement. The view being propagated in this analysis is that matters of social construction are what, in many cases, have caused women and men to behave differently as candidates.

The women in this study often had deep interests in substantive issues that were important to the community in which they were living. This is consistent with studies showing that women are more likely to get involved in politics through community-level interests and causes (Burrell 1994, 66-80). The men in this study also had deep interests in helping the community but they were often not linked to specific objectives. Men have been socialized to conceive of public service in terms of office holding. The socialization patterns of men and women go a lot further in explaining motivational differences than the notion that women and men differ along moral lines.

Levels of Political Ambition

The other gender difference that emerges in Table 2.1 is that male candidates express higher levels of direct political ambition. Bledsoe and Herring (1990), in a panel study of city council members, found similar differences in the political ambitions of women and men. Their study attempted to determine under what circumstances council members would attempt to pursue higher office. They found that women were more likely to be influenced by the "strength of their current political position" and "their perception of vulnerability" (221). Men were more likely to be "self-motivated—guided by political ambition" (221).[1] Similarly, the male candidates in the California congressional elections were more likely than the female candidates to make winning the election and attaining a position of political power their top priority. For instance, one manager commented,

> [The candidate] has always wanted to move from the state legislature to Washington. When he learned [the incumbent] was retiring he moved quickly—almost a year and a half before the election—to secure his party's nomination. He wants to keep moving up.

Another manager more clearly stated his candidate's motivation:

> He loves the idea of being a Congressman and has always wanted to be a Congressman. It has been his dream for a long time. He has been talking about it for years.

In addition to these statements of political ambition, male candidates were also more likely to say they entered the race because of the favorable political opportunity that the race presented. The manager for a central California candidate noted,

> When the lines were redrawn, our city fell into a brand new district and he thought this might be the best chance he would ever have to win a seat. So he took the plunge.

Another candidate said he had been waiting a long time to make a run:

> I thought it was a good year to take a shot at Congress. The district had changed a little with redistricting. . . . The congressman had become a little inattentive so I thought I would do it. I have had my eye on the seat just waiting for the right time to give it a try.

One possible explanation for the male candidates' greater emphasis on political opportunism and ambition is that the female candidates in the study were less ambitious than the male candidates. In addition to the Bledsoe and Herring (1990) study, a number of additional investigations have found that male political actors may have higher levels of political ambition than women. Carroll (1994, 123-24) found that the majority of women in her 1976 survey of female candidates did not see themselves staying in politics beyond twelve years. Certainly more than twelve years is required to successfully acquire top elective positions. Further, Burt-Way and Kelly (1991, 23), in a mail survey of Arizona elected officials, found that female elected officials believed that they had fewer career choices. Thus the women in their study were more likely to retain local office than similarly situated men (see, also, Fowler and McClure 1989; Carroll 1985). These studies measure ambition in a fairly narrow manner. Ambition is defined as the desire, expressed as a decision-making process, to choose to seek higher offices. Ambition is operationalized in terms of how badly one wants to climb the political ladder. This is a one-dimensional way to measure political ambition that would tend to discount the efforts of politically ambitious people who chose not to run for office. Thus, there are several other possible explanations for the lower levels of stated ambition by the female candidates in this study. First, women have not been socialized to express ambition in such a direct manner. The traditional socialization of the sex roles does not encourage women to be openly calculating and aggressive in the professional political arena. A second explanation, one that seems most applicable to the candidates in this study, is that men and women are ambitious in different ways. Men view politics and elections as a means to acquire power and to "serve" their country or community. Conversely, women view politics as an opportunity to forward a cause and fight for an issue (see, also, Astin and Leland 1991).

The different motivations exhibited by men and women in this study may provide a valuable explanation for why women have been slow to break into the upper echelons of elective office. Women can fight for their cause or issue without running for office, whereas male ambition is more likely to be fulfilled by seeking to hold positions of political power. This leads to the assessment that the full incorporation of women in the electoral process is not something that will occur soon. Similarly, Bledsoe and Herring (1990), in their study of city council members, write, "the barriers women face in achieving anything approaching proportionate political representation are certainly more numerous, and probably more onerous, than previously recognized" (221). They are in essence arguing that gender comparisons of attitude-based indicators about political ambition are not accurate in measuring the differing goals of women and men, because women and men conceive of ambition in different ways (220). Thus, in comparing the motivations and ambitions of congressional candidates in California with those found in other recent investigations, we see that women and men often have strongly differing orientations toward political involvement. However, what appears to be happening, particularly in 1992, is that women are beginning to use races for electoral office as a means of fighting for their causes instead of staying out of the electoral arena and only remaining active in community and single-issue groups.

 ## Campaign Organizations

After deciding to enter the race, the next concern for candidates is assembling a campaign organization. In competitive races the effectiveness of the campaign organization is of crucial importance.[2] One potential explanation for why women have not succeeded in electoral politics in greater numbers is that they have not had the same experience assembling effective campaign organizations (Darcy, Welch, and Clark 1994, 36-44). There is still a great deal we do not know about what makes an effective campaign. As the old political adage goes, "fifty percent of all money spent in a campaign is

Table 2.2   Scope and Size of Campaign Organization, by Gender and Challenger
Status

	Female Challengers		Male Challengers		Male Incumbents	
	1992	1994	1992	1994	1992	1994
	(16)	(9)	(28)	(13)	(16)	(19)
Active volunteers[a]	387	128	188	120	263	138
Paid staff	6.7	3.3	3.3	4.2	3.6	3.2
Political consultants[b]	1.7	2.1	1.1	2.0	1.4	2.1
Campaign offices[c]	.9	1.5	.8	1.2	1.1	1.2

NOTE: The entries represent the mean for each category.
a. Active volunteers were classified as individuals who put in a minimum of ten hours' work on the campaign.
b. Political consultants include pollsters, fund-raising, media, and direct mail.
c. Campaign offices were considered those that were set up specifically to run the campaign and had open access to the public. Candidates who used their home or place of business as a campaign office were not counted.

wasted; the only problem is, we do not know which fifty percent." Although measuring the effectiveness of a campaign is difficult, we can look at some indicators, such as the size of the campaign and the type of professional staff. Table 2.2 compares the size and professionalization of the campaign organizations for male and female candidates in 1992 and 1994.

Table 2.2 shows that the campaigns of female challengers were far more extensive than the campaigns of male challengers in 1992, but that the campaigns of all challengers had similar characteristics in 1994. We would expect incumbents to have larger pools of volunteers and more professional campaigns. Incumbents are established in their districts and are able to attract more district-level support. The level of professionalization should remain constant for the incumbents as their reelection campaigns become routinized. However, the extent of the campaign organizations for female challengers in 1992 was substantially larger than those of both male challengers and incumbents. The larger size of the professional staffs for women in 1992 can be explained by the fact that female challengers had more money than male challengers (see Chapter 4). However, more money cannot account for the staggering difference in the number of volunteers in 1992. The heightened excitement over female candidates in 1992 is clearly illustrated by the number of volunteers female candidates were able to motivate. Female challengers in 1992 had twice as many volunteers as male challengers and 50 percent more volunteers than male incumbents. The explanation for why women were able to attract so many volunteers in 1992 emerged in several of the interviews. Two managers for female candidates directly mentioned the effect of the Thomas/Hill Hearings:

> Many more women are coming forward this year to volunteer for the campaign, and many of them said that the spectacle of the Thomas/Hill hearings was largely responsible. In many ways you can feel the buzz or excitement around the candidate. It was not like this last year.

> [A great number of] women came to our campaign in the wake of the Thomas/Hill hearings and asked what they could do to help. There was a tremendous outpouring of support from women in our district; it was really something—women wanted more women in Washington.

Another manager stated,

> Women in the electorate, at least the activists, seemed more galvanized and energetic than ever. They wanted to get more women elected. We had all the volunteers we needed and they were almost all women.

In 1992, the Thomas/Hill hearings and the media focus on female candidates energized female voters. However, by 1994 the enthusiasm that brought volunteers to the campaigns of female candidates in 1992 had disappeared. The campaign manager for a female candidate who ran in both 1992 and 1994 saw the difference: "It was completely dead out there this year [1994]." We must not forget the historical uniqueness of 1992. This was probably the only election cycle in history where, for some areas of the campaign such as attracting volunteers, it was a definite advantage to be a woman.

Organizational demographics such as those in Table 2.2 do not offer insight into the overall effectiveness of men's and women's campaigns. However, if female candidates are assembling campaigns of a similar magnitude and making use of political professionals in the same proportions as male candidates, then it certainly suggests that their campaigns are comparably sophisticated. Darcy, Welch, and Clark (1994) have investigated the possibility that women run less effective campaigns. In local-level elections they found that female candidates were as likely as male candidates to receive campaign support from labor, business, and political parties (39). In another measure of campaign effectiveness, Darcy, Welch, and Clark, used 1982 American National Election Study Post-Election Survey data from congressional districts to explore how effective male and female congressional candidates were in establishing name recognition and contacting voters during the course of a campaign. They found that there was no difference in the level of voter name recognition for male and female candidates and that voters were in fact significantly more likely to recall having been contacted by a female candidate than a male candidate (85-87). These indicators and the organizational demographics of the women in this study certainly suggest that women and men are running comparably sophisticated and effective campaigns. Thus any speculation that women have less ability to wage effective campaigns may be discarded.

Strategic Priorities and Communicating With the Voters

Once the candidate has made the decision to run and begun setting up the campaign organization, the next set of questions involve strategy and campaign techniques. The goals that a campaign must pursue are clear. Darcy, Welch, and Clark (1994) view campaigns as striving to accomplish two goals: one, achieve recognition for the candidate, and two, establish a favorable image for the candidate. Jacobson (1992) adds a third objective by noting that a campaign must also get the pool of citizens favoring the candidate to the polls. Thus, the question for this analysis is whether men and women strive to achieve these election goals in the same manner.

In pursuing these goals, campaigns must make several decisions. What are the strategic priorities of the campaign? How will the campaign communicate with voters? To answer the first question, the campaign managers in this study were asked to identify what they viewed as the central strategic goals of their campaign. Several recurring objectives emerged in the interviews, and the results are reported in Table 2.3. Each entry indicates the percentage of campaign managers who stated that a given item was a central strategic objective. The table is divided into three categories of candidates: female challengers, male challengers, and male incumbents. There were nine objectives that were mentioned by more than one campaign manager (most campaign managers mentioned two or three central strategic objectives). The nine objectives were categorized into three general areas: message, organization, and tactics.

Although there were some statistically significant differences, for the most part men and women had similar strategic objectives. In the first category, organizational objectives, there were no substantial differences between

Table 2.3   Central Strategic Objectives of Candidates, by Gender and Challenger
Status

	Female Challengers (25)	Male Challengers (41)	Male Incumbents (35)
Organizational priorities			
Build a strong organization	4%	0%	11%
Raise funds	16	12	6
Receive party support	4	10	3
Message priorities			
Focus on opponent's record	52	41	17
Focus on own record	48*	32	57
Tactical priorities			
Establish name recognition	32	32	3
Target specific voter groups	8**	32	11
Get out the vote	4	12	17
Utilize free media	8	2	0

NOTES: Each entry indicates percentage of candidates who employed this tactic as a central aspect of their
campaign strategy. Difference of means test comparing the female and male challengers.
*$p < .10$; **$p < .05$ (one-tailed t-test).

female and male candidates. Female and male candidates were equally likely
to emphasize raising money, building an organization, and seeking party
support. There is nothing surprising about these similarities because the
central components of what it takes to win an election are the same for
women and men and thus it would be expected that their organizational
priorities would be the same. However, what is obscured by the similar
results for women and men presented in the "organizational priorities"
section of Table 2.3 is the different feelings and perceptions women and men
have about engaging in these campaign activities. These differences, particularly in terms of party support and fund-raising, are examined in Chapter 4.

Table 2.3 shows some difference between women and men in the second
category, message priorities. Women were more likely than men to focus the
message of their campaigns on the opposing candidate's record and their own
record. Over half of the women in this survey made focusing on their
opponent's record a priority, and around 40 percent of men did the same (this
difference was not significant). Women were also more likely than men to
prioritize presenting their own record to the voters (this difference was of
borderline significance). These differences suggest that women are some-

what more likely to make the campaign a battle over political records. This finding contradicts much of the popular wisdom suggesting that women are less likely to aggressively go after their opponent's record (Woods 1992).

In the final category, tactical priorities, there were no statistically significant differences between female and male challengers in terms of establishing name recognition, getting out the vote, and using free media. Again, these similarities are not surprising because these are basic components of running a successful campaign. However, male challengers were significantly more likely than female challengers to make targeting a specific group of voters a strategic priority. The most persuasive explanation for why female candidates were less likely to prioritize targeting voters is that they may have viewed their candidacy as a natural link to certain voting blocs such as women and minorities. Campaign managers for fifteen of the twenty-nine (52%) female candidates in this study believed that they had a significant advantage in appealing to female voters. Furthermore, nineteen of the twenty-three (83%) men running against women believed female candidates had an advantage with female voters. Therefore, male candidates may have felt a greater need to target particular groups of voters. The subject of targeting voters deserves more attention and is discussed on the following pages.

Once the campaign has clarified its objectives, it must determine how it will communicate with voters. The central decision in presenting the candidate and the candidate's message to the voters is selecting the means of political communication.[3] As mentioned previously, Darcy, Welch, and Clark (1994) have shown that women reach out to voters as effectively as men during the course of a campaign. In this study, the campaign managers were asked to list, in order of importance, which modes of political communication they employed in the campaign. The top half of Table 2.4 illustrates the modes of communication employed by the candidates and the bottom half identifies which mode of political communication the manager regarded as the campaign's top priority. The candidates were categorized by challenger status and gender. Again, there were no differences based on party, so a breakdown by party was excluded from the analysis.

The top of Table 2.4 illustrates that men and women do not differ in the types of media they use to reach voters. Of the seven most widely used modes of political communication, television ads, radio ads, phone banks, direct mail, walking literature, personal contact, and free media, there were no significant disparities between female and male challengers. As expected,

Table 2.4   Forms of Media Candidates Used to Communicate With Voters, by Gender and Challenger Status

	Female Challengers (25)	Male Challengers (41)	Male Incumbents (35)
Political communication employed by each campaign			
Television advertisements[a]	40%	41%	57%
Radio advertisements	28	24	54
Phone banks	44	35	37
Direct mail	76	73	89
Walking literature	36	43	37
Personal contact	80	80	66
Free media	48	34	14
Most important form of political communication			
Television advertisements[b]	12	15	20
Radio advertisements	4	2	9
Phone banks	4	2	3
Direct mail	20*	39	49
Walking literature	4	5	6
Personal contact	48**	24	9
Free media	8	5	3

NOTE: Difference of means test comparing the female and male challengers.
a. Each entry indicates percentage of candidates who employed this medium as part of their means of communication.
b. Each entry indicates percentage of candidates who said this medium of communication was their top priority.
*$p < .10$; **$p < .05$ (one-tailed t-test).

incumbents, who have more substantial financial resources than challengers, made greater use of radio, television, and direct mail. Both female and male challengers were more likely than incumbents to adopt a free media strategy to communicate with voters.

However, for the bottom half of Table 2.4, where the most important mode of political communication is listed, there were important differences between female and male challengers. Female challengers, by a ratio of two to one over male challengers, made personal voter contact their number-one priority. Personal contact was defined as any campaign activity where the candidate met with or spoke directly to voters, such as speeches, handshaking events, canvassing door to door, and so forth. Whereas female challengers emphasized personal contact, male challengers were significantly more likely to use direct mail as their most important form of political communication. Direct mail is rapidly becoming the most commonly used type of paid political communication in district-level elections. Almost 50 percent of incumbents said direct mail was their most important form of communication. In district-level races in heavily populated areas, direct mail is the most practical form of mass media. Television and radio are too expensive and congressional districts and television and radio markets rarely overlap.

The finding that women were more likely to prioritize personal campaigning might be suspect because the mode of political communication chosen by campaigns often depends on the amount of money and resources a candidate possesses. If women raised less money they would be reliant on less expensive means of getting their message out, such as personal contact. However, as shown in Chapter 4, for the most part the female candidates in this examination had greater financial resources than their male counterparts.[4] Thus, women in this study were more likely to emphasize grassroots campaigning in which meeting as many voters as possible was an important strategic objective. For instance, during her primary campaign, one candidate spent every weekend standing by herself in front of supermarkets meeting voters and passing out literature:

> Every Saturday and Sunday I would gather up a big stack of campaign flyers and go to supermarkets in the district. My opponents don't understand how I won the primary . . . but it is because I actually spent time meeting with people.

Or as the manager for another female candidate noted,

> Our campaign was a grassroots effort from beginning to end. Having the candidate meet as many voters as possible was our top objective. We built an outreach program with phone banks and precinct walking—we wanted to visit every house in the district at least once.

Several male candidates made precinct walking an important part of their strategy, but clearly a larger percentage of women in the study took an interest in meeting constituents and bringing them into the campaign.

Female candidates' emphasis on contact with voters is consistent with Dodson and Carroll's (1991) study of female and male state legislators. Dodson and Carroll found that women were much more likely than men to look to the input of "concerned citizens" in determining their legislative priorities (77-78). They further found that both women and men believed that female officeholders permitted economically disadvantaged groups greater access to the legislative process (79). Similarly, Abrams Beck (1991), in interviews with city council members, found that female council members were more likely than male council members to show greater attention to constituent services (107). The attitude of the female legislators and council members in those studies parallels the desire of the female candidates in this study who wanted to get out, meet the voters, and consider their input.

What is the importance of female political actors' desires for greater community and constituent involvement in the political process? On a broad level it suggests that the women in this study were more likely than the men to encourage democratic principles. The women apparently wanted more citizen involvement and were more likely than men to want to debate the issues. Female candidates seemed to have a greater desire to take their case directly to the people. This certainly suggests a preference for grassroots campaigning as opposed to presentations coming purely through the paid media. Ultimately, the best explanation for female candidates' greater desire to engage the voters directly is rooted in their politically socialized belief in community-based politics. Beginning with the first rumblings of the suffrage movement in the U.S., women have shown a tendency to engage in politics at the local level (McGlen and O'Connor 1995, 75-76). Local-level politics undoubtedly requires more direct interaction with people than does national- or state-level politics. Whether the preference by female candidates for greater voter contact is really having much of an affect in electoral outcomes is difficult to determine. Referring back to the top half of Table 2.4, we see that male and female candidates are using the same campaign tools in roughly the same proportions; therefore, women's greater desire for "personal contact" with voters may only be an attitudinal preference with little real effect on how the campaigns are waged. Nonetheless, one could assume that if enough women became involved in politics, it could change the norms of how campaigns are waged.

Style of Campaigning

Although a great deal of literature has documented differences in the behavior of female and male legislators, gender differences on the campaign trail are much more difficult to systematically assess. The activities in an election are not recorded in ways that allow methodical compilation and comparison. There are no records of decisions made in campaigns and we are often left with only personal accounts and anecdotal evidence about what transpired. For this study, campaign managers in races with female candidates were asked an identical set of questions about how their candidate campaigned. The managers were first asked the question: "Do you believe women campaign in ways different from that of men?" Of the fifty-two campaign managers who were involved in a race with a female candidate, thirty-nine (75%) believed that female candidates did in fact campaign differently from male candidates. But these same managers often had a difficult time pinpointing what the differences were. In many cases, the managers felt something was different about the race, but they were not exactly sure what it was. During the course of the interviews it became clear that campaign managers were often reticent about discussing these differences because they did not want to convey the perception that they were sexist. Further, the complexity of gender dynamics in the campaigns often eluded some of the managers. Despite the hesitancy of the campaign managers, two differences between the campaign styles of women and men came through in the interviews: the use of life experiences while campaigning and the degree of negative campaigning.

"Personal Campaigning" and Different Life Experiences

One of the most prevalent expectations about female candidates preceding the 1992 elections was that they would bring a different style of campaigning to the electoral arena (Woods 1992). As it turned out, the female candidates in this study engaged in more personal campaigning. *Personal campaigning* is defined as campaigning in which a candidate spends time interacting with and openly discussing his or her experiences with the voters. For the candidates in this study, women on the campaign trail were more likely than men to discuss what have traditionally been considered private issues. Male candidates, even when discussing their private lives, tended to focus on experiences that have traditionally been suited to the public realm, such as military and business experience. These differences indicate many of the different life experiences of women and men. This difference in the level of personal campaigning is one of the most prominent gender differences in the campaign styles of women and men. In conducting the interviews in this investigation, the idea that women and men bring different styles and experiences to the campaign trail was initially confirmed by a campaign manager who had worked for several female candidates in California:

> All the women I have worked for have tended to use their own intimate experiences in discussing issues and speaking with voters. They will talk about their kids or they will talk about preparing meals or how they faced sexual harassment. . . . They connect with voters by talking about their personal lives. This seemed to just come naturally for the female candidates I have worked with. A woman can interact with or reach voters in certain ways that a man cannot.

Another campaign manager, who had worked for and against female candidates, commented,

> I have always felt that women candidates have an easier time connecting with voters and being more personable. It is easier for voters to relate to a woman on a personal level.

One female candidate from northern California, a longtime working mother, discussed her experiences with child rearing on a one-to-one basis with the voters. Her manager commented,

> When she is speaking about day care and children's health issues, she always talks about what she did with her kids when they were younger—how she had to juggle family and her career. I saw her several times with voters, mostly women . . . exchanging stories about when their kids were babies.

This female candidate was able to connect with voters, particularly female voters, in ways a male congressional candidate usually would not. Examples of personal campaigning are evident throughout the campaign messages of female candidates discussed in Chapter 3. Overall, managers for twelve of the twenty-nine female candidates in this study believed that the women for whom they were working engaged in personal campaigning.

However, although women could more easily connect with voters by being personal campaigners, it became clear that many women on the campaign trail were conscious of the problems associated with being one's self. This reinvokes Jamieson's (1995) notion of the double bind. The *double-bind* refers to the burden women face in having to fulfill at least two social roles—roles that often border on incompatibility. Women have to simultaneously embody the stereotypical "female" and "male" traits. For instance, they must appear caring, nurturing, and soft, while at the same time coming across as tough and assertive. Several of the female candidates were highly cognizant of the fine line they were traveling between being feminine and being perceived as unprofessional. The female candidates had to be more conscious of their physical presentation to voters. For instance, some of the candidates said they often had to consider their appearance and professional mannerisms in ways that male candidates did not. Several of the female candidates attempted to make certain that they did not appear "too feminine." One candidate noted,

> My campaign manager told me to stop wearing floral dresses. She was worried that they made me appear too frilly and housewife-like, especially if we had a joint appearance with our opponent, who was always wearing a sharply pressed suit.

Another candidate commented,

> One weekend I was walking precincts, and I was dressed very casually . . . a skirt and a plain shirt . . . and one older woman voter told me that I did not look professional. I remember thinking at the time that she would have never said that about a male candidate.

A number of the female candidates reported difficulty striking a balance between appearing feminine and appearing professional. A political consultant working for a female candidate in northern California noted,

> You have to be careful in presenting the candidate. She must appear as a likable feminine figure . . . but at the time she must appear tough and ready to fight political battles . . . women have to play two roles as politicians.

Almost every female candidate in the study acknowledged some moment or instance when someone came up to them with either advice or criticism of their physical appearance. This is a phenomenon a male candidate would never face and in an important way is illustrative of the "double bind" faced by female candidates (see also Witt, Paget, and Matthews 1994, Chapter 4).

Significantly, the increase in the number of women running for office in California in 1992 and 1994 helped to ensure that the life experiences and different campaign styles of women were included in the political process. As more women enter the electoral arena and discuss many of their distinct experiences, the experiences of women will begin to become part of the accepted dialogue within campaigns. Ideally, this will eventually lead to a political process and an electoral environment with a more inclusive notion of what qualities should characterize a politician. In the meantime, the important question is whether the different styles of women and men on the campaign trail hurt or help the credibility of female candidates. How are voters and the media responding to women's differing styles? The subtleties involved in answering this question make it extremely difficult to clearly determine what women's differences in this area means. Chapter 5 examines polling from the California elections to try to determine whether voters accept the different campaign styles and messages of male and female candidates.

Negative Campaigning

Most political consultants believe that negative campaigning is one of the most effective tools available in a campaign (Kern 1989). In what is often cited as one of the most effective uses of negative campaigning, George Bush was able to portray Michael Dukakis as soft on crime and unpatriotic in the 1988 presidential election. The negative image of Dukakis came to dominate the election (Pomper 1989). George Bush demonstrated that skillful attacks on an opponent's character can effectively alter the course of an election. Congressional elections have a different atmosphere from statewide or national elections. Image creation in local-level elections requires different strategies of image presentation (Fenno 1978). Congressional personas are often created over long periods of time. The tone of a congressional campaign varies greatly from district to district depending on geography and the media market. Nonetheless, the majority of political consultants and professionals in this study believed that negative campaigning was the most effective way to gain ground in an election. As one of these consultants commented,

> I believe in just pounding the opponent. Digging up any scandalous past behavior or hammering away on any issue positions that help us with the voters. Negative ads are the only thing that move the voters. I like to go 90 percent negative and 10 percent positive about my candidate.

This was a common sentiment among the political consultants running the congressional campaigns in this study.

However, political consultants disagree over what constitutes negative campaigning. Some consider negative campaigning to be any attack focusing on the opponent's personal background and political record. Thus, any discussion of the opponent's past actions and behaviors exemplifies negative campaigning. Other consultants believe that focusing on a candidate's personal background or past scandals is negative and "dirty," but that the opponent's policy positions are fair game. The 1992 and 1994 elections gave challengers ample ammunition to "pound away" on the incumbents. Personal attacks in congressional elections across the country centered on such things as the House banking and post office scandals, payment of personal income taxes, and past acts of insensitivity toward women and minorities. Female candidates in the 1992 election were expected not to engage in the typical negative campaign tactics of male politicians (Woods 1992).

In the interviews, campaign managers were asked several questions to determine the images their candidates sought to create of their opponents and of themselves. Campaign managers reported the percentage of their public campaign message that was spent focusing on the opponent. In addition, campaign managers were asked to state which aspects of their opponent's behavior they attacked. Ultimately, responses to that question were coded into two categories: whether attacks were based on the opponents' policy positions or on their past personal behavior.

Contrary to speculation about the behavior of female candidates, Table 2.5 suggests that the female candidates, almost all of whom were Democrats, were as likely to focus on their opponent's record as their male Democratic counterparts. Women were more likely to focus attacks on their opponent's issue positions. Women's propensity to attack their opponents illustrates a combativeness and assertiveness that women are often thought to lack. Further, a comparison of the men running against women (all but one a Republican) with the Republican men running against Democratic men shows that the men running against women were much more likely to attack their opponent on the issues. This suggests that the women in this study were more likely to be attacked than their male counterparts. This despite the fact that many men running against women said they were afraid to attack their female opponent (see following pages). The bottom half of Table 2.5 shows strong similarities between female and male challengers in the level of personal attacks. However, female candidates were again more likely than male candidates to attack on the issues. To help disentangle the effects of party, gender, and incumbency, Table 2.6 employs logistic regression mod-

Table 2.5   Degree and Focus of Negative Campaigning Estimates,
             by Gender and Party Affiliation

	Women Versus Men Races		Men Only Races	
	Women (25)	Men (20)	Democrats (22)	Republicans (21)
Percentage of campaign activity[a] focusing on the opponent	40%	25%	45%	19%
Types of attacks on opponent[b]:				
Issues positions	92	70	82	38
Personal qualities	64	45	82	38

	Challengers	
	Women (21)	Men (37)
Percentage of campaign activity[a] focusing on the opponent	43%	38%
Types of attacks on opponent:		
Issues positions	95*	76
Personal qualities	67	73

NOTES: Table includes only the candidates who said they discussed their opponent in their campaign message.
Difference of means test comparing the women and men in the neighboring column.
a. Should be read: 40% of the campaign message used by female candidates focused on the opponent.
b. Should be read: 92% of women attacked opponents issue positions.
*$p < .10$ (one-tailed t-test).

els. The year of the election is also included in the equation to determine
whether the use of attacks differed between 1992 and 1994.

   Democrats and challengers were more likely to use personal attacks
against their opponents. Personal attacks were more prevalent in 1994. This
may be explained by the fact that the 1994 election was less issue-driven
than the 1992 election—widespread concern about the economy and health
care had subsided. Although we might expect that the presentation of *The
Contract with America* by many Republican congressional candidates would
have made 1994 an issue-driven election, few if any managers identified the
Contract as a major issue in the campaign. To return to Table 2.6, male
candidates were more likely than female candidates to engage in personal
attacks (significant at $p < .05$); women appeared more likely to use issue-
based attacks, although this was not statistically significant. Women's re-

Table 2.6   Logistic Regression Estimates of Campaign Attacks,
by Party, Gender, Challenger Status, and Year of Election

	Personal Attacks	*Issue Attacks*
Constant	2.38**	4.30**
	(1.15)	(1.50)
Gender of candidate	1.27**	−.95
	(.64)	(.74)
Party affiliation	−1.98**	−.24
	(.57)	(.53)
Incumbency status	−1.72**	−1.47**
	(.15)	(.52)
Year of the election	.82*	.57
	(.20)	(.51)
Log likelihood	139.26	122.45
N	(105)	(105)

NOTES: Party was coded 1 for Democrat and 2 for Republican. Incumbency was coded 1 for challenger and 2 for incumbent. Gender was coded 1 for female and 2 for male. Year of election was coded 1 for 1992 and 2 for 1994. Standard error in parentheses.
$*p < .11$; $**p < .05$.

luctance to use personal attacks supports the expectation cited by Woods (1992) that women would be less negative and cynical in their approach to politics. Also, the Staton/Hughes Research Groups, in conducting a study for EMILY's List, found that female congressional candidates showed a strong resistance to attacking their opponents (1992). They interviewed over thirty female Democratic congressional candidates in 1992 and found that although women resisted attack strategies, successful female candidates ultimately went after their opponents' record publicly. As with the results of the Staton/Hughes interviews, most women in this study did go after their opponents, although there was some resistance and hesitancy among a number of the female candidates.

Although the majority of women in this study appeared to be willing to aggressively "go after" their male opponents' records, several managers for female candidates stated that their candidate demonstrated strong reservations about publicly attacking their opponent. This resistance to attacking the opponent was described by one female candidate's campaign manager:

When she hired me to run the campaign, she told me I had control of the campaign, and she wanted to do whatever it would take to win. So I had some thorough opposition research done, and it turned up some great stuff to use against the opponent. When I presented the materials to the candidate she said she did not want to use them. My jaw dropped. She said she had thought it over and she was not comfortable campaigning that way. I have never had a candidate do something like that before. . . . We ended up losing badly, but I still believe if she had used the material and campaigned vigorously against the opponent we could have won.

In a similar vein, another woman chose not to use some of the "attack points" her staff prepped her with prior to a debate with her opponent. The manager described what happened:

We made out the candidate's note cards for the debate and discussed when she could use the attack points. The moment came, and then came again and again— she had some perfect opportunities to nail him and she didn't do it. . . . After the debate I asked her what had happened and she just said she didn't want to use the stuff.

Another manager noted,

She believes she should take the high road. Even if it will cost her the election she will not go negative. We have tried to get her to go after him [her male incumbent opponent], but she just will not campaign that way.[5]

Several male candidates chose to limit their negative campaigning for strategic reasons but no men in this study openly acknowledged that they would not engage in negative campaigning because they believed it was unethical or immoral. The greater likelihood that female candidates are going to demonstrate angst (or at least admit angst) about using negative campaigning is most likely a by-product of the separate socialization patterns of men and women. Until quite recently, women have not been competing in rough-and-tumble electoral politics and thus have not been accustomed to employing some of the more manipulative and negative tactics now so pervasive in electoral politics. However, most female candidates' eventual willingness to attack their opponents demonstrates that they are acclimating to the political environment. A likely explanation for women's eventual willingness to use negative tactics lies in the fact that they want to win and political consultants who are working for women have been schooled to believe that negative ads are one of the key instruments in the modern campaign (Kern 1989).

Table 2.7   Voter Targeting, by Gender and Challenger Status

Groups Targeted	Female Challengers (24)	Male Challengers (32)	Male Incumbents (27)
Women	67%	59%	37%
Men	25*	9	15
Democrats	29	41	22
Republicans	50	63	51
Independents	29	28	11
Seniors	33	25	22
Ethnic and racial minorities	4*	16	19
High-propensity voters	25	22	37
College students	8	3	0
Geographic areas	0**	22	30

NOTES: In coding the survey responses, for every voter characteristic mentioned by the campaign manager, a corresponding category or categories were checked off. For instance, if a candidate targeted "Republican Women," both women and Republicans were checked off. Difference of means test compare the female and male challengers.
*$p < .10$; **$p < .05$ (one-tailed t-test).

 ## Strategies in Targeting Voters

Reaching out to specific voter groups and courting their support is one of the primary strategies in putting together a winning campaign. Sophisticated blueprints of voter targeting form the basis of the modern campaign. Voters may be targeted specifically with a piece of direct mail or a phone call, or less directly when a candidate speaks to certain groups of voters. For instance, an incumbent in this study represented a district that was composed of rural and urban areas. The rural voters received mailers discussing agricultural policy and the urban voters received mailers outlining the congressman's tough stance on crime. In another example of targeting, an incumbent male candidate sent all the female voters in his district a piece of mail voicing the need to crack down on crime. The candidate targeted women with this mail because his internal polls showed that female voters were more concerned with crime than male voters.

Although almost all of the candidates in the sample engaged in some voter targeting, more male candidates than female candidates made this practice a primary objective of their campaign (Table 2.3). Table 2.7 illustrates the groups of voters that were targeted by the candidates.

Women were the most highly targeted voting bloc in the state of California. Two-thirds of female candidates turned to female voters as a primary source of support. In contrast, male voters were rarely isolated as a voting bloc by either men or women, and when they were, female challengers targeted them at higher rates (borderline significance, $p < .10$). That female candidates would be likely to turn toward women as a source of support is not surprising. There were indications that female candidates and voters, at least in 1992, demonstrated some level of group consciousness. There is considerable evidence that a sense of group consciousness forms within political "out-groups" (Verba and Nie 1972). Tolleson Rinehart (1992) has effectively argued that there is gender consciousness among women. She offers the following definition:

> Gender consciousness, like other forms of group consciousness, embodies an identification with similar others, positive affect toward them, and a feeling of interdependence with the group's fortunes . . . gender consciousness is also potentially empowering, imbuing the gender conscious woman with a sense of the validity of her world view. (14)

If this consciousness exists, as Tolleson Rinehart persuasively posits, then it would be logical for female candidates to look to female voters as a base of support.

However, female voters were also the second most highly targeted group by both male challengers and male incumbents. Thus, female voters are much more likely to be treated as a group than male voters. Campaign strategists perceive the existence of a stereotypical set of "women's issues" (e.g., abortion, children's issues, parental leave, etc.) that have a greater appeal to female voters. As one manager noted,

> There is a clear sense of what women's issues are. It is easy to put together a package of things for women only. It doesn't work that way for men.

As further indication of the role "women's issues" play in targeting strategies, 38 of the 108 (35%) candidates in the study targeted Republican women. The majority of these candidates were Democrats hoping to lure Republican women with favorable stances on "women's issues." By contrast, Democratic female voters were only targeted specifically by 10 percent of the candidates. An important change in the practice of targeting women occurred between 1992 and 1994. Among female candidates who targeted female voters there was no difference across the elections—ten out of fifteen female candidates

(67%) targeted women in 1992 and six out of nine (67%) targeted women in 1994. However, there was a dramatic increase in the targeting of female voters by male candidates over the two elections. In 1992, ten out of twenty-three male challengers (43%) targeted women; in the 1994 race, all nine male challengers (100%) who engaged in voter targeting went after women. For male incumbents, three out of fourteen (21%) targeted women in 1992 and seven out of thirteen (54%) did the same in 1994.

These targeting patterns suggest that the attention placed on female candidates and "women's issues" in 1992 forced male candidates to consider women's concerns more seriously. Even if the targeting of female voters is purely a strategic decision by male candidates, male candidates are still considering female voters in ways they had not done before. As discussed in Chapter 3, most of the targeting of female voters addresses issues that the candidates believe appeal to women. This may be considered a positive development because women and women's issues may be receiving more political attention as a result. However, both the reliance of female candidates on female voters and the treatment of women as a distinct political group by male candidates are important indicators that women are not equal players within the political system. In this system, the policy concerns of male voters are the norm and female voters are often sold a special plate of "women's issues." Similarly, female candidates rely more on female voters, which further suggests that they do not feel fully accepted by male voters.

Table 2.7 also shows that male challengers were more likely than female challengers to target voters by race (borderline significance, $p < .10$) and the geographic area they live in (significant at $p < .05$). No clear explanation for these differences emerged in the interviews. In terms of minority voters, this might be explained by the larger number of minority men in the sample; there were twelve minority male candidates and only five minority female candidates. The gender difference in use of geographic targeting is difficult to explain. Political consultants are usually responsible for devising the targeting schemes and there is no readily apparent explanation for why the consultants for female candidates did not use or acknowledge the use of geographic targeting. One possible explanation is that the male candidates were more likely to be running in large rural districts with more diverse types of communities. Many of the female candidates were running in urban areas where geographic targeting is less prevalent. However, this is only speculation and any gender-based explanations for these differences do not clearly come through in this analysis.

Female Candidates Transforming the Electoral Arena: How Male Candidates Respond

> When she won the primary we became very concerned. Even though we knew she was a weak candidate with few resources and we were running in a district we had won easily before, we prepared for the general election much differently than we otherwise would have.
>
> *—Manager of long-time incumbent*
> *running against his first female opponent*

This section tries to broaden the ways in which the effect of female candidates on the electoral arena is examined. Studying the reactions of male candidates to female candidates demonstrates that the presence of women is transforming the political arena in important ways. The question of how the presence of a female candidate affects the behavior of her male opponent has received little attention in the literature. To have a broad understanding of the role of female candidates and their overall influence in an electoral campaign, the behavior of the candidates running opposite them must be understood. Although there are currently no systematic examinations of the behavior of women's opponents, there are some indicators and studies of individual races that suggest female candidates affect the behavior of their electoral opponents in significant ways. Renner (1993), in a study of the 1992 Pennsylvania Senate race between Arlen Specter and Lynn Yeakel, shows how Yeakel's gender and the gender-related issue of the Thomas/Hill hearings caused Specter to change his strategy. Renner found that Specter consciously avoided making direct public attacks against Yeakel. This was especially apparent in a series of television advertisements that raised questions about Yeakel but never directly attacked her. Also, Renner argues that Specter made additional efforts to demonstrate support for "women's issues" such as breast cancer and day care. Specter's altered strategy was an attempt to offset Yeakel's appeal to female voters.

In the 1992 California Senate race between Bruce Herschensohn and Barbara Boxer, Herschensohn made several efforts to offset any possible "year of the woman" advantage Boxer might have had. Herschensohn organized several campaign events that were intended to demonstrate that he also had support from female voters. These included special "women

Table 2.8   Strategic Reactions of Twenty-Three Male Candidates Running
Against Women

18 of 23	Made some changes in their campaign strategy because they were running against a woman.
15 of 23	Expressed concern or reservations about attacking their female opponent.
12 of 23	Organized some form of campaign activity with the intention of reaching out to female voters.
10 of 23	Said they raised certain "women's issues" only because they were running against a woman opponent.

only" campaign luncheons and speeches to women's groups. In addition, Herschensohn often spoke negatively and bitterly about "the year of the woman" (Tolleson Rinehart 1994). Thus, part of Herschensohn's campaign strategy was an attempt to minimize the effect of running against a woman. Boxer's gender and her use of the gender issue led Herschensohn to alter his election strategy.

The examples of the California and Pennsylvania Senate races provide some insight into how a woman affects her opponent during a campaign. This study includes twenty-six male candidates who ran against women, offering an opportunity to systematically examine a large sample of men running against women. The campaigns of these male candidates exhibit patterns that are consistent with the behavior demonstrated in the California and Pennsylvania Senate races. The managers for the male candidates running against women in this study were asked if they approached the race differently because of a female opponent. Eighteen out of twenty-three (78%) campaign managers for male candidates acknowledged in the interviews that they changed their campaign strategy because they were running against a woman. Table 2.8 lists some of the common strategic alterations made by the campaign managers of male candidates running against women.

Overall, the male candidates changed their campaign strategy in two ways. One, they were hesitant to engage in negative campaigning, and two, they went to extra lengths to demonstrate that they were in touch with the interests of female voters. These patterns help establish a framework for understanding how the presence of female candidates alters the behavior of male candidates in the electoral process. If we turn to the specific responses of the managers for male candidates running against women, it clearly demonstrates that these male candidates are carefully weighing what it means to run against a woman.

Fear of Negative Campaigning

In the twenty-three campaigns in which men ran against women, fifteen male candidates altered or downplayed any publicly negative treatment of the women they were running against. If men are afraid to attack their female opponents, this could have important consequences for the electoral process. This could change the way issues are debated in elections. Most of the campaign managers for these male candidates believed that it was more difficult to attack a woman because of the way this could be perceived by voters. The fear of a negative reaction from the electorate stemmed from the traditional notion that it is not "gentlemanly" to attack a woman. Tolleson Rinehart found this traditional reluctance to attack present in studies of California (1994) and Texas (with Stanley, 1994). For instance, one campaign manager of a male candidate running against a woman noted,

> Oh, he would never attack a lady, he just does not believe in that. He will treat the opponent graciously and with respect in the campaign.

Another campaign manager of a male candidate, who was running against the daughter of a popular incumbent, stated,

> You can't go around bashing his little girl. The appearance of being mean to the congressman's daughter would be devastating.

One male candidate was even more open in his chivalry (or sexism):

> I don't think it is proper to attack a woman. I was completely constrained in how I went about campaigning. It was a constant struggle to show the proper politeness toward my opponent. Women cannot handle criticism or high stress so I had to watch what I said closely so that I would not appear to be causing my opponent any grief.

The fear of attacking a female opponent will undoubtedly be historically situated. As women become less of a novelty as candidates, men will realize that to win elections they will have to attack their opponents, and voters will become more accustomed to women running for high elective office. There have already been several instances of men and women engaging in extremely nasty races, such as the 1994 Senate race between Huffington and Feinstein in California. In this race it did not appear that Huffington was stigmatized for harshly attacking Feinstein. However, this was a large-scale, statewide race. Most of the campaign managers in this study believed that attacking a woman was not appropriate for district-level elections because the candidates are much closer to the voters and need to create an amiable district persona (Fenno 1978).

Male candidates' reluctance to attack their female opponents exhibited itself in candidate debates and public forums. Eight campaign managers for male candidates stated that when the opponent was a woman, their candidate was less aggressive during a debate or public forum than they would have been against a male opponent. One candidate went so far as to send a representative of his campaign to debate his female opponent. The aide commented on why he was sent to debate the opponent:

> She was a nice elderly woman—having the candidate hammer away on her record and issue positions would not look good. Instead I went to debate her. I am much older than the congressman and could get away with a lot more.

By and large, male candidates were careful not to present the image of a man "bullying" a woman in public. Several male candidates demonstrated that they were gentlemen by treating their women opponents in traditional ways. As one manager noted,

> We feared we had been a little too harsh in some of our TV ads, so in the upcoming debate we wanted [our candidate] to appear kind and gentlemanly. We had him pull out her chair for her at the debate and made sure he referred to her very respectfully over the course of the debate. We were always a little concerned about how our interactions appeared.

The attempt to appear "gentlemanly" at various points in a campaign did not mean that male candidates did not attack their female opponents on issues or past indiscretions, rather that they tended to present these issues more carefully. These "gentlemanly" acts also reinforce the idea that women are weak and in need of special treatment and thus might present a subtle way for the male candidates to discredit their female opponents. Significantly, none of the fifty-six male candidates who ran against men mentioned any fear of a negative public reaction if they chose to attack their opponent.

Although many campaign managers of male candidates felt that it was more difficult to attack female opponents, others felt that they could attack through alternative strategies. For example, one manager insisted that they wait for their female opponent to attack first:

> [waiting for the woman to attack first] averted the problems associated with attacking a woman because you were only responding to attacks. . . . Also, when a woman attacks first she demonstrates that she is not above the typical fray of electoral politics.

A political consultant working for a candidate in northern California explained why he believed it was bad strategy to attack a woman first:

> If you attack her first you look like you are brow-beating a woman. You have to let her cast the first blow, and once she has done that, the perception of unfairly beating up a helpless woman is minimized.

Another attack method with subtle implications was used by six of the male candidates, who noted that their female opponent was inconsistent in her policy positions. Attacking an opponent for flip-flopping on issues is by no means a tactic exclusive to men running against women. However, in this study, men running against women were much more likely to employ this strategy: six of the twenty-three male candidates charged that their female opponent had a tendency to "flip-flop" or be "wishy-washy" on the issues. As one campaign manager stated,

> By simply pointing out that our opponent had adopted one position and then later changed it, we look like we are reporting facts instead of attacking her.

In addition, one of the managers for a female candidate who was accused of being "indecisive" or "wishy-washy" believed that the opponent's attacks were sexist:

> I have no doubt that the opponent was trying to make her look like a typically fickle woman. In the debates he would take on this condescending and patronizing tone about how she was always changing her position on the issues.

Male candidates used this attack strategy to play up the stereotype that women are more indecisive and fickle. Notably, only one out of fifty-six male candidates in this study attempted to portray a male opponent as "wishy-washy."

Does the reluctance to attack a female opponent directly change the dynamics of the electoral process? Because negative campaigning has become such an important tool in the modern campaign, this is an especially important question to address (Kern 1989). Male candidates reluctant to attack their female opponents may have a more difficult time highlighting the defining issues in the campaign or raising issues of personal character. If male candidates are not at ease confronting female candidates on issues they would raise against a man, this may have a number of consequences. The tone of the campaign may become less harsh as the candidates are less likely to exchange negative accusations. Also, the issue agenda of the campaign may be slightly altered if male candidates are not raising issues as vociferously as they otherwise would have. The presence of a female candidate in an election may change the nature of political discourse in that election. Perhaps more important, however, is that the high percentage of male candidates who changed their campaign strategy shows that a number of these male candidates are demonstrating stereotypical attitudes about the political involvement of women. With so many of the male candidates ready to adopt different strategies in reaction to a female opponent, it shows that some men do not treat women as equals in the electoral arena and that they are employing strategies that they believe will help them win.

Building Bonds With Female Voters

The second prominent reaction of male candidates running against women was to engage in some affirmative campaign activity designed to appeal to female voters. A perception within the media is that female candidates have greater appeal to female voters than male candidates (see Rosenthal 1995). Many of the male candidates running against women operated under this principle. The male candidates in this study usually sought to offset this perceived advantage by attempting to reach out to female voters. Typically, the goal of men's efforts to reach out to female voters was to convey the impression that the candidate was sensitive to women's needs. Twelve of the twenty-three male candidates running against women engaged in campaign behavior designed to illustrate the candidate's connection with the concerns of women. Male candidates tried to reach out to female voters in a variety of ways but their tactics can be classified into one of two groups. The first were campaign activities that tried to demonstrate that the candidate cared about the needs and interests of women just as much as those of men. For instance, one campaign manager noted that in his candidate's television commercials about constituent service, the incumbent was seen helping female constituents. The manager continued,

> We had never really thought about women and the constituent service ads before, but this year with all the "year of the woman" stuff going on, we wanted voters to see that the congressmen was there for women too.

Similarly, another candidate's campaign commercials and literature always showed the congressman engaged in conversations with women, so the candidate would appear concerned about the interests of women. Another male candidate attempted to recruit more women into his campaign organization:

> The congressman decided that this year we would have a separate group of women supporters. This way, if his woman opponent ran around claiming she was the candidate for women, we could combat this by demonstrating our support from women.

In another example, a longtime incumbent visibly endorsed other female candidates, intending to show his support for women:

> We endorsed a woman in a neighboring district. We would have endorsed her even if it wasn't the "year of the woman," but this time we released the endorsement to the press and talked it up a bit. . . . We just wanted a little positive "year of the woman" coverage.

In all four of these situations it is important to note that the male candidates were long-term incumbents who had never run against a female candidate before. Thus, it is possible that the incumbents' involvement with women could change their political behavior in future legislative and electoral action. These congressmen's increased interaction with women in the political arena could make them more aware of and more sensitive to women's concerns. This was the case with one male incumbent whose manager admitted that the formation of a women's support group helped his candidate become more involved with certain woman-specific issues, such as sexual harassment and abortion. The candidate formed the group only because he was running against

Table 2.9 Summary of Differences Between Men and Women on the Campaign Trail

	Differences	
Aspect of Campaign Behavior	Female Candidates	Male Candidates
Motivation for entering the race	Concern over a specific policy	Desire for political power
	Desire to forward a cause	A good political opportunity presented itself
Campaign objectives	Emphasized own political record	Prioritized targeting of voter groups
Communicating with voters	Most important mode of communicating with voters was personal contact	Most important mode of communicating with voters was direct mail
Campaigning style	Emphasized "personal campaigning"	More likely to make personal attacks
	More likely to attack an opponent's issue positions	Men running against women modified their attack strategy so that they would not appear to be bullying women
		Men running against women made special efforts to appeal to female voters
Voter targeting strategies	More likely to target male voters	More likely to target by ethnicity and geographic area

a woman. Although there appeared to be an important substantive outcome in this instance, it is quite possible that any alterations in campaign behavior may only be campaign tactics used by male candidates and have no lasting effect beyond the election.

The second method men employed to reach out to female voters was to alter the substantive message put forth by the campaigns. This was potentially the most important change of behavior seen in the male candidates, because it goes straight to the question of representation. Ten of twenty-three male candidates running against women chose to address policy issues that they otherwise would not have raised had they been running against a man (the issue agendas used by the campaigns is discussed extensively in Chapter 3). This change in the issues that male candidates focus on is significant because elections help set the issue agenda of the election's victor (Arnold 1990; Kingdon 1989). If male candidates running against women, and even male candidates running against men, raise more "women's issues" because of the increased number of women in the electoral process, the interests of women may be more fully represented in the legislative process. This is especially important when we consider that six of the ten male candidates who made special efforts to raise women's issues were incumbent congressmen who were reelected.

Conclusion

There are similarities and differences in the campaign strategies and styles that women and men bring to the electoral process. Women and men candidates exhibited several important differences in terms of motivations, priorities, and behaviors. Table 2.9 summarizes the important differences between female and male candidates discussed in this chapter.

The women in this study were motivated by a sense of mission, emphasized a strategy of personally reaching out to voters, sought the support of female voters, and faced the constraints of the "double bind." The men displayed more open political ambition, relied on less personal means of communicating with voters, and were more likely to use personal attacks against their opponent. The findings in this chapter corroborate some of the literature on gender differences in political orientation (Bledsoe and Herring 1990; Gilligan 1982). These differences in behavior can for the most part be attributed to how women and men have historically been socialized to conceive of the political process. The persistence of traditional beliefs about the role of women in the political arena still exists within a substantial portion of the electorate. The larger question is whether the presence of more female candidates changes the election process and the nature of political representation. Women bring many traits to the campaign process that have not traditionally been prominent in congressional campaigns. Women's alternative styles were embraced in 1992. However, women's styles were met with indifference in 1994, although this may be partially explained by the partisan shift in the electorate. Gender differences in campaign style add to the likelihood that women's perspectives and interests will receive greater attention through the broader incorporation of female candidates into the electoral process.

Notes

1. For other analyses of gender and political ambition see Costantini (1990) and Sapiro (1982).

2. The extent to which a campaign strategy can determine the outcome of an election is still largely unknown. This is especially true of congressional elections, where it has been well established that incumbency and the district's party registration usually dictate election outcomes (Mayhew 1974; Fenno 1978; Jacobson 1992). However, a number of studies seem to confirm that campaigns and strategic behavior have an important effect on who wins and who loses (Holbrook 1996; Jacobson 1992; Hershey 1984; Agranoff 1980; Atkins 1973).

3. For a comprehensive examination of the most modern techniques used in political communication, see Trent and Friedenberg (1995).

4. This calculation excludes the candidacy of Michael Huffington. Huffington set a record for spending in a House election. He spent over $5.6 million in the course of the 1992 election. In addition, almost all of the money came from Huffington's personal wealth.

5. This particular candidate received some national attention for her refusal to engage in negative campaigning. These refusals to attack her opponent are quite notable, considering that the district in which she was running had recently been one of the most competitive congressional districts in the country.

Gender and Strategy
in Campaign Messages

D o female and male candidates present different campaign messages to
the electorate? This chapter compares the campaign messages of male
and female candidates in three areas: personal traits, central themes, and
policy issues. Major academic studies of female candidates have largely
ignored their strategies and agendas (e.g., Burrell 1994; Darcy, Welch, and
Clark 1994). Comparing the campaign messages of female and male candidates deserves attention for a number of reasons (see Williams 1994; Benze
and DeClercq 1985). First, campaign messages provide a window into the
dynamics of candidate behavior in an election. Examining the messages
allows us to determine how men and women strategize about campaigns.
Second, the agendas presented in a campaign are the primary indicators of
the issue priorities of the candidates. As argued in Chapter 1, the issues raised
in campaigns are likely to become the basis of the legislative agenda of the
election winner. The question of whether women and men raise different
issues is important because if female candidates have different issue priorities, women's presence as candidates may have an important effect on the
substantive representation that emerges from an election. Finally, the campaign messages employed by candidates reveal a great deal about the political atmosphere of a given election.

58

The salient political issues in an electoral environment are important in light of evidence that women and men have different levels of credibility in addressing different issues. For instance, in 1987 the National Women's Political Caucus commissioned a poll that found that voters prefer the leadership of women on issues "dealing with children," "protecting the interests of consumers," "dealing with health problems," and "improving the educational system." Male politicians have advantages on issues such as "foreign trade," "taxes," "arms control," and "the farm situation" (see Burrell 1994, 24). Thus, depending on which political issues dominate an electoral environment, the campaign messages being put out by female and male candidates may have a significant effect on their ability to win.

Further, the three areas of the campaign message that are examined in this chapter, personal images, central themes, and policy issues, are individually important. Each of these areas may have a significant effect on voter decision making. Most models and assessments of what determines the vote have been based on examinations of presidential voting. Although there is large-scale agreement over the factors that contribute to how citizens cast their ballots in presidential elections—party identification, candidate image, candidate issue positions, and personal economic well-being—the emphasis of each of these factors is greatly debated. Analysis of vote determinants in congressional elections has been much less explored. Nonetheless, three factors have historically been central to examinations of congressional voting patterns: party identification, incumbency, and presidential approval ratings (Davidson and Oleszek 1994, 101-110; Jacobson 1992, 132-136).

In terms of candidate appeal and personal traits, much has been written on how incumbents have tried to cultivate personalities that are in sync with their districts. Fenno's (1978) landmark study of contrasting congressional behavior in the home district and in Washington demonstrated the care with which members of Congress develop their personal image (see also, Parker 1986). We know that candidate image matters to voters in presidential elections (Lodge, McGraw, and Stroh 1989; Fiorina 1981; Page 1978). Image also undoubtedly matters in lower-level elections when the campaigns are visible enough for voters to be able to form opinions about the candidates. Because partisanship has declined over the past thirty years, the importance of issues and personal characteristics may be increasing in House races. Davidson and Oleszek (1994, 111) have noted that in an era of heightened competition in House elections, candidate image is playing an increasingly large role in candidate performance.

With regard to the central themes and issues put forward in campaigns, a growing body of evidence shows that substance does matter in how people vote. Early assessments of voting in congressional elections suggested that voters knew next to nothing about the issue positions of House candidates (Stokes and Miller 1962). Since that time, some analyses have posited the importance of issue voting at both the presidential and congressional level. At the presidential level, Luttbeg and Gant (1995, 78) have documented a marked increase in issue-oriented candidate evaluations by voters. The picture at the congressional level is not as encouraging. However, a study of the 1990 congressional elections found that one-third of voters were able to identify an issue that they said was important to them in their House vote (Miller, Kinder, and Rosenstone 1992). Thus, the central themes and issues candidates present in House elections may resonate with a significant portion of the electorate.

Although issues and themes presented in House elections certainly do not play as substantial a role for voters as party identification and incumbency, they are important in other ways. Davidson and Oleszek (1994), in a recent assessment of issue-voting in congressional elections, noted,

> issues motivate that segment of voters who are opinion leaders, who can lend or withhold support far beyond their single vote. Issues are carefully monitored by organized interests, including political action committees, in a position to channel funds, publicity, or volunteer workers to the candidates' cause. It is more than superstition, then, that makes legislators devote so much time and attention to promoting issues and explaining them to attentive publics. (111)

Thus, the issues and themes candidates stress in House elections are at the very least important to a broad number of potential support groups who play a major role in the success of any campaign.

In examining the campaign messages of male and female candidates in this study, two sources of information are relied on. First, and most important, is the data from the interviews with campaign managers. The managers were asked both closed- and open-ended questions about the contents of their candidates' message. Second, campaign literature was collected for most of the candidates and a content analysis of the literature is presented to supplement the interviews. The images and issues candidates chose to present help to further advance the central argument in this book that the socialization process explains many of the differences in the behavior of female and male candidates. However, before moving on to explore the messages, it is first important to understand how candidates select campaign messages.

Selecting a Campaign Message

The candidates in this investigation varied substantially in the amount of material and the method of presentation that their congressional campaigns used to communicate with voters (see Trent and Friedenberg 1995). Campaign messages in this investigation were conveyed through any of the following activities: speeches, precinct walking, passing out campaign literature, direct mail, signs and bumper stickers, radio advertisements, television advertisements, and phone banks, to name the most common methods. Some of the less competitive races did not have highly visible campaign efforts. Several poorly financed challengers running against safe incumbents could not afford paid media and relied on personal contact with the voters. The more competitive and well-financed campaigns were able to make certain that they delivered their message. For instance, one well-financed campaign had a thirty-two piece direct mail program and more than a dozen different television commercials.

Most of the candidates and campaign managers taking part in this survey employed one of two considerations in selecting the various components of their campaign message. Some candidates used their campaign message as a platform for articulating their personal convictions and presenting their true selves to voters. These candidates based their campaign message on the themes and issues of sincere importance to them. In contrast, other candidates selected their messages on the basis of what images they believed would get them elected. These candidates made calculated strategic decisions about what messages would appeal to voters. Most candidates undoubtedly select their campaign message by combining both of these factors. Some aspects of the message will reflect those subjects important to the candidate and other parts will be selected because of their strategic importance. Indeed, in some cases these factors relay the same message. Of importance to this investigation, gender considerations may be a factor in either means of constructing a campaign message. In the case of personal convictions, female and male candidates may demonstrate differences in political attitudes and priorities, such as those found in male and female legislators (see Thomas 1994; Dodson and Carroll 1991). In the case of the strategic message, male and female candidates may use their understanding of gender stereotyping by voters to help further their election efforts. Both types of decisions reveal the importance of traditional socialization. Differences in personal convictions may reveal that men and women have unique conceptions of politics and policy priorities. Differences in strategic messages reveal that stereo-typical conceptions of women and men motivate and guide campaign man-agers and political consultants in developing a message. These two types of potential gender differences in campaign messages require greater explana-tion because they serve as the analytic framework for examining the cam-paign messages of candidates running for Congress in California.

Personal Convictions

When candidates select campaign issues based on personal convictions, they are selecting issues that are their own issue priorities. For instance, the campaign manager for a female candidate from northern California described a personal passion of his candidate:

> Everywhere we went she spoke about First Amendment rights. I tried to get her to stop doing this, but she has this obsession with free speech and the idea that all groups need to be able to address government. This is all well and good, but voters are not thinking about free speech rights. I don't think they could care less. The voters in our district were worried about crime and the educational system.

In a southern California district, the campaign manager for a longtime Con-gressman commented,

> He is always talking about illegal immigration. Sometimes he goes down and helps work on the wall himself [the wall is a fence being erected on the California/ Mexico border]. I cannot even tell you how strongly he feels about preventing illegal immigration. He mentions it in every campaign speech and in every piece of literature.

These are clear illustrations of candidates placing issues on their agenda because of deep personal interest in the subject matter. Despite the cynicism that shrouds the modern election, there were examples throughout this inves-tigation of candidates building campaign messages based on the issues they believed in.

The more difficult yet important task for this examination is assessing whether the personal convictions evident in campaign messages are different for female and male candidates. A number of investigations have explored the policy agendas of male and female officeholders, uncovering evidence (such as that discussed in Chapter 1) that women and men pursue different policy agendas (Thomas 1991; Boles 1991; Schumaker and Burns 1988; Carroll 1984). These studies help lay the groundwork for an understanding of the gender differences we might expect to find in the issue priorities of female and male candidates.

Strategic Decisions

The second type of gender-related difference in campaign messages is in the use of strategic decisions. To illustrate a strategic decision we can turn to the campaign message of a male challenger running against a popular incumbent:

> I stressed abortion at every turn in the campaign. My opponent was quietly pro-life and I thought by playing up abortion I might win over a lot of votes. This district is very progressive on social issues. In the end abortion did not seem like much of a draw and I probably should have selected some other issue, maybe the environment or guns. I am not sure what would have worked.

This candidate, although strongly favoring abortion rights, was in reality not overly concerned with the issue of abortion; he was merely looking for an issue to weaken the support of his opponent. In another district, illustrative of the political environment in California, one campaign manager noted,

> Our polling said crime and illegal immigration were the top issues this year [1994]—so we focused on crime and immigration. Two years ago our polls said jobs and health care were on top. The congressman much prefers those issues, but we must address the issues the voters want to hear about. In 1994 health care fell off the face of the earth and we barely mentioned it, even though the congressman has spent most of his time in office on this issue.

These examples depict the role of strategic decision making in creating a campaign message. They are both situations in which candidates chose issues not because of personal interest but to advance their campaigns.

Strategic decisions are usually based on the input of political professionals who have conducted polls and opposition research. Thus, it is important to consider that the actions and decisions of candidates are often filtered through the strategic designs of campaign consultants. The conception of political consultants as a group of shrewd image manipulators who have little allegiance to particular candidates and a cynical conception of voters was often on the mark in this investigation. One direct mail consultant, working for Democratic congressional candidates across the state of California in 1992, commented,

> The voters are not interested in what is going on. When I devise a piece of mail all I hope is that a person pulls it out of their mailbox and looks at it, maybe if we're lucky, even flips it over. When they do that, I have to hit them with something—bright colors, stark letters, or a startling visual. In that fleeting moment I do not have time to explain things to voters and I would be foolish to try. It is crazy when candidates send out detailed policy positions or videocassettes. Those things go right into the circular file.

This consultant advises candidates on what they must do to win the election, showing no regard for presenting the candidate in an open or thoughtful manner. Another campaign consultant, who was brought out to California from Washington to manage the campaign of a Democratic male challenger in a tight race, commented about her candidate:

> He is no rocket scientist. . . . He is a nice guy who would rather be with his kids and family than worry about the campaign. . . . I devise the campaign message . . . and most of our message is an attack of our opponent. We have done extensive polling to determine where our opponent is vulnerable and we have researched his record fully. The policy preferences of my candidate aren't really part of the message.

In this example, the message being presented to voters may only faintly resemble any real beliefs or attributes of the candidate. In a final illustration, when a political consultant working for an incumbent Congressman from southern California was asked about the policy issues included in the campaign message, he laughed and replied,

> Issues? . . . There were no issues in this campaign. We stayed away from issues. We wouldn't want to mention those. What mattered in this campaign was character. The entire campaign was spent trying to discredit our opponent, repairing our own image and avoiding issues. There was no agenda being put forward in this race.

Given such attitudes, which are commonplace in the electoral arena, an important question arises: What happens to the role of candidate gender when candidates turn over the reins of their campaigns to political professionals?

When political professionals are brought in to run campaigns they will make strategic decisions about formulating a campaign message. Of the 109 congressional campaigns that took part in the interview process in this study, seventy had hired political professionals. In approximately thirty of these cases it appeared that most of the control about how to present the campaign message had been turned over to the political professionals. Campaign consultants are concerned with putting forward a winning message and not with presenting a sincere and complete picture of the candidates. Therefore, the role of gender in devising a campaign strategy is only important to consultants when they believe that gender or gender stereotypes might be used to further their clients' candidacy. As the following analysis makes clear, the role of gender dynamics in the formulation of campaign messages is often based on strategic considerations.

Personal Traits Used by the Candidates

What personal traits do candidates attempt to convey about themselves to voters, and do they vary by gender? The personal characteristics incorporated into campaign messages are perhaps one of the clearest indicators of the effect of gender in campaigns. There are many sociologically ingrained stereotypes about male and female sex roles that candidates have to consider when presenting themselves to voters. Huddy and Terkildsen (1993b, 518-22), in surveys of college students, have found evidence that stereotypical "male traits," such as aggressiveness, rationality, and assertiveness, are considered crucial for holding higher office. They further determined that stereotypical "female traits," such as sensitivity, warmth, and caution, although not a liability, did not offer the same benefits for the candidates as the "male traits" (see, also, Kahn 1993). In addition, polling data on the images and personal attributes of women and men have revealed some important differences. Female politicians have been characterized by voters as more likely than men to be "caring," "honest," "moral," and willing to "compromise." Male politicians, on the other hand, have been characterized as more likely than women to be "tough," "emotionally stable," "better at handling a crisis," "knowledgeable about the system," a "fighter," and "decisive" (see polls summarized in Burrell 1994, 24-25). These stereotypes, held in varying degrees by a sizable portion of the electorate, are clearly linked to traditional conceptions of sex roles (see Bennett and Bennett 1996). Thus, male and

Table 3.1   Personal Traits in the Campaign Messages of Male and Female
Candidates

	Female Challengers (N = 39)	Male Challengers (N = 37)	Male Incumbents (N = 25)	Significance of Chi-Square Male/Female Challengers
Personal qualities				
Integrity/honesty	28%[a]	32%	51%	.717
Ties to local community	40	24	36	.093*
Family-oriented	36	36	56	.880
Caring	20	14	3	.441
Professional qualities				
Leadership	4	8	10	.659
Credentials	68	24	18	.000**
Gets things done	40	30	23	.251
Intelligence	8	11	15	.771
Ideology	0	14	15	.093*

a. The column percentages do not total 100% because most respondents listed two or three character traits in the campaign message.
*p < .10; **p < .05.

female candidates, but particularly female candidates, must be wary of the damaging stereotypes and attitudes voters possess.

In exploring the use of personal qualities by candidates in this study, campaign managers were asked which personal traits they emphasized in the campaign message. Most managers mentioned two or three important traits; a total of nine personal traits were mentioned by more than one campaign manager. The traits fall into two general categories: personal qualities and professional qualities. Personal qualities focus on the individual characteristics of the candidate and professional qualities focus on the characteristics considered necessary for holding office. Table 3.1 shows the responses of female challengers, male incumbents, and male challengers. The male candidates were divided into incumbents and challengers to allow better comparisons with female candidates, all of whom were challengers. Because there were only four incumbent women in the study, they were dropped from the analysis in Table 3.1.

Three differences of at least borderline statistical significance emerge in Table 3.1. Female candidates, by a wide margin, were more likely than male candidates to tout their "credentials." If candidates stressed their professional accomplishments or qualifications, they were placed into this cate-

Table 3.2   Regression Estimates of Personal Traits Used in Campaign Messages, by Gender and Incumbency Status

	Personal Qualities	*Professional Qualities*
Constant	1.09**	1.22**
	(.15)	(.14)
Gender of candidate[a]	−.13	−.35**
	(.19)	(.16)
Challenger status[b]	.32*	−.10
	(.17)	(.16)
Adjusted R^2	.03	.03
Number of cases	105	105

NOTES: Personal qualities include honesty, ties to the local community, family-oriented, and caring. Coded 0 to 3 for the number of traits used. Professional qualities include leadership, credentials, gets things done, intelligence, and ideology. Coded 0 to 3 for the number of traits used.
a. Gender of candidate was coded 0 if a female and 1 if a male.
b. Challenger status was coded 0 if a challenger and 1 if an incumbent.
Chi-square test, *$p < .10$; **$p < .05$; standard errors are in parentheses.

gory. Also, female candidates emphasized "ties to the local community." Male candidates were more likely to emphasize their political ideology. To further disentangle the effects of gender and incumbency, a regression analysis was conducted. All but four of forty-three incumbents were men, so the incumbency variable is primarily testing the behavior of male incumbents. The dependent variables were grouped into the two categories from Table 3.1—personal qualities and professional qualities. The results are presented in Table 3.2.

There are two relationships in Table 3.2 of at least borderline statistical significance. Incumbents were more likely than challengers to stress personal qualities. The desire of incumbents to stress more personal qualities may be attributed to the scandals and low popularity ratings that engulfed Congress in the 1992 and 1994 elections. Many members needed to reestablish their personal connection, or what Fenno (1978) would call "home style," with their districts. Table 3.1 supports this by demonstrating that male incumbents were far more likely than female and male challengers to stress their honesty and integrity. In terms of gender, female candidates demonstrated a greater likelihood than male candidates to stress professional qualities. To explain these general findings, four areas of gender difference in the use of personal traits require further exploration.

Credentials and Professional Qualities

Female candidates were much more likely to tout their qualifications and accomplishments than their male counterparts. In the same vein, women were also more likely, although to a lesser extent, to present themselves as someone who "gets things done." Female candidates wanted to portray themselves as achievers and spent a great deal of effort in their campaigns chronicling their qualifications. Female candidates running for Congress in California in 1992 and 1994 believed that they encountered credibility problems in the election process. Fifteen of the twenty-nine (52%) campaign managers for female candidates felt that their candidate had a "credibility" problem regarding either certain issues or certain groups of voters. In addition, twenty of the twenty-nine (69%) managers believed that female candidates were held to higher standards by voters, the media, and the election process in general. The campaign managers of female candidates believed they were operating in a skeptical political environment.

To counter the perception that they were not credible, female candidates emphasized experiences that were prototypical qualifications for holding office. Female candidates pursued this strategy *despite* the fact that more female than male challengers had previously held an elected position. Twelve of the twenty-five female challengers (40%) in the study had held office prior to running for Congress, whereas only thirteen of the forty-eight male challengers (27%) were previous officeholders.[1] Women touted their qualifications because they encountered in the electoral environment what one manager referred to as a "subtle yet pervasive questioning about the suitability of women for public office." This same manager described the experiences of her female candidate:

> Everywhere we went we told voters how [the candidate] had started her own business. We felt under pressure to show that she had done more with her life than simply having been a good mother, an activist in the community, and a member of city council. That did not seem like it was enough for voters . . . we felt showing business acumen and entrepreneurial spirit gave voters more confidence in her. . . . In reality, the business she started was a home business with modest success, but by presenting her as a businesswoman it made her seem more substantial.

Another female candidate stressed her credibility problem a little more directly:

I never felt I was taken seriously. I was portrayed as a wealthy novice by my opponent and the media. Even though he is a dumb [expletive], he was always taken seriously. He can barely talk about issues and seems to know very little about the issues. But the fact remains, if you take a female challenger and put her next to a sitting congressman, she will come across as having no stature. This was really frustrating when I think of my opponent.

In working around these perceived credibility problems, women tried to present themselves as competent and able candidates. As Table 3.1 illustrates, more than two-thirds of female challengers discussed their credentials actively in their campaign, whereas less than one-quarter of male challengers did the same.

In addition to general credibility problems, female candidates also believed they had to work harder to establish their expertise on issues that are traditionally considered "male" policy interests. Several campaign managers for female candidates believed their candidate was not perceived as credible when discussing the economy, crime, or defense. One of these managers noted,

> I get the sense that whenever we are in a public forum with the opponent, that he is taken more seriously when discussing economic issues, and that we have the burden of trying to prove we are competent in these areas. This was apparent from the questions she was asked and the tone in which they were asked. . . . I remember one public forum where a man asked the congressman what he was going to do about possible base closures in the district. After the congressman replied, the man thanked him and then turned to our candidate and doubtingly said: "Do you have any ideas?" That's the kind of thing you see all the time.

The campaign staff of this female candidate countered the credibility problem by coaching their candidate so she would come across as an authority on "male issues." Similarly, the campaign staff of another female challenger spent a great deal of time developing specific economic and military proposals, with the goal of offsetting the disadvantage women have in discussing these issues. Yet another female candidate, from northern California, began her campaign by distributing a short book that contained her economic prescription for the country:

> Early in the primary season we wanted to establish our credibility, so we littered the district with 80,000 copies of [the candidate's economic plan]. She was . . . running in a crowded primary and she needed to do something to establish herself.

This particular candidate had run for office before and, based on her previous experience, wanted to counter what she perceived as biased presumptions that women were less qualified to handle certain issues. Her manager further described the effectiveness of having a written plan:

> When somebody would ask, what is she going to do about the budget? We would say: Have you seen her plan? Then we would hand them a copy. It was a great way of cutting off potential credibility problems and it seemed to silence the doubters.

A final example of how female candidates spent time establishing their credibility was reaching out to older voters. Campaign managers for five of the twenty-nine female candidates in the survey mentioned problems appealing to senior citizens. This problem was not mentioned by any male candidates. One of these managers commented,

> I came out from Washington to run this campaign, and I was totally unprepared for and surprised by the reactions of older voters to our candidate. We were running in a district with a lot of seniors and I could always sense some of their uncertainty about voting for a female candidate. This was not to mention the several or so older women who came up to the candidate during the course of the election and told her that politics was better left to men.

In a race in the Orange County area, another campaign manager for a female candidate sounded a similar sentiment:

> Older voters do not have confidence in a woman to fight and protect their interests. This is really ironic considering we were much stronger advocates of protecting Medicare and social security than was our [male] opponent.

These comments are not surprising in light of voter surveys that show that older voters admit to the highest levels of bias against female candidates. The 1993 General Social Survey (GSS) shows that 22 percent of voters over sixty-five say they would not vote for a woman for president (Davis and Smith 1993). That is compared with the national average of 9 percent. The number of seniors in a district will continue to be an important concern for female candidates. Campaign managers of two female candidates running in very competitive districts both believed their credibility troubles with older voters may have been decisive in their eventual defeat.

A central problem in assessing the credibility problems of female candidates in this analysis is the reliance on the perceptions of candidates and campaign officials. Unfortunately, it is difficult to document effectively the nuances of an election atmosphere. For instance, in pressing one campaign manager for specific examples of the credibility problems faced by female candidates, the manager replied,

> Listen . . . I cannot really think of any concrete examples, but I have worked for many female candidates and this year I am working for a man. There is no question in my mind that the electorate looks at the two differently. You can see it in the voters or the faces of the reporters. There is a clear sense the women are being judged—women have to be better; any little mistake is seized upon; there is a different standard.

Most of the managers felt that credibility problems were subtle yet pervasive, but often had trouble pinpointing specific examples. Williams (1994), in studying the television commercials of male and female Senate candidates in the 1992 election, found further evidence that women perceive a credibility problem. Williams systematically analyzed fifty-nine commercials, thirty-three for male candidates and twenty-six for female candidates. In terms of the production values of the advertisements, female candidates were more likely than the male candidates to be dressed formally and to have a male narrator (201). Williams posits that these differences illustrate that female candidates "felt the need to appear business-like, tough, and in-control" (203). Williams further notes that these qualities are almost always assumed to be true of male candidates.

Women's concerns over credibility was equally present in both the 1992 and 1994 elections. The persistence of a credibility problem for female candidates is often related to electoral circumstances. For instance, Alexander and Anderson (1993, 534-543), in a survey of Syracuse voters, found that when voter knowledge about the candidates is sparse, voters have a tendency to rely on gender role stereotypes. Their findings suggest that stereotypes can be overcome when the candidates are known to the voters. This is particularly important considering that voter knowledge about House candidates is usually quite low. The female congressional candidates in this examination fought to present themselves as professional and qualified politicians. They had to do this to avoid the possible consequences of having many voters rely on preestablished stereotypes of men and women in the political arena. Although the female congressional candidates in California worked to establish credibility and win the respect of a skeptical electorate by touting their qualifications, male challengers did not feel the same pressure. Not a single campaign manager for a male candidate in the survey expressed concerns about overcoming questions of credibility with voters. In emphasizing credentials in their campaigns, women were making a strategic decision in response to traditional societal beliefs concerning sex roles. Female candidates continue to have additional burdens in presenting themselves to voters. Ultimately, for the electoral process to be fair to women, women must feel free to compete in elections without these additional considerations and burdens. There is a basic unfairness in the extra lengths women must go to in order to convince voters that they are qualified. Despite the success of women in 1992, we have still not reached the point where female candidates are judged fairly by the voters.

Family Traits

Female and male candidates portray their family lives differently. Although both men and women used references to their family life in roughly equal amounts, they used family characteristics in very different ways. Several female candidates in 1992 stressed the aspect of being a single parent. The centerpiece of one female candidate's campaign involved her personal story of raising children as a single mother on welfare. The following quote is from a piece of her direct mail. Under the bold headline "WORKING MOTHER," it read,

> It's not been easy . . . [she] . . . became a single mother with three children ages 1, 3 and 5. She had very little money and they moved into a tiny cottage. . . . Although she worked, she was forced to turn to federal assistance (AFDC) to support her children. Determined to build a better future for herself and her family, she took a job as office manager . . . earned her business degree at night. She wanted to open her own business. . . . It's now a twelve-year success story.

Similarly, another female candidate from southern California made many references in her campaign to the challenges of being a single parent and putting her daughter through school. Presenting the challenge of being a single parent accomplishes two things for women. One, it demonstrates that they have succeeded, under difficult conditions, at what is often viewed as one of their primary responsibilities. Two, it demonstrates that they are tough and can handle difficult life situations. Toughness and the ability to successfully handle difficult situations are personal characteristics desirable in political leaders. Female candidates were able to use their particular life experiences to create a powerful personal image. Using family in this manner combined both the personal and strategic components of devising a campaign message.

In addition to emphasizing their status as single parents, several other female candidates also discussed their roles as mothers. For instance, a piece of campaign literature for a female candidate had one simple word on the cover: "Mother." This piece of literature was about environmental protection and on the inside cover was a quote from the candidate:

> Any mother knows why we call her 'mother' earth. Our life springs from her. She feeds us. And too often, she allows herself to give more than she has. We cannot behave as her spoiled children.

A piece of direct mail from a female candidate that discussed health care read,

> We walk the floors with our kids when they're sick. Then we care for our parents. Those experiences taught me that we need to control health costs and make care universally available.

Several campaign managers who had experience running the campaigns of female candidates all noted that women, as these quotes indicate, are much more likely to incorporate their personal family experiences into the way they discuss issues and how they campaign. Similarly, Williams (1994, 209) found that female Senate candidates were more likely to stress "feminine qualities" in their campaign commercials, although he did not mention such specific traits and experiences as were picked up in the interviews in this study. The nurturing images presented by female congressional candidates in California were nowhere to be found in the campaigns of male candidates. Child-raising and other intimate family experiences would appear to be messages that only women use. The ways that female candidates used the personal quality of motherhood corresponds well with the social psychological literature emphasizing the developmental effect of different life experiences for women and men (Belenky et al. 1986; Gilligan 1982). As with the discussion of personal campaigning in Chapter 2, it is difficult to infer the practical effects of women's propensity to discuss experiences that are usually considered personal.

Although many women were referring to qualities such as motherhood and nurturing, particularly in 1992, the male candidates referred to family experiences in different ways. Male candidates used family traits with the same frequency as women (see Table 3.1) but they tended to discuss their "family" experiences in a more traditional manner. Most male candidates attempted to convey the portrait of a good "family man." One male challenger in northern California always had his family with him and visible at campaign events. His goal was to demonstrate his upstanding and virtuous "family values." Another male candidate often had his wife introduce him at speeches and rallies to illustrate the strong support he had from his family. None of the campaign managers for female candidates acknowledged any public role for the husbands of their candidates.

This largely superficial and abbreviated use of the family trait was most evident in the campaign literature of male candidates. Almost all the male candidates had at least one piece of literature that showed a picture of the candidate with his family. However, these pictures were not usually accompanied by any written discussion of the family. This was in sharp contrast to the literature of female candidates, which often displayed a family picture accompanied by text discussing her family. In one example, a female candidate had a section in a piece of her campaign literature titled, "It's a Family Affair." Underneath the title was a lengthy discussion of the role her family played in the campaign, part of which read,

[Her] campaign is a family affair. And her children take their roles very seriously. Last week saw [two of her children] furiously working with their mother in their downtown campaign headquarters. . . .

One of her children is quoted in the text:

I am working full-time for Mom. She dedicated her life to us and now it is our time to give back.

The male candidates did not discuss their family in such personal terms. In reviewing all the campaign literature collected for this investigation, seventy-eight pieces (for 53 candidates) of literature from male candidates contained a picture of their family. In only six of these pieces of literature (8%) was there any description or discussion of the family beyond a brief sentence identifying the pictured people. For female candidates in this investigation, thirty-one pieces (for 24 candidates) of literature were collected showing a family portrait; fourteen of these portraits (45%) had accompanying text discussing the family in some detail. Male candidates used "family" to convey that they were good providers with a closely knit family. Women used "family" to help define their life experiences and qualifications for holding office.

The gender differences in the use of family traits is a combination of both the strategic and personal aspects of campaign messages. Women used family traits to establish the strength of their character. The male candidates used family traits as symbolic gestures. For male candidates, the family relationships represented in campaign messages embodied long-held stereotypes of what a family should be. Despite the reality that less than 20 percent of families in the United States are consistent with the traditional structure of a male breadwinner and female homemaker, many of the male candidates in the California congressional elections were reinforcing this stereotype (McGlen and O'Connor 1995, 250-58). The perceptions by the male candidates that came through in the interviews was that voters are very comfortable with the idea of a traditional family and that any other presentation by the candidates may cause concern or skepticism on the part of the voters.

Finally, it is important to note that the use of parenting and motherhood as personal images by female candidates was much more prevalent in the "year of the woman" elections in 1992. Three of the female challengers who won in 1992 and employed "mother" themes abandoned them as incumbents in 1994. This may be explained by drastic changes in the political environment between the two elections. Female candidates were acting strategically by using the stereotypical "female traits" in 1992, a political environment that welcomed these traits, and by abandoning them in 1994, an environment that was not responsive to these traits. This suggests that female candidates will have to be in tune with the political environment in ways that male candidates will not; the presentation of stereotypical male traits such as toughness and assertiveness are traits that will be desirable in almost any political environment.

Intelligence

A third important area for consideration is the use of "intelligence" as a personal trait. As seen in Table 3.1, few candidates made use of the characteristic of "intelligence" in their campaign messages. Ten out of seventy-six male candidates (13%) and only two out of twenty-five female candidates

(8%) stressed their intelligence as personal attributes. However, three male candidates who emphasized their intelligence and were running against women said they used this trait in an attempt to discredit their female opponent. One of the managers of these male candidates stated,

> Everywhere we had a joint appearance with her, we made a point of having the candidate list his advanced academic degrees to show he was more qualified than her. We wanted to highlight her flimsy intellectual record.

When asked whether this was an attack on the woman opponent's intelligence, the manager responded,

> You bet. We wanted people to know we were from the ivy leagues and she only had an A.A. from some nothing little college.

Another manager of a male candidate expressed a similar strategy:

> We wanted voters to know that he was smart and that she was not. At debates we would always use lots of specific facts in answering questions. We wanted to overwhelm her and hopefully show the voters that she did not know much about anything.

The last of these three male candidates was much less subtle in his attacks and during a radio interview directly stated that his woman opponent "was not smart enough" to serve in Congress. In another instance, a longtime male incumbent referred to his female opponent at a public forum as a "naive young woman." His opponent was a forty-year-old woman who was a practicing lawyer. The campaign manager for this female candidate definitely thought the incumbent was trying to embarrass and demean the intelligence of the female candidate:

> In the debates he would say things that were dripping with condescension, as if he were talking to a five-year-old. . . . He would always patronizingly call her by her first name—he wanted to make her look stupid.

The campaign manager for this male incumbent denied that they were trying to attack the intelligence of the opponent.

Although a candidate's strategy of highlighting educational and intellectual differences between him- or herself and the opponent may not appear unique, it is important to note that of all the candidates in this investigation, only men running against women made public attacks on the intellectual fitness of their opponents. Men running against men made no such attacks, and women running against men made no such attacks. When asked about this phenomenon, a longtime political consultant who was working for one of the female candidates whose opponent tried to attack her intelligence commented,

> It seems to me that men are more likely to think of intelligence in terms of achievements, as if there is a pecking order. . . . The higher the academic degree you have, the better equipped you are to be in Congress. The more posts you have held, the more qualified you are. In my experience with women [candidates], they think of qualifications in relation to the individual, and not the number of degrees.

This explanation of the behavior of male candidates is more accommodating than the possibility that these male candidates were making strategic decisions to perpetuate the stereotype that women are less intellectually and emotionally suited for political endeavors. From these male candidates' own accounts, they were attempting to frame the election as a choice between a well-educated, experienced man and a less intelligent woman. This was a choice they felt would produce a favorable result with voters. In the end all three of these male candidates were defeated, although in the postelection interviews, two of the three vowed to run again the following year, both believing that their superior qualifications would eventually allow them to prevail. Although ultimately the behavior of these male candidates seems minor considering the other factors going on during an election, it still suggests that there is some resistance to women winning and taking positions of high electoral power.

Ideology and Community

A final area of difference between women and men pertains to the traits of "ideology" and "ties to the local community" listed in Table 3.1 (both were of borderline statistical significance). These differences are consistent with social psychological and political science literature that has suggested that men and women may have differing political orientations (Kathlene 1995; Sherry 1986). In the first instance, male candidates were more likely to advertise their political ideology than female candidates. Several male challengers and incumbents touted their political ideology but no female challengers did the same. For instance, the campaign manager for one incumbent male Republican noted,

> He wants people to know that he is a conservative. One of our pieces of campaign literature refers to him as Mr. Conservative. He stresses his conservatism because he believes this is something voters should know about him.

Similarly, a male challenger from northern California stated that he always lets people know that he is a "libertarian on social issues, and a fiscal conservative on economic issues." Another Republican candidate was so wedded to his conservatism that he gave a speech denouncing Republican gubernatorial candidate Pete Wilson in the 1994 election for his false conservatism. He remarked about the speech:

> I believe in traditional conservatism. A conservatism that is rooted in family and morality. In a speech to the Republican convention I told my party members that I could not support Pete Wilson because he had violated so many tenants of conservatism.

Interestingly, this male candidate delivered this speech to a room full of Wilson supporters and was roundly booed and even physically assaulted by several Wilson supporters who wanted to remove him from the microphone:

> I was really shaken up about what happened at that speech. I could not believe words could make people so angry, but I knew I had to speak up for my beliefs and principles. Wilson's conservatism is phony.

There were no female congressional candidates who made it a clear point to advance a political ideology. This is not to say that women were in any way less passionate about their positions. As we will see when we turn to a discussion of issues and themes, women were dedicated to particular agendas but did not tie their message to a particular ideology. Also, it was noted in Chapter 2 that several women entered their races to combat the "religious right." However, these women did not make their concerns over the religious right major parts of their campaign message. Male candidates' greater adherence to an ideology is supported by Sherry's assessment that men in the political process demonstrate a greater adherence to abstract principles (1986).

An equally good fit with the literature on men's and women's different political orientations is the evidence in this study that female challengers

Table 3.3   The Central Themes of the Candidates, by Gender and Challenger
Status

Theme	Female Challengers (N = 39)	Male Challengers (N = 37)	Male Incumbents (N = 25)	Significance of Chi-Square Male/Female Challengers
Change	64%[a]	27%	10%	.000*
Reform congress	8	19	10	.298
Economy	24	41	28	.312
Serving local interests	12	24	28	.191
Outsider	32	19	10	.183
Choice (abortion)	8	8	0	.898
Opponents' record	8	3	26	.367

a. Percentages signify the number of candidates who said they used that theme. Columns total more than 100% because some candidates had two central themes.
*p < .01.

were more likely than male challengers to stress their "ties to the local community." Forty percent of female challengers stressed their closeness with the community, whereas less than a quarter of male challengers did the same. As discussed previously, the best explanation for this difference is the socialization patterns of women and men. Women are more likely than men to begin their political involvement with grassroots activity that links them to the community (Darcy, Welch, and Clark 1994). These two differences in the presentation of personal images—ideology and ties to the local community—are best explained by small differences in the personal convictions of men and women. Both of these differences may be attributed to the socialization of men and women in how they view political involvement.

 ## Presentation of Campaign Themes

In the media age, campaigns are often reduced to simple presentations of symbols or themes. These themes often come to dominate the message of the campaign. As the campaign manager for a challenger running in the Los Angeles area noted: "The entire campaign was fought over two words: *choice* and *change*." In light of the limited knowledge voters possess about House candidates, central themes may be the only thing that campaigns can hope to convey to the disinterested congressional electorate (Luttbeg and Gant 1995,

184). Campaign managers in this investigation were asked open-ended questions about the themes of their campaigns and how they used them. Themes were defined in the interviews as "broad or general messages—not specific policy positions." Managers usually mentioned one or two themes that were foremost in their campaign's message. Across the 1992 and 1994 election there were seven campaign themes that were mentioned by more than one campaign manager. These are listed in Table 3.3.

The most striking difference and the only statistically significant item in Table 3.3 concerns the theme of "change." Female challengers were more than twice as likely as male challengers to use change as a central theme. Along similar lines, female candidates were more likely than men to emphasize their status as an "outsider." Over the elections of 1992 and 1994, when many Americans were dissatisfied with the performance of Congress, a relatively small number of male candidates were stressing change as a central theme. Female candidates in 1992 were able to present themselves as the agents of change despite the fact that in many cases they had more political experience than their male counterparts. Women were able to capitalize on the stereotype that they were a different type of politician, even though many of them had career paths similar to those of male candidates. The 1992 election afforded women the opportunity to sell themselves as different. There has been no other election in history that has provided this kind of electoral advantage for women. During the course of the 1992 general election, Senate candidate Dianne Feinstein, who had lost a close gubernatorial election in 1990, commented about the 1992 elections that "this is the first time I feel that running as a woman isn't a disadvantage" (Witt, Paget, and Matthews 1994, 12). Colorado Senate Candidate Josie Heath also commented about the dynamics of 1992: "It's about change and they [voters] see women as the agents of change . . . people see us as outsiders, as agents who can really come in and bring an agenda that isn't the same-old, same-old and I think that's what they are looking for" (Crier & Co. 1992).

The only other sizable, although not statistically significant, difference occurs in the use of the "economy." Male challengers were more likely to use the economy as a general theme. Over 40 percent of male candidates stressed the economy as one of their foremost themes and less than a quarter of female candidates did the same. Kahn (1993) found that male candidates were significantly more likely to use the economy as a campaign appeal. This finding is also consistent with the literature on legislative agendas, which suggests that female officeholders are less likely than men in similar positions to place high priority on issues of economic growth (Thomas 1991; Schumaker and Burns 1988). This difference may also be partially explained by the fact that Democrats are less likely to discuss the economy. Most of the female candidates in this study were Democrats, which suggests that both gender and partisan considerations explain the difference in the use of the economy theme.

not true in 1992 Pres. ele.

"Change" as a Campaign Theme

There is little doubt that female candidates felt more comfortable trying to sell themselves as agents of change. The ability of women to use change as a theme was more apparent in the 1992 elections than in the 1994 elections. The use of the change theme by women speaks to the uniqueness of the 1992 elections. Many female candidates in 1992 imbued the theme of change with a gender component; several stressed the idea that their sex presented an important form of change. For instance, in the sample of female candidates from the 1992 election, eight out of sixteen made either direct or indirect appeals to voters, asking them to vote for them because they were women. In the two U.S. Senate races in California in 1992, Dianne Feinstein and Barbara Boxer led the way by using the underrepresentation of women as a theme in their campaigns. A Feinstein campaign slogan read, "Two percent may be good enough for milk, but it is not good enough for the U.S. Senate." Many of the female candidates running in the House races followed suit. As one female candidate stated,

> Every time I am in front of a women's group or any group that I think will be receptive, I mention how few women there are in Congress. I never actually say vote for me, I am a woman, but where appropriate I discuss the need for more women in politics.

Another female candidate made a reference to the need to "bring more women to Washington" in all of her speeches.

Five other female candidates, all in 1992, used direct mail to highlight the underrepresentation of women in Washington. The cover of one mailing read in bold letters: "It's Time to Change The Face of Congress." Beneath this caption was the picture of seven white men conducting a congressional committee hearing, an obvious reference to the Senate Judiciary Committee in the Anita Hill/Clarence Thomas hearings. On the bottom of the mailer it read, "Vote for The Only Pro-Choice Democratic Woman on The Ballot." Another female candidate used a piece of direct mail that featured a picture of Anita Hill testifying at the Supreme Court confirmation hearings of Clarence Thomas. Beneath the picture the caption read, "Last Year, She Spoke Out. Now It's Your Turn." On the reverse side of the mailing it stated, "We can send a strong . . . pro-change woman to the U.S. Congress." A third female candidate discussed the need for change in greater depth; a piece of her campaign literature read,

> We need more women . . . in Congress to change "The Good Old Boy" system in Washington. [She] has challenged the good old boy system her entire life. Time and time again when she was told that change wasn't possible—she set her mind and energy to work and made change happen.

Women clearly wanted to capitalize on the idea that they represented a different kind of politics.

Although half of the female candidates in 1992 associated change as a theme with gender, only one out of fifteen female candidates examined in 1994 made gender-based appeals. Of the five female candidates in the study who ran in both elections, all five used a gender/change theme in 1992 and only one of these women used the theme again in 1994. Women who ran in 1992 used the gender theme as a matter of personal conviction; they believed it was important to increase the number of women in Washington. However, by 1994 the political environment forced women to drop any direct appeals to change based on gender—a strategic consideration.

In using the themes of "change" and being an "outsider," women were able to capitalize on the heightened perception by voters and the media that female candidates represented something different. In playing up the theme of change, women were strategically capitalizing on the political environment. This was particularly true in the 1992 election. In 1992, the campaign managers were asked if there were any advantages women had in the campaign; twenty of the twenty-nine managers in a race with a female candidate felt that women had a much easier time selling themselves as agents of change. As one incumbent Congressman's campaign manager noted,

> It is a built-in advantage that women seem to have this year, they appear to be something new and different, and whether they are or not is not that important.

Another campaign manager stated,

The people want something different, and the voters seem to think that female candidates will do things differently. People are fed up with Washington and they see that men dominate the politics in Washington.

A number of other campaign managers expressed similar sentiments. However, by 1994, of the twenty-three managers surveyed who were involved in races with women, only one viewed being a female candidate as an advantage. In sharp contrast to 1992, six of these managers believed that female candidates were at a disadvantage in 1994. The honeymoon for women congressional candidates ended abruptly. One manager and long-time political operative in California noted,

> Everything changed in 1994. In 1992 voters wanted to try something new, and women, or pardon the expression, mommies, running for office provided that. However, 1994 was the complete opposite, the issues worked against women— voters had heard enough about women in the previous year and they felt that the change they had voted for in 1992 did not materialize . . . women were really hampered in 1994.

With several factors working against them, female candidates were forced to strategize differently about the elections in 1994.

This discussion of campaign themes leads to two conclusions. One, that women's ability to present themselves as new and different kinds of candidates was very short-lived. There is little reason to think that female candidates as a group, possibly with the exception of the first viable female presidential candidate, will ever be as clearly viewed as agents of change as they were in 1992. The second conclusion is that the political environment may have a great deal to do with the types of central themes female candidates can effectively present in their campaign message. The effect of the political environment can be more clearly seen in turning to the issues that dominate the political agenda.

The Policy Issues in the Campaigns

Recent studies of the issues presented in the campaign messages of women and men have found greatly contrasting results. Kahn (1993), in focusing on the campaign commercials used by candidates for the U.S. Senate in 1984 and 1986, found striking differences in the issues emphasized by male and female candidates. The differences were consistent with the stereotypical strengths of women and men identified in other analyses (see Thomas 1994). Female Senate candidates were more likely to discuss social programs and social issues, whereas men were more likely to discuss economic issues, farm issues, and getting a fair share for their state (490). Kahn concluded that women and men "do have distinct issue priorities that they pursue in their quest for election to the U.S. Senate" (489). Williams (1994), examining campaign commercials of U.S. Senate races six years later in 1992, found no issue differences between men and women. Of the five issues frequently mentioned by the candidates, governmental reform, the economy, the opponent, social welfare, and energy or the environment, Williams concluded that "male and female Senate candidates did not exhibit any significant differences when it came to the issues mentioned in their ads" (205). Thus we are left with an unclear picture of the issue-based campaign messages of female and male candidates. However, we must remember that the sample of female candidates surveyed in both of these studies was quite small. Williams examined the political ads for eight female candidates and Kahn examined the ads of ten female candidates.

In turning to congressional elections, our knowledge of gender differences in the campaign messages of House candidates is almost nonexistent. The studies by Kahn (1993) and Williams (1994) give us some insight into what we might expect; however, House races certainly have different dynamics from statewide elections. In turning to California, we must consider what issues were important in 1992 and 1994 because the issues presented by candidates are often influenced by the political environment. The issue agenda in California differed greatly between the 1992 and 1994 elections. In 1992, Clinton and the Democrats ran on two major issues: reviving the economy and enacting health care reform. In California, with the state's unemployment rate hovering around 10 percent, job creation was the central issue in the election. By 1994, with the U.S. economy moving along at a steady pace and health care reform having died in the U.S. Congress, the issue priorities of voters had changed. In California in 1994 the top two issues in most congressional districts were crime and illegal immigration (see Table 5.7).

The change in agendas posed some interesting dilemmas for female and male candidates. The 1992 elections in California focused on jobs and health care, two issues that fall comfortably near the realm of traditional "women's interests." However, the 1994 election turned to crime and immigration, two issues for which voters have expressed greater confidence in male leadership. A poll conducted by Celinda Lake demonstrated voters' preference for men to tackle issues such as crime and immigration (see Berke 1994). To investigate the issue agendas of the candidates, campaign managers were first asked to identify the four most important policy issues in the message of their campaign. The intent was to determine the top issue priorities of the candidates. The responses are listed in Table 3.4. In examining gender differences in policy agendas, two comparisons are important. First, comparing the female candidates (column 1), all of whom were Democrats, with the Democratic male candidates (column 3) allows distinctions to be made between gender and party differences. There were only four Republican women and only two Democratic men opposing Republican women who participated in the interview process for this study. These candidates were dropped from analysis in Tables 3.4 and 3.5 to permit more accurate comparisons. The other important comparison is between two categories of male Republican candidates, those running against a woman (column 2) and those running against a man (column 4). This comparison helps to determine whether running against a woman causes a male candidate to change his issue message. Table 3.4 has been broken into three sets of issues: those the literature classifies as traditionally "women's issues," "men's issues," and non-gender-specific or general issues. As mentioned previously, these classifications are based on studies of policymakers that have identified differing agendas for women and men.

The 1992 and 1994 elections were dominated by "men's issues" and general issues. Only three of the issues mentioned as main issues—abortion, health care, and education—could be classified as "women's issues," and there was no significant gender-related difference for any of these, although female candidates appeared more likely to stress abortion and education in their campaigns. All three of these issues were part of the national debate and there is no surprise that they were among the main issues the candidates stressed. Thus, female candidates were not running on a central platform of "women's issues." For instance, none of the candidates used parental leave, day care, or gender-based employment discrimination as main issues.

Of the fifteen issues mentioned by campaign managers as main issues, there were gender differences (columns 1 & 3) of at least borderline statistical significance for four of them. Female candidates were more likely to stress the environment and family values as main issues in their campaigns. Male candidates were more likely to focus on free trade and the character of their opponent. The differences on family issues and free trade are consistent with studies of the legislative priorities of men and women policymakers.

Table 3.4   Main Issues in the Message of Each Campaign, by Gender, Party, and
Type of Opponent (1992 and 1994 Combined)

	Female versus Male Races		Male Only Races		Significance of Chi-Square	
	1 *Women* *(N = 25)*	*2* *Men* *(N = 21)*	*3* *Democrats* *(N= 27)*	*4* *Republicans.* *(N = 26)*	*Columns 1 & 3*	*Columns 2 & 4*
Women's issues[a]						
Health care	44%	24%	41%	23%	.961	.911
Education	48	10	33	12	.379	.873
Abortion	32	5	15	0	.244	.371
Men's issues						
Crime issues	44	48	37	62	.554	.206
Tax policy	12	52	11	35	.762	.215
Deficit	16	24	4	8	.102	.161
Defense	4	10	7	12	.511	.743
Government regulation	4	29	4	15	.959	.354
NAFTA/GATT						
free trade	0	10	19	4	.015**	.480
Immigration	12	33	7	27	.700	.786
General issues						
Job creation	76	67	67	69	.640	.539
Reform	8	19	11	39	.580	.103
Family values	12	24	0	15	.086*	.566
Environment	48	5	15	8	.028**	.898
Opponent's character	8	14	30	12	.070*	.873

NOTES: Percentage signifies the candidates who included that issue as one of their four main issues. Listed are
all the issues that were mentioned by more than one campaign manager.
a. The headings "women's issues" and "men's issues" were determined based on the categorizations of issue
priorities that emerge in the gender politics literature on female candidates and policymakers.
*$p < .10$; **$p < .05$.

For instance, Schumaker and Burns's (1988) study of city council members
found that women tended to emphasize issues of social welfare and men
tended to emphasize issues of economic development. In California, environmental protection emerged as the issue with the largest differ in
emphasis between female and male candidates. The environment has not
generally been categorized by the gender politics literature as a woman's
issue. None of the major studies of women in legislative office have identified a gender gap on the issue of the environment (Thomas 1994; Dodson
and Carroll 1991; Saint-Germain 1989). Further, Williams's (1994) study of

Table 3.5   Issues (Selected List of 16) Appearing in the Message of
Each Campaign, by Gender, Party, and Type of Opponent
(1992 and 1994 Combined)

	Female Versus Male Races		Male Only Races		Significance of Chi-Square	
	1 Women (N = 25)	2 Men (N = 21)	3 Democrats (N = 27)	4 Republicans (N = 26)	Columns 1 & 3	Columns 2 & 4
Women's issues[a]						
Abortion	84%	29%	70%	4%	.149	.026**
Parental leave	52	5	44	8	.586	.626
Education	72	33	70	46	.866	.419
Health care	72	52	82	69	.422	.357
Thomas/Hill hearings						
sexual harassment	40	0	0	4	.001**	.342
Children's issues	64	24	27	15	.018**	.354
Men's issues						
Defense spending	64	48	52	58	.299	.490
Crime issues	72	81	74	80	.672	.828
Tax policy	64	91	33	96	.030**	.241
Government regulation	8	81	22	77	.087*	.866
NAFTA/GATT						
free trade	48	48	48	42	.992	.934
Immigration	32	67	33	58	.700	.590
General issues						
Gay rights	48	24	12	8	.013**	.161
Family values	28	48	15	31	.418	.357
Environment	84	48	54	62	.086*	.336
Job creation	96	95	89	96	.266	.480

NOTE: Percentage signifies candidates who included that issue in the message of their campaign.
a. The headings "women's issues" and "men's issues" were determined based on the categorizations of issue priorities that emerge in the gender politics literature on female candidates and policymakers.
$*p < .10;$ $**p < .05.$

gender differences in campaign commercials did not find any gender difference on the emphasis of the environment. However, Kahn (1993, 490) classified the environment as a "woman's issue," placing it in the category of social
issues. In addition, in polls, voters have tended to favor the leadership of
women in protecting the environment (Burrell 1994, 24-25). The final
difference emerging in Table 3.4, the greater tendency of male candidates to
make a central issue of the opponent's record, is somewhat contradictory

with the findings in the last chapter in which women said presenting their opponent's record was a top strategic priority. We might conclude that, although women said it was a priority, they did not make it one of their main issues or central themes.

In the comparison of male candidates (columns 2 & 4) there were no issues with a statistically significant relationship, although the difference on the issue of congressional reform is descriptively large. Men running against women were less likely to raise the issue of congressional reform. Most of this difference comes from the 1992 election. The difference in emphasizing congressional reform is consistent with the earlier discussion of the use of change as a campaign theme. Focusing on congressional reform is a means of emphasizing the general theme of change. Some of the men running against women, particularly in 1992, did not feel credible using issues that were directly related to change. For example, when one campaign manager for a male candidate running against a woman was asked why their campaign did not emphasize congressional reform, he explained,

> We just did not think we could credibly sell ourselves as reformers. Women were getting so much media attention about how they were going to shake up Washington. . . . With all the hoopla, and undeserved attention our opponent was getting, we did not feel we could credibly say: We are really the ones who are going to reform the system. We had to focus in on other things.

Women only dominated the "change" theme in 1992. By 1994 none of the male candidates in the sample were expressing these types of concerns.

To assess the substantive agendas of the candidates beyond the main issues, campaign managers were asked directly about sixteen wide-ranging issues. The list was composed of what were thought to be the most important issues on the political agenda. Also, six of the sixteen issues were "women's issues," to test the hypothesis that female candidates are more likely to raise these issues. The campaign managers were asked whether each issue appeared in the message of the campaign. In other words, was the issue addressed in speeches, TV and radio advertisements, or campaign literature? The goal was to determine whether the candidate sought to raise the issues. Table 3.5 lists the sixteen issues and the candidate responses. The table is organized in the same manner as Table 3.4.

Table 3.5 shows gender differences on six of the sixteen individual issues (columns 1 & 3). Women were more likely to emphasize sexual harassment, children's issues, tax policy, gay rights, and the environment. The greater emphasis on sexual harassment and children's issues is consistent with the literature on gender differences in issue priorities of male and female legislators (e.g., Thomas 1994). Women were also more likely to raise the issue of gay rights. Although gay rights has not generally been classified as a "woman's issue," Havens and Healy (1991, 23), in a study of cabinet appointees in Connecticut, found that female cabinet members were more supportive of gay rights than male cabinet members. This is also consistent with Kahn's (1993) finding that female candidates place a greater emphasis on social policies. Surprisingly, women were more likely to address tax policy, an issue generally considered to be a "male" policy priority. There appears to be no clear explanation for this. In the comparison of male candidates (columns 2 & 4), abortion was the only statistically significant issue. Men running against women were significantly more likely than men running against men to use the abortion issue in their campaign message. The best explanation for this is that the presence of a female candidate encouraged the male candidate to raise the issue. Male candidates' use of the abortion issue is addressed on the following pages.

To further examine the relationship between gender, party, incumbency, and the issues used in the campaign messages, regression equations were developed. The year of the election was also included in the equation to test whether the year of the election affected the issues presented by candidates. For the equations, the dependent variables were grouped into three categories of issues: "women's," "men's," and "general." The groupings of issues are reported for both the main issues and the list of sixteen issues. The results are presented in Table 3.6.

The top half of Table 3.6 shows that women, Democrats, and challengers were more likely to discuss the three "women's issues" as main issues in their agenda, particularly in 1992. For the "men's issues," gender and incumbency were not significant, but Republicans were more likely to raise these issues. Female candidates were more likely to raise the "general issues." This can best be explained by the inclusion of the environment and family values in that category. In terms of the main issues in the campaign messages, the year of the election emerges as one of the most important factors in determining when particular issues will dominate the electoral environment. "Women's issues" and "general issues" were used prominently as main issues in 1992, and "men's issues" were more prevalent in 1994. This further indicates the changes in the political environment between the two elections. The equal likelihood that female and male candidates employ

Table 3.6   Regression Estimates of Grouped Main Issues and Sixteen Selected
Issues, by Gender, Party Affiliation, Incumbency, and Year of Election

	Women's Issues[a]	Men's Issues	General Issues
Main issues:			
Constant	1.84**	.66**	1.83**
	(.14)	(.17)	(.15)
Gender of candidate[b]	−.66**	.09	−.28
	(.13)	(.19)	(.17)
Party affiliation[c]	−.45**	.86**	−.12
	(.14)	(.17)	(.16)
Incumbency status[d]	−.27*	.17	.50**
	(.14)	(.18)	(.16)
Year of the election[e]	−.66**	.30*	−.74**
	(.13)	(.16)	(.14)
Adjusted R^2	.46	.29	.15
N	105	105	105
List of 16 issues:			
Constant	4.07**	2.49**	2.42**
	(.24)	(.25)	(.16)
Gender of candidate	−1.03**	−.03	−.44**
	(.27)	(.29)	(.19)
Party affiliation	−1.32**	1.45**	−.22
	(.25)	(.27)	(.17)
Incumbency status	−.56**	−.04	.34*
	(.26)	(.27)	(.17)
Year of the election	.01	.54**	.00
	(.23)	(.24)	(.16)
Adjusted R^2	.46	.29	.08
N	104	103	104

a. The headings "women's issues" and "men's issues" were determined based on the categorizations of issue priorities that emerge in the gender politics literature on female candidates and policymakers. The main issues, women's issues, and men's issues were all coded from 0 to 5 depending on the five main issues used by each campaign. The list of 16 issues was coded 0 to 6 for the women's issues, 0 to 6 for the men's issues, and 0 to 4 for the general issues.
b. Gender of candidate was coded 0 if a female and 1 if a male.
c. Party affiliation was coded 0 if a Democrat and 1 if a Republican.
d. Incumbency status was coded 0 if a challenger and 1 if an incumbent.
e. Year of election was coded 0 for 1992 election and 1 for 1994 election.
Chi-square test, $*p < .10$; $**p < .05$; standard errors are in parentheses.

"men's issues" in their campaign messages may be explained by female candidates' strategic decisions to emphasize these issues to offset some of the credibility problems they were experiencing.

Turning to the list of sixteen issues in the bottom half of Table 3.6, the patterns here were very similar to the use patterns for the main issues. Democrats, women, and challengers were again more likely to raise the "women's issues," and Republicans were more likely to raise the "men's issues." Significantly, there were no gender differences between women and men in the use of "men's issues." With regard to the year of the election, again, "men's issues" were more prominent in 1994. However, the year of the election made no difference in the use of "women's issues." This is important because it suggests that women are more likely to raise "women's issues" regardless of the electoral environment. The six "women's issues" placed on the list of sixteen issues were raised in equal amounts in both elections. This ultimately suggests that female candidates place a strong priority on making "women's issues" part of their campaign agenda.

Yet looking at the overall picture for 1992 and 1994, female candidates were acting as strategic politicians; they were more likely to place "women's issues" at the forefront of their agenda only when the political environment was favorable toward these positions. The greater incorporation of "women's issues" in the campaign messages may lead to the fuller representation of these issues in the legislative process. As discussed in Chapter 1, the literature on the decision making of members of Congress suggests that issues raised during the course of an election are likely to become part of the legislative agenda of the election winner (Arnold 1990; Kingdon 1989).

Gender Differences in Policy Usage

Two additional aspects of policy and issue usage in campaign agendas require examination. The first concerns the ways in which men and women discuss the issues. Gender differences in the manner and context of the presentation of issues does not come through in Tables 3.4-6. However, what became apparent with regard to a number of issues is that female and male candidates tend to discuss issues differently. Many of the female candidates addressed issues in a broader context than their male counterparts, often discussing an issue in relation to other issues. Male candidates were more likely to see issues in isolation and identify issues in terms of rights. Kathlene (1995) found similar patterns in how female and male state legislators in Colorado conceptualized the issue of crime. In summarizing female legislators' assessments, Kathlene writes, "women emphasized the societal link to crime, which led them to speak about long-term preventative strategies as well as intervention measures" (720-21). In comparison, the men in the sample "emphasized individual responsibility, which led them to propose stricter sentencing and increased prison space" (721). This different conception of issues was apparent in some of the behavior of the congressional candidates in this study. For instance, compare the following two candidates' responses to the question of how they used the issue of health care in their campaign. Both are from liberal Democratic candidates, one a woman and the other a man. The female candidate responded,

> In discussing health care, I tried to explain to voters that improving health care services was linked to their personal economic stability. If they don't have health insurance, their job could be in jeopardy if they get injured or sick. Like many of the people in this district, they could find themselves on welfare, continuing the poverty which is prevalent in this part of the city. I used health care to try to educate voters about how reforming the system was also about family and job security.

The male candidate responded,

> Citizens need to begin viewing health care as a right that belongs to everyone. I explained to people in speeches and at breakfasts that the current system is grossly unfair. Wealthy people have health care and poor people do not.

In this example, the male candidate tells voters that health care is a fairness issue, whereas the female candidate tries to get voters to consider health care in the context of their lives.

Another illustration of the broader consideration with which many women viewed issues can be seen in the differences between how a male and a female candidate used the issue of the Family and Medical Leave Act. The campaign manager for the male candidate explained how they used the issue:

> The congressman proudly discussed his vote for the Family Leave Act. He always listed it with his other major accomplishments of the last two years . . . his vote for the crime bill, his work to reduce the deficit, and his support of NAFTA.

The campaign manager for the female candidate stated,

> She talked about the benefits of parental leave in conjunction with a group of related issues. These issues included increased funding for breast cancer, sexual

harassment, abortion rights. . . . She always treated these issues as a package of issues that were linked in their effort to allow women to be full partners in society.

The male candidate considered parental leave as an independent issue. The female candidate viewed the issue as part of a broader, connected agenda.

A final instance of male and female candidates discussing issues differently occurred with the abortion issue. Differences in the use of this issue were common among a number of male and female candidates. The managers of male candidates described their candidate's view on abortion in simple and narrow terms:

> The candidate believes abortion is murder. That is his view and he states it whenever the issue is raised.

> Our candidate has always supported a woman's right to choose.

> The congressman believes that this not a political issue and the government should not be involved.

Female candidates tended to view the issue in a larger context. When asked about her campaign's use of the abortion issue, the manager for one female candidate shot back,

> It is about choice. It is not about abortion. I do not like questions that refer to abortion. Choice is what is important. Women must be allowed to have choices for themselves, their careers, and their families. The choice issue speaks to the entire issue of opportunity for women.

The differences in how men and women discussed issues in the campaigns demonstrate a subtle dynamic. Nonetheless, in interviewing campaign officials and candidates from over 100 campaigns, it was evident that female candidates were more likely to discuss issues in relation to their broader effect on people's lives. This difference came through in how the candidate discussed issues with voters but was usually lost in the text of campaign literature, which is often not written by the candidates. The effect this may have on the outcome of an election and on how voters perceive the candidates is difficult to determine. Yet these differences between female and male candidates are consistent with Kathlene's (1995) analysis of male and female legislators' attitudes toward crime. The female legislators in Kathlene's study tended to think about policy issues as they related to other decisions or concerns. Conversely, the male legislators were more likely to conceive of an issue in abstract terms and not in relation to other potential facets of the issue. These same patterns are evident in the preceding quotations, which show that on issues such as health care, parental leave, and abortion, male and female candidates often think about policy issues in different ways. Again, the existence of this difference offers the potential for a different brand of representation if more women become involved in the political process; a type of policy representation that is potentially more contextual.

Men Running Against Women

The final area to be addressed concerns how men running against women changed their campaign messages because of the sex of their opponent. This question was touched on in Chapter 2. If it turns out that male candidates are altering their agendas to be more inclusive of a broad range of women's issues, it indicates that the presence of women may be transforming the political arena in ways we have not before considered. The comparisons of male candidates running against men with male candidates running against women (Tables 3.4 and 3.5) revealed only one statistically significant difference. Men were more likely to raise the issue of abortion when running against a woman than against a man. The campaign managers of male candidates running against women were also asked directly if they raised any issues that they otherwise would not have if their candidate were running against a man. Ten of the twenty-three managers for male candidates running against women admitted that they raised certain issues because of the sex of their opponent (see Table 2.8). Several managers of male candidates were reticent in discussing how they changed their strategy in facing a female opponent. Four of the managers answered the question of whether they changed their message with an immediate "yes," but then backtracked, saying that they actually did not do much differently. Along these lines one manager responded,

> We did a lot of things different from last election when we ran against a man. There are a bunch of considerations when running against a woman.

Asked if he could say whether different issues were raised because of the woman opponent, he answered,

Well . . . we had a very complex targeting strategy for men and female voters. I mean we didn't treat them differently. We used a wide range of issues . . . but I really could not go into the specifics. I don't think the congressman would want me to discuss this.

This was also one of the few campaigns that refused the request for copies of campaign literature and direct mail. A number of the campaigns were leery of admitting different treatment for male and female voters. Nonetheless, several managers revealed issues that they raised solely to counter their female opponent.

One manager noted that her candidate spent more time establishing his support for RU-486, the "abortion pill." Two campaign managers said that their candidates emphasized "caring" as a campaign theme with the hope of appearing more sensitive to female voters. Along these lines, Huddy and Terkildsen (1993a, 120) have argued that male candidates often try to adopt stereotypical "female traits" with the hopes of appearing kind and sympathetic. Another candidate, who had written an "anti-stalker" bill as a state legislator, spent a great deal of time discussing his work on this bill with the intention of showing his concern for issues that directly affect women. Several incumbents publicized and discussed their support for increased funding for women's health care issues, particularly breast cancer research. One incumbent congressman used his franking privilege to help his image with female voters:

Right after the primary we did some polling that showed we had very low ratings with women in the district. So we sent out a piece of mail from the office that was intended to show our concern for the safety of women. The piece offered some suggestions on safety tips for women. Little suggestions to encourage women to protect themselves from crime. We sent that out before the franking deadline.

When I asked whether the congressman put forth any legislation in conjunction with his mailer on women's safety, the manager responded,

Oh God, no. We just needed to do something to boost his approval rating. And boy did it work, in the next poll after the mailer went out, our support from women really jumped.

These comments illustrate that in some cases, male candidates may only be using "women's issues" or showing concern for women as a strategic ploy to win votes.

In addition to raising additional "women's issues," a number of male candidates worked to reverse what they perceived as voter stereotyping on the abortion issue. Abortion was the one "women's issue" men running against women were significantly more likely to raise than men running against men (see Table 3.5). There are two explanations for the greater use of the abortion issue by men running against women. The first has to do with using issues to try to reach out to female voters. As discussed in Chapter 2, men running against women were often attempting to find ways to appeal to female voters. Thus, raising more "women's issues" is part of a strategic tactic. The other reason for raising the abortion issue was to counter what the male candidates perceived as stereotyping by the electorate. "Pro-choice" men running against women believed voters assumed that the female candidate was the only "pro-choice" candidate in the race. As one frustrated manager noted,

> Voters just assumed she was pro-choice and we were not. She is one of those right-wing candidates that receives perfect ratings from the Christian Coalition, yet we had to spend an enormous amount of resources pointing out that we were for women's rights and she was not.

Asked to explain this phenomenon, the manager continued,

> I think it has to do with people's perceptions of strong women. Voters view women running for office as strong and aggressive, therefore they assume that these women must be for women's rights. Abortion has been made a woman's rights issue, thus they make the connection that any woman running for office must favor abortion rights.

Similar problems were mentioned by three "pro-choice" Republican male candidates running against "pro-choice" Democratic women. The manager for one of these candidates commented,

> The women voters in the district were very skeptical of our position on abortion. Even though we had a long history of favoring abortion rights, many of the female voters who care deeply about this issue did not trust our position. I am sure this was because our candidate was a man.

In the case of the abortion issue, voter perceptions worked against male candidates. The issue of abortion became a credibility problem for male candidates in much the same way female candidates had credibility problems

Table 3.7   Summary of Differences in the Campaign Messages of Male and Female Candidates

	Differences	
Aspect of Campaign Message	Female Candidates	Male Candidates
Presentation of personal characteristics	Emphasized qualifications and ties to the community	Emphasized political ideology and intelligence
	Discussed family in personal terms	Discussed family in stereotypically traditional ways
Central campaign themes	Emphasized change and outsider status	Emphasized the economy
Main campaign issues	Greater focus on "women's issues"	Emphasized free trade and the opponent's character
	Emphasized the environment	
	Worked to establish credibility on "men's issues"	
Lesser campaign issues	Raised the issues of gay rights, children, sexual harassment, and tax policy	Raised government regulation
	Raised "women's issues" regardless of the electoral environment	Men running against women emphasized the abortion issue
	Discussed issues in the context of other issues	Tended to discuss issues in "black and white" terms

on many "men's issues." Although certainly male candidates are rarely the victims of harmful gender stereotyping in the electoral process to the extent women are, the experiences of male candidates on the abortion issue shows that stereotyping can in some instances be a sword that cuts both ways. Perhaps the 1992 "year of the woman" elections was the first time that a significant number of male candidates have been at a disadvantage to women in some aspects of presenting their campaign message. Further, this analysis is instructive because it shows that the presence of women has made male candidates rethink their campaign message. For the most part, male candidates' increased use of women's issues were strategic decisions and not indicative of any transformation in the personal convictions of the male candidates. This suggests that gender is in some cases simply being used as a strategic tool in the electoral process.

Conclusion and Summary

The framework put forward in the beginning of this chapter, which suggested that decisions about a campaign message are based on strategic decisions and personal convictions, proved to be a useful tool for analyzing the presence of gender differences in the campaign messages of female and male candidates. Throughout this analysis of campaign messages, real and strategic differences were apparent in much of the decision making of male and female candidates. Table 3.7 offers a summary of the message differences between women and men.

In terms of the personal images and central themes the candidates presented, gender differences are best explained by the candidates making strategic decisions based on many of the traditional gender role stereotypes. In almost all of these instances, except perhaps for female candidates' abilities to capitalize on the "change" theme in 1992, the stereotyping makes the campaign process more difficult for women. The role of traditional socialization in appraising the personal characteristics of candidates is something that will continue to work against women. Almost all of the characteristics that we have typically ascribed to competent politicians are traits on which women have to work to establish their credibility. The most troubling example of this dynamic that came through in this chapter concerned the female candidates' emphasis on stressing their credentials. Women's perceived need to focus on their qualifications in their campaigns illustrates the unfair environment that exists for female candidates. In many cases, the female candidate had considerably more experience and expertise than her male opponent, but at the same time she often felt that she had to prove herself to the voters. The experiences of the female candidates in this study show that in terms of stereotyping about credibility and qualifications, women are still not on a level playing field in the electoral arena.

Turning to candidates' use of policy issues, this analysis shows that there are important differences in the issue agendas of women and men in campaigns. These differences were not as great as some of the media speculation and candidate rhetoric may have suggested. There was not a gulf between the sexes in terms of the issues they raised. However, there were clearly discernible differences in the issues that were part of the campaign agendas of male and female candidates. There are a number of issues listed in Tables 3.4 and 3.5 for which male and female candidates, regardless of party affiliation, had different agendas. The clearest explanation for these differences would appear to be differences in personal convictions. These findings have two potentially important ramifications. First, if elections do help to set the election agenda, as some analyses suggest (see Arnold 1990; Kingdon 1989), then the increase in the number of women participating as candidates in the political arena may change the policy debate in elections and in legislative chambers. Changes in the policy debate as a result of the presence of women were clearly illustrated by the male candidates running against women who raised particular "women's issues" only because of their female opponent. The presence of female candidates appears to in some ways transform the policy debate in an election. The second important consequence of the differences in issue agendas follows directly from the first. The agendas of the female candidates in this study add further evidence to the growing body of literature that has found that male and female political actors have differing issue priorities (Thomas 1994; Dodson and Carroll 1991). This turns us to the question of representation, more specifically to the role of symbolic and substantive representation that was raised in Chapter 1. The more evidence that reveals that men and women bring to the political process a different set of legislative and policy priorities, the more urgent the need to elect more women. These findings demonstrate that the small number of women serving in the U.S. House is more than symbolically unjust and appears to be substantively unjust as well. There is a set of issues that do not receive the attention they would receive if women composed a more substantial portion of the U.S. Congress.

Note

1. The candidates' prior occupations are based on the short biographies listed in the *Congressional Quarterly Almanacs* for 1992 and 1994.

The Gender Dynamics of Fund-Raising, Party Support, and Media Coverage

As recently as the late 1960s, one of the surest means by which a woman could become a member of Congress was to have a husband who was a Congressman die while in office.[1] If her husband was a Senator, she could be appointed by the governor to finish out the term. If her husband was a member of the House, a special election could be called and she would become the sentimental choice for election (Gertzog 1980; Kincaid 1978; Bullock and Heys 1972). The difficulty women have had breaking into high elective office on their own is undeniable. The first Republican woman elected to the U.S. Senate completely on her own merits was Nancy Kassebaum in 1978.[2] The first Democrat was Barbara Mikulski in 1986. The extremely low percentage of female candidates who have been elected without the help of a dead relative is testimony to the social and institutional road blocks that prevent women from entering into and succeeding in electoral politics. The "matrimonial connection" no longer offers the quickest route to Congress for women but many fundamental questions persist as to whether the congressional election process is open to female candidates. This chapter examines how female and male congressional candidates in

100

California in 1992 and 1994 were treated by the institutions in the electoral process. This chapter focuses on the experiences of female and male candidates in the areas of fund-raising, party support, and media coverage.

In the years leading up to the 1992 elections, the proportion of women serving in the U.S. Congress was shockingly low. Between 1975 and 1992, the number of female Representatives ranged from 4 to 7 percent. In the U.S. Senate over the same period, there were either zero, one, or two female Senators serving full terms. In the early 1990s, of the twenty-five leading democracies in the world, the United States ranked 22nd in percentage of women serving in the national legislature. This placed the United States above only Japan, Malta, and Greece (Norris 1994, 116). Each of the Scandinavian countries had over 30 percent women in their national parliaments and most of the other western democracies had between 8 and 30 percent. The United States was lagging behind countries such as Spain and Portugal, where traditional attitudes about women's roles would seem to be even more pervasive than in the United States (Darcy, Welch, and Clark 1994, 81). Thus, the high number of women running for federal office in the United States in the 1992 elections seemed long overdue. The infusion of female candidates was historic not only across the country, but in California as well. California had never had more than three (out of forty-five seats between 1982 and 1992) female members of the House of Representatives serving at one time and had never sent a woman to the U.S. Senate. The only woman to have won a statewide election in California between 1974 and 1990 was Democrat March Fong Eu, who served as secretary of state from 1975 to 1994. Table 4.1 illustrates the effect of 1992 on selected electoral positions nationwide and in California.

The figures in Table 4.1 demonstrate a clear increase in the number of female officeholders following the 1992 elections. Women in California and across the country made substantial gains. Women almost doubled their representation in the California House delegation. The increase of female senators nationwide in 1992 was in large part aided by the victories of Dianne Feinstein and Barbara Boxer. In 1994, women held on to the seats they had won in 1992 but made few further gains. However, despite the success of female candidates in 1992, the number of women holding high elective office has only been upgraded from shockingly low to alarmingly low. The United States is on the threshold of the twenty-first century but the progress and fair access of women to positions of high elective office remains in question.

Table 4.1   Effect of the "Year of the Woman" on Officeholding in Selected
Elective Positions

Elective Office	1990	1992	1994
U.S. House	7%	11%	11%
U.S. Senate[a]	2	6	8
State legislatures	18	21	21
California U.S. House Delegation[b]	7	13	15

SOURCE: Compiled from fact sheets provided by Center for the American Woman in Politics (CAWP), Rutgers University.
NOTE: Percentages indicate the ratio of women serving in those elected positions.
a. Only one new female senator was added in 1994; this figure includes Texas Senator Kay Bailey Hutchison, who won a special election in 1993.
b. The California House delegation gained 7 seats after the 1990 census, increasing from 45 to 52 seats.

Explaining Women's
Numerical Underrepresentation

Three general explanations have emerged in the literature on female candidates to explain the low levels of female officeholders: direct discrimination, sex-role socialization, and institutional inertia. First, a great deal of analysis has argued that, to varying degrees, direct discrimination against women exists in the electoral process. Aside from a broad range of feminist analysis that argues that the entire political, economic, and social structure of the country is male-dominated and inherently discriminatory (MacKinnon 1993, 1989; Kendrigan 1984; Amundson 1971), numerous investigations have found discrimination against female candidates in the specific components of the electoral process. A number of studies, even recent ones, have found voter bias against and stereotyping of female candidates. Several recent examinations of voter behavior have focused on the stereotypes voters use to evaluate male and female candidates (see Rosenthal 1995; Huddy and Terkildsen 1993a, 1993b). These analyses have shown that male and female voters often have different impressions of male and female candidates. (The role of voter stereotyping in California is covered extensively in Chapter 5.) Other recent examinations of voting have dismissed the importance of voter bias against female candidates (Burrell 1994, 140-150; Chaney and Sinclair 1994, 125-127). Further, although Darcy, Welch, and Clark (1994, 77-82) argue that women in general elections perform as well as men with the voters, they do note the existence of substantial anti-woman bias in the attitudes of many voters.

In addition to the possibility of voter bias, other scholars have found discrimination in the structure of the election process. Some analyses suggest that women do not fare as well in single-member plurality elections as they do in multimember elections. Darcy, Welch, and Clark (1994, 161-69) have found that in states that employ or have employed both methods, a higher portion of women are elected in multimember electoral systems (see also Welch and Studlar 1990). Norris (1994, 116), in a comparison of different electoral systems worldwide, has found that parliamentary systems with proportional party lists have a much greater share of women serving in national legislature than those with single-member districts such as the U.S. Congress. Bias against female candidates has also been found to varying degrees in the areas of campaign finance (Mandel 1981), party support (Baer 1993; Kendrigan 1984), and media coverage (Kahn 1993). The literature in these three areas is discussed more fully in the ensuing analysis.

The second explanation for the low numbers of women in elected positions centers on the idea that women and men have different patterns of political socialization. Many of the behavioral differences of the candidates discussed in Chapters 2 and 3 support this explanation. From early ages women and men are taught either overtly or through inference that politics is a business best left to men (Lee 1976; Costantini and Craik 1972). The traditional roles of women as homemakers and primary caretakers of children have histori-cally made their involvement in high-level electoral politics much more difficult. Although certainly the conception of a rigid set of sex roles as an expected norm is on the decline, the effects of traditional socialization remain quite strong. Thus, at the age when most male politicians receive their first taste of politics, women are often encumbered with family responsibili-ties. Several scholars have demonstrated that women are more likely than men to enter politics at advanced ages (Burrell 1994; Fowler and McClure 1989; Kirkpatrick 1974). In addition, some research shows that women tend to have less ambition to hold office than men and are less likely to view their first elective office as merely a stepping-stone to higher office (Bledsoe and Herring 1990; Bernstein 1986).

Further, the socialization of women and men has historically led them to different career paths (Simon and Landis 1989; Andersen and Cook 1985; De Boer 1977). The professions from which most politicians are drawn are dominated by men. Careers in business or law have usually been the precursors to political involvement. In 1980, male lawyers outnumbered female lawyers by six to one (Darcy, Welch, and Clark 1994, 109). By 1988 the disparity was down to five to one and by 1994 the gap was down to four to one, but that is still a substantial difference (Jones 1995, 3B). Women have also been less likely than men to be business managers, administrators, and entrepreneurs. In 1970, only 16 percent of "managers or administrators" were women (Darcy, Welch, and Clark 1994, 109). By 1988 women made up 39 percent of all "managers and administrators" and by 1994 the number had grown to 43 percent (Jones 1995, 3B). Occupational socialization patterns are offered by Darcy, Welch, and Clark (1994) as one of the best explanations for the continued paucity of women serving in high elective office; they conclude, "The fact that women have less education and lower occupational status than do men accounts for a significant part of their underrepresentation in office" (118).

A third explanation for the slow rate of women's progress into the political process is what might be labeled *institutional inertia*. This explanation minimizes claims of discrimination and sex-role socialization by focusing on the contention that change in American institutions is slow. In terms of the U.S. Congress, the focus of this study, the incumbency advantage has been identified by some analyses as one of the primary reasons for the small number of female members of Congress. Again, Darcy, Welch, and Clark state, "A major reason for the slow entrance of women into political office, particularly at the national level in the United States, is the power of incumbency" (1994, 176). Slow turnover in a male-dominated institution makes gender parity lag behind changes in the social structure. The argument emanating from these analyses is that if more women run, more will be elected; over time, as open seat elections occur, women will achieve equal levels of representation (see also Burrell 1994; Chaney and Sinclair 1994). These studies contend that the electoral system in place is for the most part operating fairly.

All three theories provide explanations for the limited inclusion of women in the political process. In employing these theories in this analysis, several important questions arise. Is there evidence that the election process in the California House elections worked to hinder the inclusion of women in 1992 and 1994? Is there evidence of substantial discrimination in the political process? Does the political socialization of women and men work against women? Also important to consider is whether the 1992 elections were an aberration in terms of the success of female candidates, or whether the 1992 elections represented a major turning point in the electoral environment. In answering these questions and assessing the general experiences of women and men in the election process, this chapter relies on the perceptions of campaign managers and their firsthand accounts of the experiences of male and female candidates.

Throughout the chapter a number of findings emerge.[3] First, there were low but clear levels of direct gender bias and discrimination in the electoral process for California's congressional seats. The bias that does exist is usually subtle and difficult to document. Another finding is that men and women compete in the electoral process by facing different sets of challenges. As with the experiences of the candidates discussed in Chapters 2 and 3, these differences are usually the result of traditional socialization and usually work against female candidates. Finally, and potentially of greatest interest, is that female candidates are much more likely than male candidates to perceive that the various components of the electoral process are unfair. The perception of unfairness exists even when objective indicators seem to suggest otherwise. This perception of unfairness often results in female candidates having a more negative perception of the electoral arena, which may have important consequences for their willingness to engage in electoral politics as candidates.

Advantages and Obstacles
in the Electoral Process

Did men and women confront different challenges in the electoral process? To ascertain how female and male candidates perceived the challenges they faced, campaign managers were asked a series of questions to uncover how they believed their candidate was treated by the electoral process. In an open-ended question, the managers were first asked to describe their campaign experiences with fund-raising, party support, and media coverage. In a closed-ended question they were then asked whether each of the three areas posed a "major obstacle to the campaign." Table 4.2 presents the responses to the closed-ended questions.

In the perceptions of the campaign managers of challengers, female candidates were significantly more likely than male candidates to view the media as an obstacle to their campaigns. In terms of party support and fund-raising, there were no statistically significant differences, although men

Table 4.2   Perceptions of Campaign Obstacles, by Gender and Challenger Status

Major Obstacles	Female Challengers (25)	Male Challengers (39)	Male Incumbents (33)
Fund-raising	48%	59%	9%
Media coverage	64*	44	30
Party support	52	49	6

NOTE: Numbers indicate the percentage of campaign managers who responded "yes" to the question, "Did fund-raising [or media coverage or party support] pose a major obstacle to your campaign?"
$*p < .05$; one-tailed t-test comparing the male and female challengers.

appeared to have a slightly tougher time with fund-raising. These are important findings because there has been wide speculation that women receive less party support and have more difficulty raising money. All three of these areas are explored in greater detail on the following pages. As expected, incumbents faced almost no obstacles in terms of fund-raising or party support. Several incumbents had a difficult time with the media but most of these candidates (eight out of ten) were from the 1992 elections, when a number of congressional scandals received prominent coverage (e.g., the House Bank scandal).

To look beyond these three areas, campaign managers were also asked an open-ended question to identify both the obstacles they faced and the advantages they possessed in the election process. The responses to this question are listed in Table 4.3. Incumbents were dropped from the analysis in this table because they named few obstacles and had fundamentally different electoral experiences from challengers.

For the most part, male and female challengers confronted similar obstacles and advantages. Both women and men listed the "electoral environment," the "difficulty of running against an incumbent," and "party registration in the district" as the top three obstacles they had to overcome. Most of the complaints about the "electoral environment" came from male and female Democrats running in 1994. For instance, the manager of a male Democratic challenger running in a very competitive district noted the intense level of anti-Clinton sentiment he encountered:

I was not ready for the degree of hatred for Clinton in this district . . . it was unbelievable. Back in May [of 1994] we did some polls and we thought we had a

Table 4.3   Obstacles and Advantages of Male and Female Challengers in the Electoral Process[a]

Obstacles	Advantages
Female challengers (25)	
Party registration in district (5)	More volunteers (3)
Electoral environment (5)	Smarter than the opponent (2)
Running against an incumbent (4)	Opponent was scared (2)
Absentee ballots (1)	Good name recognition (2)
Opponent in hiding (1)	Support from feminist groups (2)
Level of name recognition (1)	Connections among the political elite (1)
Size of the district (1)	Electoral environment (1)
Male challengers (41)	
Electoral environment (10)	Smarter than the opponent (5)
Running against an incumbent (7)	Electoral environment (2)
Party registration in district (6)	Support from unions (2)
Low voter interest (4)	Great organization (2)
Level of name recognition (4)	More hard-working than the opponent (2)
Needed more time (1)	Good name recognition (1)

NOTE: Number in parentheses represents actual number of candidates giving that response.

a. Represented in the table are all obstacles and advantages mentioned by candidates other than fund-raising, party support, and media coverage. Not all candidates offered obstacles and advantages in addition to those three.

real good shot at winning this district. We ended up getting killed [his candidate lost by 20 points]. . . . There was no winning this year. . . . This district is winnable for a Democrat, just not this year.

The campaign manager for a female candidate expressed similar disbelief in how poorly her candidate fared:

We ended up with under thirty percent of the vote. I was devastated. Last year [1992] in this district . . . [the Democratic opponent] barely waged a campaign and received about thirty-five percent of the vote. This year we went all out, campaigning hard and ended up doing worse. There was a huge anti-Clinton and anti-Democrat surge in the San Diego area this election [1994].

The candidates' concerns about the electoral environment were dominated by partisan considerations and not gender considerations.

Female and male candidates also mentioned the incumbency advantage as an important obstacle to overcome. The incumbency advantage makes it harder for women as a group to increase their numbers because it works to the benefit of the male incumbents who dominate the system. In discussing the advantages of the incumbents, several managers mentioned the franking privilege. As one manager commented,

> I counted three mass mailings he [the incumbent] did leading up to the election deadline. The amount of money you would have to raise to compete with that makes it almost impossible. . . . It is so blatant how they abuse the franking privilege.

Several House members used their franking privilege to introduce themselves to voters they were not even representing at the time. One manager described the practice:

> After the redistricting in 1990 almost every district in the state was redrawn. . . . Most incumbents were gaining some new voters as all of the district lines shifted. . . . So what many of them did was to send franked mail to voters in the new districts . . . before they were even officially representing that district.

The campaign manager for a female challenger running against a female incumbent mentioned an even more dubious usage of incumbency:

> She [the incumbent] tried to freeze us out of fund-raising in the district and in Washington. She warned many local interests and Washington groups that she would punish them if they funded her opponent. Sometimes it felt like a race for us to get to the donor before her staff did.

Incumbents' use of congressional resources to help ensure reelection has received considerable attention by scholars of congressional politics (Jacobson 1992; Fiorina 1989; Mayhew 1974). The use of office resources reported by the managers in this investigation lends credence to the institutional inertia explanation for women's continued numerical underrepresentation. The resources incumbents possess make it exceedingly difficult for newcomers.

In addition to the electoral environment and incumbency advantage, candidates also battled the structural feature of party registration in their district. Although the 1990 redistricting made many California congressional districts more competitive, the majority of the districts still present considerable advantages to either one or the other major party. One Republican manager, who began the election thinking he could pull off an upset in a traditionally Democratic district, was far less optimistic after the race was over:

We were constantly fighting the registration of the district—always thinking of how we could bring some Democrats over to our side. I thought we could win, but we ran a good campaign [losing by fifteen points] and now I don't know if a Republican can overcome the registration.

At the end of the campaigns, the managers for male and female challengers both viewed district registration as the number-one obstacle they faced.[4] The important conclusion to draw from this analysis of campaign obstacles is that female and male candidates generally saw themselves confronting similar obstacles in the election process. The responses from the campaign managers indicate that the structural barriers in elections are viewed similarly by both male and female candidates.

In the second half of Table 4.3, the campaign managers listed fewer electoral advantages than obstacles and again there were no systematic differences in the reported experiences of male and female candidates. Both campaign managers for female and male challengers listed support from particular groups, intellectual superiority over their opponent, good name recognition, and the electoral environment as advantages. Again, there were no readily apparent gender differences in how the candidates viewed their electoral advantages.

The general perceptions of the campaign managers depicted in Tables 4.2 and 4.3 suggest that women and men have similar experiences in the electoral process. However, as is often the case with examinations of gender and politics, important differences are often obscured within quantitative compilations. Responses to "yes" or "no" questions such as those in Table 4.2 often present an oversimplification of the candidates' experiences. Further exploration of the experiences of men and women in the areas of fund-raising, party support, and media coverage reveal that the women and men in this examination had to employ different strategies in confronting gender stereotyping and socialization patterns.

Gender and Campaign Finance

Raising money has become the most essential aspect of waging a modern campaign. Complex strategies involving electronic media, direct mail, computerized voter analysis, and get-out-the-vote campaigns have enormous costs. Brilliant strategies lie dormant on notepads if there is not enough money to carry them out. If women are going to compete effectively in

elections, it is imperative that they be able to raise money at levels compa-
rable to those of male candidates. Ann Richards, writing in 1987 as the Texas
state treasurer, believed that women clearly had disadvantages when it came
to fund-raising. Richards asserted that to raise money successfully you must
present yourself as a "credible" candidate, have "contacts" in the political
and business world, and have the "courage" to ask for money. Richards
believes women have historically lacked two of the three necessary components for successful fund-raising: credibility and contacts. Several early
studies have indeed argued that women run campaigns with lower levels of
funding than men (Mandel 1981; Baxter and Lansing 1980).

However, these claims about gender differences in campaign financing are
not supported by more recent systematic examinations of campaign receipts.
Two studies of campaign contributions in congressional elections found little
evidence of gender differences in fund-raising. Burrell (1985), in a study of
Congressional candidates from 1972 to 1982, found a "very weak" relationship between gender and the ability to raise campaign funds. Similarly,
Uhlaner and Schlozman (1986) determined that female incumbents in the
U.S. House, on average, raised about $24 thousand less per race than male
incumbents. However, they explain the difference by noting that male
incumbents generally held positions of greater political power and were thus
more likely to attract large contributions. In a more recent analysis of House
candidates (using data up through the 1992 elections), Burrell (1994, 128)
concludes, "Whether we look at totals, sources, or timing, female candidates
in similar situations as male candidates generally do as well and sometimes
even better in financing their campaigns for national office." The most recent
compilations and comparisons of fund-raising that include the 1994 House
and Senate elections, confirm the trends that Burrell has documented
(McCormick and Baruch 1994, 16-17). All of these investigations of campaign finance focus on the net receipts of the candidates and to some extent
the sources of the campaign contributions. They almost all overlook the
process by which men and women raise money. This analysis of fund-raising
tries to go beyond the numbers and ask the candidates about their fund-
raising experiences.

The female candidates in this examination were highly successful fundraisers. Table 4.4 displays the total net receipts of all the candidates and a
breakdown of the sources of the campaign receipts. The candidates are
categorized by party, incumbency, and gender. Two candidates, both running
in 1992, were outliers and were dropped from the table—Jane Harman, a

Table 4.4   Campaign Receipts, by Gender, Party, and Challenger Status for All Congressional Candidates in California, 1992 and 1994

	Total Receipts	Individual Contributions	PAC Money	Candidate Contributions[a]
Democratic challengers[b]				
Men	$207,215	45%	38%	24%
(33)				
Women[c]	384,197	57	30	10
(20)				
Republican challengers				
Men[d]	250,711	57	16	16
(48)				
Women	358,032	50	25	18
(8)				
Democratic incumbents				
Men	586,409	45	49	0
(41)				
Women	572,511	53	46	0
(9)				
Republican incumbents[e]				
Men	625,621	62	31	0
(35)				

SOURCE: Compiled from Federal Election Commission Reports.

NOTE: Dollar figures are average amounts raised by congressional candidates of that particular type. Percentages represent the ratio of campaign receipts derived through that manner. Percentages across each column do not add up to 100 because there were other miscellaneous sources of campaign funding not included in the table (such as money on hand from previous campaigns).

a. Candidate contributions includes candidate loans and outright candidate contributions.

b. Challengers includes the combined candidacies of challengers and candidates running for open seats.

c. Candidate Jane Harman was dropped from the sample of Democratic women.

d. Candidate Michael Huffington was dropped from the sample of Republican men.

e. There were no female Republican incumbents in the California delegation.

Democratic challenger in the 36th District, contributed $1,496,000 of her own money to her campaign, and Michael Huffington, a Republican challenger in the 22nd District, contributed $5,191,728 of his own money to the campaign. Huffington set the record for the size of a candidate contribution in a district-level election. The figures for female Democratic challengers and male Republican challengers are calculated without these candidates.

Overall, female candidates in California raised considerably more money than their male counterparts.[5] The female Democratic challengers raised almost twice as much money as their male counterparts. This is partially explained by women's greater likelihood of running for open seats, which are funded at higher levels. Female Republican challengers also raised considerably more than male Republican challengers but this finding needs to be regarded cautiously because there were only eight Republican women in the sample. Still, female challengers in California ultimately had a considerable advantage in fund-raising. Among incumbents, there were only minor differences in the net receipts of men and women. Female Democratic incumbents raised 98 percent of what male Democratic incumbents collected. There were no female Republican incumbents running in California in either 1992 or 1994. These findings are inconsistent with the studies cited earlier, which found that female challengers generally raised campaign funds in equal or lesser amounts than male candidates (Uhlaner and Schlozman 1986; Mandel 1981; Baxter and Lansing 1980). However, the fund-raising performance of the female candidates is consistent with Burrell's (1994, 128-30) recent assessment that women fare as well or better than their male counterparts.

Are women's sources of funding different from men's? Three types of contributions are reported in Table 4.4: individual, PAC/party, and candidate. Female Democratic candidates, both challengers and incumbents, received a larger portion of their total campaign receipts from individual contributors than did male challengers. Also, male Democratic challengers were more likely than their female counterparts to rely on personal wealth to fund their campaigns.[6] The finding that female Democrats received a larger portion of their contributions from individuals suggests that female challengers may not be as successful at obtaining institutional money that requires connections to traditional fund-raising networks (Richards 1987). Several of the campaign managers supported this contention. Many of the female Democrats felt cut off from some institutional support. This was despite the fact that women Democrats on average received more PAC money than male Democrats in net receipts. Burrell (1994, 115) also found that female House candidates appeared to have no disadvantage in acquiring PAC contributions.

A possible explanation for women's higher level of funding may be that women are more successful at attracting individual contributors. Women's success in attracting contributions from individuals, many of them small contributors, is consistent with one of the themes running throughout this analysis: women are more likely to be connected to the community in which they are running. Receiving money from small contributors and making those contributors a base of support suggests that a candidate has greater contact with local constituents. Women's greater emphasis on personal campaigning and their preference for direct voter contact, as discussed in Chapter 2, also indicate that women may be better at winning over small contributors.

Discrimination in Fund-Raising

Although the data presented in Table 4.4 suggest that women do not suffer any disadvantage and may even have greater success than men in raising money, several important differences in the fund-raising experiences of men and women emerged in the interviews. First, consistent with Richards's (1987) contentions, though not supported by the net receipts, several of the campaign managers for female candidates did not believe that women had the same access as men to traditional fund-raising networks. One manager who had worked for many female candidates across the country noted,

> Women do not have the ties with the business community and they are in many ways still excluded from the serious power networks. . . . When I take over a campaign I want my candidate doing two things, either out meeting voters or on the phone asking people for money. In the early days of a campaign a candidate needs to spend six or seven hours a day on the phone asking for money. . . . The women I have worked for did not have the comfort level or list of contacts to do this well.

The female Democratic candidates who were part of the Staton/Hughes interviews for EMILY's List also expressed a great dislike for the process of raising money (1992). Other campaign managers shared similar sentiments in terms of women's connections with fund-raising networks. One female Democratic challenger who was counting on the financial support of labor in her district met with unexpected resistance. Her campaign manager assessed it this way:

> Our candidate was the natural labor candidate [favored worker rights and opposed NAFTA and GATT], but for no clear reason they were lukewarm towards us. I called them and went to meet with them and they promised money and volunteers,

but after that it was like pulling teeth getting any kind of support from them. . . .
I just think certain sources, particularly labor unions, are hesitant to support
female candidates. . . . Union leadership is still a male enclave.

Another manager, who had worked for both male and female candidates,
summed up the fund-raising dilemma for women:

Men have much better access to the individual contributions of executives and
businessmen. I don't want to be so trite as to say that this is sexism pure and
simple—it is just that businesspeople, mostly men, are accustomed to dealing with
the congressman, a man.

A final example illustrates the clearest display of direct discrimination found
in this examination: A woman running in northern California was denied
financial assistance from her national party headquarters. The national party
determines whether to financially support a candidate based on the candidate's viability in the election. The campaign manager described what happened when he contacted the party seeking financial support:

I talked to the party leaders and I tried to sell them on the idea that our candidate
was viable. I gave them the results of a poll we conducted that showed we were
in striking distance of our opponent, but ultimately they decided that we did not
have a good chance to win. . . . Then I heard that they funded . . . [a male]
candidate running in the neighboring district. I thought this was odd, considering
we had almost identical poll numbers. I called up the party and asked why they
funded our neighbor and not us. The director of finance stated that this was the
old-boy network in action. They gave him party money because he has contacts
in the leadership and we don't.

The manager for this female candidate was told bluntly that his candidate was
being subjected to gender discrimination. This was the only instance in this
examination of an institutional component of the election process acknowledging gender discrimination.

Overall, six of the twenty-five managers of female candidates believed
their candidate was in some way unable to access the traditional fund-raising
networks. Although six out of twenty-five (24%) is not an overwhelming
proportion, it nonetheless demonstrates that a significant number of female
candidates continue to feel excluded from the traditional power structure
within the electoral process. Only one of the forty-one (2%) male challengers, a member of an ethnic minority, reported any institutional bias in

fund-raising. The experiences of female candidates who felt cut off from male-dominated fund-raising networks was similar to some of the perceptions of exclusion felt by female state legislators in Texas and Arkansas. Blair and Stanley, in a survey of state legislators, found that female legislators often believed that they were removed from the typical socializing events (e.g., drinks and golf) that took place with other legislators and lobbyists (1991). There is certainly some evidence that the "old-boy network" still excludes women or at the very least makes women feel excluded. The different experiences of female candidates in the area of fund-raising present some women with a greater burden in their approach to fund-raising. The alternative assessment is that women only perceive greater difficulty in fund-raising and that their success indicates no substantial bias. If this is the case, it still presents an important impediment to the full inclusion of female candidates. If the process continues to seem unfair to women, then it will have the effect of turning away female candidates who do not want to take on the challenge of overcoming a sexist environment (see Naff 1995).

Socialization and the Contribution
Patterns of Men and Women

Another important gender difference in fund-raising concerns the contribution patterns of male and female voters. In studying contributors to presidential candidates, Wilcox, Brown, and Powell (1993) found a clear "gender gap" in the size and number of contributors. The perceptions of the campaign managers regarding the contributors to California congressional candidates was similar. Several managers and fund-raising consultants believed that female contributors gave smaller donations than male contributors. This phenomenon was described by a campaign manager for a female candidate:

> Women candidates rely more heavily on women for support in a campaign. However, when it comes to financial support, women are not in the habit of making large contributions to political campaigns. Women contributors give less and this hurts female candidates by making them have to work harder to raise enough money.

Another campaign manager for a female candidate found the differences striking:

Women don't know how to contribute money. We would call very successful businesswomen in the community and they would send us 50 or 100 dollars, we would call men in lesser positions and we would get 250 or 500 dollars. Many of the women did not seem to understand the relation between money and political power.

Women have not been socialized to contribute to political campaigns. Thus, if female candidates are dependent on the financial support of female voters, this could have important consequences. A recent survey of voters suggests that female candidates may be more dependent on the support of female voters than male candidates (see Rosenthal 1995). This may translate into some difficulty for female candidates. Another campaign manager described what this meant for women in practical terms:

Women have to spend more time seeking money from a wide variety of small individual contributors because they have trouble getting the larger contributions.

Although some aspects of campaign contributions may be examined empirically, the important question here can not. The names and identifications of contributors under $200 are not recorded; therefore, it would be difficult to verify the contentions of these campaign managers that women tend to contribute less money. Nonetheless, the possible differences in the contribution patterns of men and women are consistent with the differing political socialization of men and women shown throughout this examination. Men have been socialized to make contributions to candidates, and up until recently, women have not.

The Role of Women's PACs

The final gender difference in fund-raising concerns the emergence of women's PACs. Although some women felt excluded from certain sources of campaign money, it is important to keep in mind that women in this study received more money in contributions than did their male counterparts. A primary reason for this was the dramatic increase in the contributions made by "women's" or "women's issues" PACs (see Nelson 1994; Boles 1993). The rising prominence of PACs working exclusively for women adds to the number of sources from which women can draw. The contributions from women's PACs reached record levels in 1992. For instance, the most prominent women's PAC, EMILY's List, raised $6 million in 1992, four times more than in any previous year. The Women's Campaign Fund raised $1.3 million, almost doubling its previous record.[7] EMILY's List and the Women's Campaign Fund were able to raise and contribute more money in 1994 than in 1992. Thus, the increasing success of women's PACs has remained constant despite the shift in electoral environments between the two elections. The continued success of these PACs after the "year of the woman" elections provide evidence that a base level of support for women exists in the political process even when circumstances may not be favoring women.

The "women's PACs" ultimately provide a counterbalance to the traditional network of campaign fund-raising. The existence of these groups is essential for female candidates. In 1992, eight of the sixteen managers for female candidates described their fund-raising as reliant on small contributions and the "women's groups." The manager for a female candidate from northern California stated,

> The contributions from the women's groups were vital. It helped us equalize the funding race with our opponent. . . . I don't know where we would have got the money we needed without EMILY's list.

A campaign manager for a woman running in the San Diego area also noted his candidate's reliance on money from "women's groups":

> The money from the women's groups was crucial for us. The money from them came in when our local fund-raising had really stalled. That money allowed us to follow through with our direct-mail program, which we were getting ready to scrap.

Similar sentiments were expressed by several other managers of female candidates. The reliance on the "women's PACs" suggest that women have not yet been fully acclimated to the network of campaign contributors and have had to create their own distinct sources of financial support.

The existence of women's groups raises some important questions about the electoral environment. The women's groups' level of fund-raising has grown dramatically over the last three elections. For the most part, these groups contribute money based on the gender of the candidate. Gender-specific groups add an unusual dynamic to the election process, as there are no corresponding PACs working on behalf of male candidates. Almost all other PACs are motivated by ideological or policy concerns. If female candidates remain reliant on the "women's PACs," this may prevent them from becoming fully socialized into the traditional fund-raising networks.

The foremost conclusion in this examination regarding fund-raising is that female candidates in California and across the country were able to raise funds at equal or greater levels than male candidates over the 1992 and 1994 election cycles. Thus, much of the mythology surrounding women's inability to compete in terms of fund-raising is not true (see also Burrell 1994, 128-30). Significantly, though, men and women rely on different sources of funding. The ability of women to gain footholds in the traditional fund-raising networks is unclear but most indicators suggest that gender bias in this area is diminishing as women in positions of high elective office become fully accepted. However, it is clear that for the immediate future, male and female candidates must approach the task of fund-raising with different concerns. Traditional socialization is clearly important in two aspects of contributing to campaigns. First, there were several instances in which women believed that they were denied access to fund-raising networks. These avenues appear to be shut down because of women's historic exclusion from politics. Second, the possible differences in the contribution patterns of women and men reveal the differing conceptualization of politics by women and men. Both of these differences make the electoral arena more difficult and burdensome for female candidates.

 ## Gender and Political Parties

As parties have lost some of their hold over voter allegiances (e.g., Sabato 1988), party organizations have expanded their roles to meet the demands of modern campaigns. Party organizations at all levels are performing a wide array of functions and tasks that they had not performed previously. The parties, particularly at the national level, are training candidates, providing media assistance, and conducting opposition research for their candidates. Parties are also playing a vital role in get-out-the-vote drives, voter registration campaigns, and absentee ballot distribution (Herrnson 1988; Kayden and Mahe 1985; Cotter et al. 1984).

Party organizations have traditionally been reluctant to promote women into positions of political power. Clarke and Kornberg (1979), in a study of local party chapters, found important differences in the roles of men and women in the organizations, with women being less likely to attain positions of political power. The most striking finding that emerges from Clarke and Kornberg's analysis is that party involvement appears to have different import for women and men. Men become involved in the party's activities to fuel their political ambitions, whereas women tend to be concerned with fighting for the party as if it were a cause. The candidates in the California congressional elections exhibited similar tendencies when discussing their motivations to enter political campaigns (see Chapter 2). Other examinations of the role of gender and party organizations have found that female party officials tend to be stuck with menial jobs (Kendrigan 1984; Boneparth 1977). The political parties have moved forward in their attempts to include women, particularly at the national level in terms of convention delegate selection (Jennings 1990). However, the important question for this examination is whether the parties demonstrated gender bias in recruiting and promoting the candidacies of women.

Biersack and Herrnson (1994), in a recent study on the role of political parties in the "year of the woman," found almost no relationship between the level of party support and gender. They determined that the candidate's viability in the election was the sole criteria used by the parties in determining the level of candidate support (178). In 1992, the parties provided money and other services to male and female candidates in roughly equal proportions. Biersack and Herrnson's study did not examine individual candidacies and only examined the aggregate level of party support for female and male candidates. The most current assessments indicate that women are not discriminated against by the party organizations. To further test the developments in the relationship between the political parties and candidate gender, two areas of party support were examined in relation to the candidates in this study. First, whether the parties made equal efforts in recruiting female and male candidates, and second, whether there were any gender differences in how the parties allocated resources to the candidates (i.e., money, opposition research, media services).

Recruitment of Candidates

Several studies suggest that, in the past, the male-dominated party structure did not recruit women to run for office (Kendrigan 1984; Kirkpatrick 1974). In relating their experiences with party recruitment, a number of U.S.

Senate candidates in 1992 discussed the difficulty they had in getting their party's support. For instance, Patty Murray, Democratic U.S. Senate candidate from Washington state, commented,

> I think we've had to prove ourselves. When I announced my candidacy, they [the party] kept looking for another guy . . . continuously, until finally, all of a sudden, I'm the front-runner. (Crier & Co, 15 July 1995)

Democratic Senate candidate Geraldine Ferraro, who ultimately lost the nomination in New York in 1992, described her experience with party recruitment:

> When I started in politics in '78, when I ran for Congress, I had to run against the party and it was only after I had the nomination that I secured some support within the party system in order to win the general. (Crier & Co., 15 July 1995)

Finally, Democratic Senate candidate Josie Heath describes how she got on the ballot in Colorado:

> I had to petition to get on the ballot, something that has not been done in Colorado Democratic politics in over 30 years. And I traveled the state in an old yellow school bus and stopped at every supermarket, day care center, factory gate to get enough signatures to fight my way onto the ballot . . . it was not the traditional route and I think many women have [problems with the party] . . . even if we're insiders, until we want something, then we are obviously outsiders. (Crier & Co., 15 July 1995)

From the comments of these Senate candidates, it is clear that, historically, women have not been recruited as candidates for high elective office. Deber (1982), in a longitudinal study of female and male congressional candidates in Pennsylvania, found that bias against women has existed in the state party organizations that often recruit congressional candidates. Other studies offer further evidence that women may receive only token party nominations to run against safe incumbents (Gertzog and Simard 1991). Even more recent examinations have found that Republican women are less likely to be running in open-seat contests with good prospects of winning (Berch 1994; Burrell 1992).[8]

In this study, evidence of a gender component in candidate recruitment surfaced in an interview with an official from the Democratic Congressional Campaign Committee. The official, who was supervising the California congressional races in 1992, was asked about his party's effort to recruit women:

We did some extensive polls in the fall of 1991 and early 1992 to determine what the public was looking for in candidates. . . . For seats in Congress the candidates who did the best in our polls were women who had local political experience—school board and city council members. The voters demonstrated the most confidence in women from the community.

When asked about what specific steps the Democrats took in California, the official continued,

In districts we thought we had a chance, and no strong candidate already decided to run, we looked for viable women in the community. As I recall there were at least two women we urged to run. One was on a city council and the other had run before and lost. We felt that this might be the year she could win.

The Republicans in California did not appear to undertake specific recruitment efforts on behalf of female candidates in 1992. Although Biersack and Herrnson (1994) assert that both parties actively recruited women as candidates in 1992, Republican efforts to recruit women were not apparent in California. Of the seventeen female challengers running in the general elections in 1992, only two were Republicans. Further, in 1992 there were 127 male Republican candidates competing in forty-five primaries and there were only seven female Republican candidates competing in six primaries. These numbers are not indicative of any broad recruitment effort. By contrast, in 1992, twenty-seven Democratic women ran in twenty-one primaries.

Ultimately, the question of candidate recruitment is not explored in great depth in this study because the primary candidates were not surveyed. Without questioning the primary candidates it is difficult to determine the extent of party recruitment. The state party organizations in California have traditionally been weak and fractious. Recruitment of candidates by state party leaders is typical of strong party states such as those in the Northeast but not of weak party states such as California (Mayhew 1986). Furthermore, recruiting candidates to run in wide-open primaries, such as those in California in 1992, is not effective, considering that there are often large fields the parties cannot control. Some of the hotly contested primaries for open seats in 1992 had as many as ten candidates from one party vying for the seat. In 1992, there were ten primaries in which seven or more candidates vied for their party's nomination. The 36th district was the most competitive, with seven Democrats and eleven Republicans running in the primary election. The ability of the parties to effectively recruit candidates in this environment is severely diminished. In addition, only nine (six men and three women) of sixty-six challengers in this study mentioned that they were actively encouraged by their political party to run for office. From the interviews with the campaign managers, there were no examples of direct bias against women in terms of party recruitment, nor was there any clear proof that male candidates were more likely than female candidates to have been recruited by their party. There is not enough evidence to draw conclusive statements about gender differences in party recruitment of female and male candidates.

Party Allocation of Resources

The level of party support candidates received during the course of the campaign comes through more clearly in this study than the role of the parties in recruitment. The level of party support and commitment of resources is usually based on the viability of the candidate. Candidates who appear likely to win easily or lose badly are generally not the focus of party support. However, regardless of the history or the party registration of the district, candidates almost always believe they have a good chance of winning. Thus, political amateurs who enter elections against safe incumbents do not usually understand why they receive little or no party support. For instance, one first-time candidate, a woman running against a very "safe" incumbent, did not understand why the party gave her little support:

> No one was interested in my race. The local party [organization] was nice and gave me some office space, but did not lend me any of their volunteers. The state party did not return my phone calls and the national party sent me a packet of information about the incumbent, but really did not help me at all. . . . I felt like I was running all alone . . . the party hardly did a thing.

This candidate, who entered the race believing she was going to win, went on to receive only 28 percent of the vote in the general election. A male challenger from northern California was also quite disappointed with his party:

> Before I decided to run I attended a future candidate's workshop put on by the Republican National Committee. . . . They encouraged us to run and gave us instructional hints on how to organize volunteers and raise money. They said the party would be there to assist us with our campaigns. . . . So after I filed the papers

to enter the race, I called the National Party Headquarters and they were almost of no help. They told me they did not think I could win.

This candidate ended up receiving less than 35 percent of the vote. Politically inexperienced candidates, regardless of gender, often did not understand two things: one, that they had no realistic chance of winning, and two, that parties allocate resources based on the candidates' chances of victory. Therefore, in assessing the candidates' perceptions of party bias, the professionalism of the candidate and the competitiveness of the election must be considered. Both of the preceding candidates complained about the level of party support they received yet neither of these cases is necessarily indicative of any unfair bias by the parties.

To address the issue of party support, campaign managers for all candidates were asked several questions about their party experiences. Managers were first asked if they felt they received adequate support in general and specifically from the three levels of party organization (local, state, and national). In addition, managers were asked if they believed there was party bias against their candidate. The topics of bias and support were differentiated for the managers in the following manner. *Party bias* was defined as any instance in which a candidate was denied support from the party because the party was biased against the particular candidate—something personal was involved. Claims of inadequate *party support* were defined as instances in which candidates had little or no contact with the party and merely felt under-supported, but were unable to link the lack of support to any particular incidents. Finally, the managers for female candidates were specifically asked whether they believed there was party bias based on the gender of the candidate. The responses to these questions are listed in Table 4.5.

The perceptions of the campaign managers did not suggest broad, systematic gender bias by the parties. On the questions of general support and bias, there were almost no differences between female and male challengers. Considering that political amateurs do not have realistic expectations about the level of party support they will receive, the important comparison is between experienced candidates running in competitive races. For this analysis, districts in which the victor won with less than 55 percent of the vote are considered marginals (for further discussion of the California congressional districts, see Chapter 5). Of the candidates running in the twenty-nine competitive races, almost none complained of an overall lack of party support. However, several strong and eventually victorious candidates did

Table 4.5   Perceptions of Party Support, by Gender and Challenger Status

	Female Challengers (25)	Male Challengers (41)	Male Incumbents (33)
Did you receive sufficient party support overall?	40%	44%	97%
Did you receive adequate support from the			
Local party?	44	39	94
State party?	32*	54	91
National party?	56*	83	100
Did you feel there was party bias directed toward your candidacy?	24	24	3
Did you feel there was party bias directed toward your candidate that was based on the gender of your candidate?	16	(asked only of female candidates)	

NOTE: Percentages indicate "yes" responses to the questions.
*$p < .05$; one-tailed t-test comparing the male and female challengers.

complain about the support from local and state party organizations. None-theless, the managers' responses indicate that overall levels of party support during the course of the election had more to do with the competitiveness of the race than with the gender of the candidate.

Gender differences in party support did emerge when the campaign man-agers were asked to appraise their support from the separate levels of party organizations. In assessing their support from the various party organiza-tions, the managers of female challengers were significantly more likely than those of male challengers to believe they were receiving inadequate support from the state and national party offices. Although support from the Califor-nia state party organization is difficult to measure, there was no evidence that the state party was biased against women. The state parties in 1992 and 1994 were generally focused on the state-wide races for U.S. Senate and governor and not on the district-level races. Many managers of Democratic candidates in 1994 commented that they received almost no state support because the state party was entirely focused on the race for governor between Kathleen Brown and Pete Wilson. The disparity in perceived support from the national party level also contradicts previous research. Biersack and Herrnson (1994, 166-70) determined that national party organizations were equally likely to financially support and recruit female and male candidates.

What explains gender differences in the perception of party support? A possible explanation is that women and men have different expectations about party support. Female candidates were more likely to assume that the party would be fully engaged in their campaigns. Male candidates discussed their expectations about party support differently than female candidates. For instance, one male candidate, when asked about the help he got from the national party, responded,

> They couldn't do anything for me, the DNC has given up on this district . . . when I entered the race I knew I was on my own. The party didn't do anything for me, but that was expected.

Another male candidate, running in the central California area, discussed his approach to the election:

> I knew I would not get any help when I entered the race. I did my own opposition research. I flew to Washington to check on the house [the congressman] was living in. I had heard reports that he was illegally living in a house owned by a PAC. I knocked on the door and sure enough he answered. . . . I looked into some of his other shady business dealings in the district. The guy is corrupt. . . . I knew if I was going to pull this off [win the election] I had to nail this guy [the incumbent] with a scandal.

Both of these male candidates received almost no party support, yet neither of them claimed that the party provided inadequate support. The attitude displayed by these male candidates—of being able to run the campaign without any party support—was not evident in the campaigns of female candidates. Women may have viewed the election process as more of a cooperative team effort, and when they did not receive extensive support from the party, they may have tended to view the parties as inadequately supporting them. This attitude is consistent with the analysis that suggests men and women have different conceptions of political behavior.

Bias and Discrimination in Party Support

In terms of bias or actual discrimination in party support, female and male challengers were equally likely to perceive bias against their campaign (see Table 4.5). The candidates who reported party bias identified specific evidence that the denial of party support was based on the party's dislike for the candidate. For instance, one male challenger, who emerged as the unexpected winner of his party's primary, noted the bias against him:

> Nobody thought I would win the primary. I beat two candidates who were supported by the local party offices. So when I won, I went to the local party leaders and asked for help in coordinating my campaign . . . [the head of the local party chapter] did not like me, we had several run-ins and disagreements and the local party did nothing for me. . . . The chair of the local party literally diverted campaign contributions away from me.

Almost 25 percent of female and male challengers believed their party showed some bias toward them. Most of these instances of bias, as with the preceding case, were perpetrated at the local levels and centered on personality clashes.

Of the six women who noted evidence of party bias, four (16% of women in the study) attributed the bias to their gender. The clearest example of party bias in this study, mentioned previously, concerned the female candidate who did not receive party funding although a male challenger running under similar circumstances was financed by the party. When the campaign manager pressed the national party for further clarification of why his campaign was not funded, he was again told that it was because his candidate was a woman. The campaign manager described what happened:

> I called the party again to pursue the issue of party money and again the finance director told me that this was the old-boy network in action. When I pressed him on how we might challenge this decision, he came clean and told me that . . . [a particular party leader] was hesitant about supporting women. . . . I was basically told that I was right, we should have gotten funding, but that I was out of luck because my candidate was a woman. The whole thing really shocked me.

This admission by a national party organization suggests that gender discrimination by parties is widespread; however, none of the other women in the examination mentioned problems with this same party organization.

The three other female candidates who identified bias cited state- and local-level party organizations. In these three cases, the claims of gender bias were based on the perceptions of the campaign managers. Unlike the preceding example, there was no direct confirmation of discrimination by the party. All three of these candidates believed that the party did not take them seriously as candidates. One of these managers, running the campaign of a female Democratic challenger in a tight race, described her campaign's experience with the local party:

Here we were in the midst of a tight race, our race was written-up as one of the top 100 races in the country . . . and the old boys running the local party office had no interest in helping us. . . . This is a district filled with Reagan Democrats and they thought . . . [our candidate] must be an old-time liberal because she was a woman . . . they hardly did anything.

When this manager was pressed to provide specific evidence of gender bias she could only identify the local party's seemingly inexplicable lack of interest in her campaign. Another manager for a female candidate described her experience with the party:

I called the state offices, I tried to work with the local party, but we got no help. You know when you are not being taken seriously, and that was the feeling I always got when I tried to work with the party here. . . . I can only think that it was because my candidate was a woman.

Again, these perceptions are uncorroborated. Nonetheless, several female candidates in this examination felt some element of hostility from party organizations. The perception of party discrimination, whether confirmed or not, is potentially as harmful as actual discrimination. Naff (1995) has shown that when female political actors perceive gender discrimination, it often has the effect of impairing their desire to climb the political ladder and acquire top positions.

In sum, there is evidence of sporadic gender bias by the parties. However, most of the evidence suggests that the parties in recent elections gave equal levels of financial and technical support to female and male candidates (Biersack and Herrnson 1994). The 1992 elections demonstrated a broad effort by the Democratic party to recruit and support female candidates. Yet support for female candidates will only be undertaken if the parties believe the women are credible candidates in the election process. As the analysis in Chapter 3 suggests, the success of female candidates may be contingent on the electoral environment. Thus, if female candidates are vulnerable in a given election, the political parties may be less likely to promote the candidacies of women. The fluctuating fortunes of female candidates and the parties' responses to them were evident in the Democratic party across the 1992 and 1994 elections. In 1992, the Democrats recruited and promoted women, both in California and across the country. In 1994, all specific efforts to promote female candidates disappeared. Thus, how parties address female candidates will need to be monitored carefully in upcoming election cycles.

Gender and Media Coverage

In elections for the U.S. House, the level of media coverage and the effect of that coverage can vary substantially across districts. For instance, in the Los Angeles area there are twenty-two congressional districts and only four to eight of them can be considered marginals or competitive. Los Angeles is covered by two major daily newspapers (*The Daily News* and *The Los Angeles Times*) and several local television stations.[9] Thus, unless there are unique circumstances (e.g., scandals), district races in the Los Angeles area receive very limited coverage. News reports about particular congressional elections are relevant for only a small portion of newspaper readers or television viewers in Los Angeles. *The Los Angeles Times's* coverage of the congressional races in California in 1992 and 1994 included single stories on only some of the competitive races. In 1992, most election news coverage focused on the two statewide Senate races. In 1994, most media attention was given to the governor's race and the record-breaking Senate race in which Republican Michael Huffington spent over $27 million of his own money. Thus, candidates running in urban areas and candidates running in what are thought to be noncompetitive districts cannot rely on the news media to deliver their campaign message.

Conversely, in highly competitive districts in which there is a synchronicity between the congressional district and the media market, the news coverage may be one of the most crucial components of election strategy. An example of a district in which the media plays a central role is California's 22nd District, which encompasses the cities of Santa Barbara, San Luis Obispo, and the adjacent communities. This district is served by two small daily newspapers (*Santa Barbara News Press* and *San Luis Obispo Telegram Tribune*) and three local television stations. These news outlets have a local focus and tend to extensively cover the congressional race. The district is also highly competitive: The 1994 race between Democrat Walter Capps and Republican Andrea Seastrand was decided by less than 1 percent of the vote. The role of the news media is of crucial importance to candidates running in this type of district.

The Extent and Scope of Media Coverage

In examining the role of the media in congressional races, we again turn to the interviews with the campaign managers. In eighteen of the sixty-one

Table 4.6   Extent and Type of Media Coverage for Congressional Races in
1992 and 1994

	Female Challengers (25)	Male Challengers (41)	Male Incumbents (33)
Extent of media coverage[a]			
No coverage	20%	29%	24%
Little coverage	40	44	45
Moderate coverage	28	20	12
Extensive coverage	12	7	21
Type of media coverage[b]			
Local television	16*	5	3
Local newspapers	80	71	79
National media	16*	2	0

a. For the extent of coverage the candidates were grouped as follows: "No coverage" is less than three news stories about the candidate over the entire election; "Little coverage" is news stories every two weeks; "Moderate coverage" is weekly reporting; "Extensive coverage" is daily reporting. The columns add up to 100%.
b. For the type of coverage, the campaign managers were asked whether they appeared in local newspapers, local television, and national media. The percentage indicates that the candidates received coverage in that forum.
*$p < .10$; one-tailed t-test comparing the male and female challengers.

races in this study, the campaign managers for both sides acknowledged that media coverage played an important role in the campaign. In assessing the coverage, managers were asked a series of questions about their candidates' experiences with the media. First, the managers were asked about the extent and type of coverage they received. The results are listed in Table 4.6.

There were no sweeping gender differences in the campaign managers' perceptions of how their candidates were covered by the media. In the eyes of their managers, female challengers were slightly more likely than men to receive "extensive" or "moderate" coverage and male challengers were more likely than women to receive "no coverage," although these differences are not statistically significant. That women were perceived as having received more coverage may be explained by the increased attention women received in 1992. Eight out of sixteen managers for female candidates mentioned that their candidate was covered in media stories focusing on the "year of the woman." One female candidate was featured on *Nightline* in a special program on female candidates. Another woman received national attention because she had once been a single mother on welfare. Another woman was part of a story on the campaign styles of female candidates. Being the frequent objects of media exposure, especially nonnegative exposure, was definitely an advantage for female candidates in 1992. However, this advantage was short-lived as the novelty of female candidates and the media's fascination with them rapidly trailed off. None of the managers for female candidates interviewed in 1994 noted any increased media attention for their candidate because she was a woman.

The second part of Table 4.6 reveals only minor differences in the campaign managers' perceptions of the types of coverage their candidates received. Overall, the congressional races received very little television coverage; most of the media coverage of the races appeared in the local newspapers. Women received higher levels of coverage in all three categories: local newspapers, local television, and national media. Three female candidates made the national news. Again these differences can be attributed to the greater media attention women received in 1992. There was no gender difference in the campaign managers' perceptions of the types of coverage received by male and female candidates in the 1994 elections.

Bias in Media Coverage

With 30 to 40 percent of all candidates reporting either moderate or extensive media coverage in Table 4.6, it is important to understand whether there are any systematic differences in the types of coverage female and male candidates receive. Is there any significant bias working against female candidates? The role of candidate gender in campaign coverage has been explored in the literature only recently. Kahn and Goldenberg (1991), in a study of the coverage of U.S. Senate candidates, uncovered some startling information about the treatment of female candidates. They conducted a content analysis of the newspaper coverage of Senate candidates in 1984 and 1986. They concluded that "female candidates receive less news coverage and the coverage they do receive concentrates more on their viability and less on their issue positions" (196). They further found that the coverage of female Senate candidates tended to be more negative. In addition, other examinations have found that media often employ traditional gender stereotypes. For instance, Kahn (1993), in a later article based on the same database of the 1984 and 1986 Senate races, also found that the media tended to cover women in stereotypical ways, often downplaying their personal qualities of leadership and effectiveness (see also Kahn 1992). No systematic research has investigated the role of candidate gender in media coverage of House races. In fact, there is almost no research at all on the role of media coverage in House elections.[10]

In this study, two types of gender bias in media coverage are explored. The first is the existence of direct media bias. This type of bias would involve intentional acts of gender discrimination in which journalists or editors choose to portray female candidates negatively because of their gender. The second type of media bias occurs when female and male candidates are portrayed in the media through gender stereotypes. In this form of bias the media depict male and female candidates in terms of the stereotypical social qualities that compose traditional sex roles (Kahn 1992). In such instances, media sources are not setting out on a course of direct bias and intentional discrimination against women but manifest sex-role stereotyping in their reporting. This unconscious stereotyping may have the same effect of discriminating against women and therefore may be just as harmful as intentional bias. However, one might also plausibly argue, as was alluded to in Chapter 3, that the media's emphasis on "feminine traits" may have made female candidates more attractive to voters in 1992. They more easily sold themselves as the "agents of change," apparently only because of their status as women. However, by 1994, as the electoral environment became indifferent to the presence of female candidates, media stereotyping of female candidates may have more clearly worked against them.

There are several ways in which media bias and negative coverage are manifested in a campaign. One type of bias occurs when the media choose to not cover a candidate; media disinterest delegitimizes a candidate. Another type of bias occurs when the opponent receives excessively favorable coverage. The final type of bias occurs when the media directly disparage the candidate and his or her policy positions. To address the question of media bias in this study, two approaches were taken. Campaign managers were asked several questions to assess the quality of media coverage. Also, newspaper coverage was analyzed for as many races as possible.[11] However, there were only ten female candidates in races who received "moderate" or "extensive" coverage. This did not provide a large enough sample of newspaper articles to analyze systematically, although some anecdotal evidence emerged. The managers' assessments of media coverage is listed in Table 4.7.

The campaign managers of female candidates were the most likely to believe that their candidate was not treated fairly by the media. Several of

Table 4.7   Perception of Media Bias, by Gender and Challenger Status

	Female Challengers (25)	Male Challengers (41)	Male Incumbents (35)
Overall, do you believe you were treated fairly by the media?	36%*	59%	71%
Do you believe there was media bias favoring your candidate?	24	12	0
Do you believe there was media bias against your candidate?	64*	41	17
Do you believe there was gender bias in the media coverage of your candidate?	36	(only asked for female candidates)	

NOTE: Percentage indicates a "yes" response to the questions.
*$p < .05$; one-tailed t-test comparing the male and female challengers.

the managers believed that some of the coverage portrayed women in a stereotypical manner. Female candidates were also more likely to perceive bias in favor of their candidacies. Six of the sixteen managers for female candidates in 1992 believed they had a media advantage because female candidates were receiving media attention in the hype surrounding the "year of the woman." The responses to the questions in Table 4.7 are only the perceptions of the campaign managers and do not indicate objective levels of gender bias. Determining the actual degree of bias is made more difficult because in eight of the fifty-five campaigns, both sides claimed that the media was biased against them.

Gender Bias in Media Coverage

Was there evidence of direct gender bias against female candidates? The female candidates in this study believed they faced significant levels of gender bias or stereotyping. The campaign managers of nine out of twenty-nine female candidates (31%, including the four female incumbents) believed that the media engaged in some form of gender bias against them. Some of the specific instances that were described correspond well with recent findings by Kahn (1993) that stereotypical "feminine" and "masculine" traits were imposed on female and male candidates. Five female candidates, all running in 1992, felt that the news media were uncertain about how to "deal with" female candidates at the beginning of the campaign. Three of these candidates' managers believed that female candidates were not taken as seriously as men at the beginning of the campaign. One of these female candidates was constantly referred to in the local papers by her first name, whereas her opponent was always addressed as "Mr." or by his last name. In another example, the manager for a female candidate running in southern California noted,

> At the start of the campaign we really had to prove ourselves. We had to prove that we were a credible alternative to the incumbent. At first the local papers were not very interested in this race, then when a poll showed we were close, they suddenly began to take us seriously. . . . Also the fact that women were a big story this year encouraged them to cover our campaign. Without the poll and the "year of the woman" going on, I don't really think the media would have given us a second look.

This manager believed that the media were predisposed to disregard his candidate and to not take her seriously. Another manager for a female candidate described what he saw going on in the election:

> The local press did not know what to make of us in the beginning; it was as if they did not know how to cover the campaign merely because she was a woman. You could really see it at the candidate forum we had with our opponent . . . [the journalist] got up and asked him a tough question about immigration. . . . Then the same guy meekly asked [our female candidate] a question about her experiences on the school board.

Media coverage presented another instance in the campaign process in which female candidates perceived a credibility problem. However, women in 1994 were less likely to report instances of gender discrimination than in 1992. The burst of female candidates in 1992 may have prepared journalists to treat women as ordinary candidates in future races. Nonetheless, for both the 1992 and 1994 elections, the managers of female candidates reported several specific instances in which they felt the media demonstrated gender bias in reporting. One female candidate spoke of her problems with the press:

> I got little press, but when I was mentioned, it was often in reference to my family, particularly the amount of money my husband and I have. . . . My identity was always associated with my husband.

Another manager, working for a female candidate who had gone through a "nasty divorce," thought the press focus on the divorce was gender-driven:

> I'll give you an example of gender bias. The press totally over-emphasized her divorce. She had a nasty divorce with child custody battles and the whole thing. The press was always bringing it up. I really don't believe a male divorcee candidate would have been subjected to as much focus on this personal issue. . . . Our [male] opponent had a host of personal and family scandals and the press stayed away from them.

This example illustrates the dual expectations society has of women in professional positions. If the traditional family unit breaks apart, this reflects more poorly on the mother than on the father. As the manager for one female candidate quipped,

> Nobody cares if a man does not stay home to fix the kids' school lunch, but if a woman appears to be neglecting her children by not making them their lunch, then the woman has a big appearance problem.

The problems female candidates have in fulfilling the many roles today's women are typically expected to fulfill—mother, wife, and career woman— are colorfully chronicled by Witt, Paget, and Matthews (1994, chapter 4).

In a study similar to this one, Poole (1993), in a set of interviews with women running for state legislative office in Illinois, found numerous examples of media bias against female candidates. One woman in Poole's study stated,

> [the media covering the race] concentrate[d] on stupid, little things such as clothes, hair, etc., which never comes up with men. They also use loaded adjectives to describe us such as feisty, perky, small, and lively. (6-7)

Another female candidate from Poole's study noted,

> Women candidates need to be aware of where they are campaigning and of the need to dress appropriately. A more presentable appearance seems to be expected. There seems to be a feeling among the media that most female candidates are bored housewives who 'dabble in politics' after their families are raised. (7)

The general conclusions drawn by Poole were that women feel they must work much harder to gain credibility with the press. Many of the female candidates in this examination had similar feelings.

The anecdotes from this study, along with the experiences of the female candidates from Poole's study in Illinois, suggest that female candidates are often held to different standards than men. Most of the gender differences in media coverage could be attributed to gender stereotyping by reporters. The effect is that many of the female candidates believed they had to fulfill two roles to compete successfully under the media eye of a campaign. They had to meet the standards of someone with high political qualifications and they also had to fulfill their stereotypical traditional roles as women. These experiences with the media are consistent with Jamieson's (1995) analysis of the "double bind" faced by women in the public eye. Women have to appear extra professional while maintaining their traditionally feminine personas. The media coverage female candidates receive places additional burdens on women in two ways. First, evidence seems to indicate considerable gender bias in coverage. This makes the system unfair and discourages women's participation. Second, many women expect and perceive a higher level of scrutiny and criticism from the media than given to men. Both of these phenomena place a greater burden on female candidates with regard to how they must strategize about a campaign and the care with which they must present themselves as candidates.

Incumbency Advantages and
Ideological Bias as Gender Bias

Although there were definitely clear instances of direct gender bias in media coverage, most claims of bias by the campaign managers were attributed to ideological considerations or unfairly favorable treatment of the incumbent. First, in terms of ideological considerations, it was typical for campaign managers to blame the "liberal press" or a "conservative paper" for bias against their candidates. For instance, one candidate running in a northern California inland district complained about the local newspaper:

> The owner of the newspaper is a friend of our opponent. He held a fund-raiser for him. . . . We couldn't get anywhere with the press, the coverage was so biased against us and completely supported the positions of our [conservative] opponent.

One explanation for ideological bias in district-level races is that one reporter is usually given the responsibility for covering the race—there is no team of reporters through which any individual biases would be evened out. Thus, several campaign managers cited ideological bias from individual reporters. One manager, working for a female candidate, offered the following example of a particular reporter's ideological bias. In referring to the ideology of the male candidate in a campaign story, he wrote,

> [the male candidate is] running as a conservative Republican who supports family values and property rights.

In referring to the ideology of the female candidate he wrote,

> [the female candidate], who has been aligned with some of the county's more liberal Democrats, claims to be running as a conservative Democrat.

The manager thought this reporter exhibited both gender and ideological bias throughout the campaign. Another manager complaining about an individual reporter commented,

> [the reporter] would beat us up relentlessly in his column. I called him, tried to make peace with him, I called his editor, but nothing changed. All the coverage from . . . [his newspaper] supported our liberal opponent.

In addition to ideological bias, another type of non-gender-related bias was reported by several challengers who felt the press was biased in favor of incumbents. As one manager put it,

> We would send out press releases, we would stage press conferences and we even had some street demonstrations. The press refused to cover us. . . . [The incumbent] would blow his nose and it would end up in the paper. It was so frustrating.

When asked if this was an ideological bias in favor of the incumbent, the manager responded,

> I think it is about legitimacy. When the congressman does something . . . makes a speech or is in the district . . . that is news, when the congressman's challenger— who most people don't think has a chance in hell—does something, that is not news.

In the races in which a challenger was running against an established incumbent, most of the challengers thought it was impossible to get any press attention. One longtime political consultant described the typical role of the media in this type of race:

> To make news you have to have credibility. Members of Congress have credibility simply because of who they are, and they develop their relationship with the local media very carefully. They have full-time press people. . . . The local press and the congressman often have very congenial relationships. So when some upstart comes along and is badgering the editor for coverage, many times the editor's sympathy and interests lie with the incumbent.

These sentiments are consistent with analyses suggesting that members of Congress cultivate a congenial "home style" in their districts (Fenno 1978) and that they use the prestige of their office to secure positive media coverage (Mayhew 1974). The fact that the "home style" discussed in the congressional literature has been the style of male incumbents should not be overlooked. Up until recently this kind of image creation and cultivation of the press has not been an option for women. This type of incumbent-favorable coverage is consistent with the institutional inertia explanation for women's slow entry into the U. S. Congress. The institutions that have served male incumbents over the past forty years are only now learning to integrate women into the process.

The managers for female challengers in this study were considerably more likely than their counterparts working for male challengers to mention instances in the news media of ideological- or challenger-status bias against them. Although the sample of female candidates is ultimately too small to allow any generalizable conclusions, there are several possible explanations for this disparity. First, some gender bias against women may be cloaked in other forms of negative coverage. For instance, newspaper editors or reporters who are either consciously or subconsciously biased against female candidates may choose to attack a female candidate based on other criteria to mask their real motivations. An alternative explanation may lie in the presumption by many female candidates that the political and electoral system is hostile toward them and thus they perceive more bias than actually exists (Naff 1995). Another possible and non-gender-related explanation is that there was more partisan bias by the news media against Democrats. This would have had an adverse affect on the responses of the female candidates in the study because there were only eight Republican women in the study. All of these possible explanations require a more in-depth study of media coverage in a larger number of campaigns. However, as noted in the discussion of party support, the perception of gender bias can have many negative consequences for female candidates. The electoral system becomes more challenging and difficult for women than men.

Conclusion

This chapter began with a discussion of three possible explanations for why women have historically had difficulty being elected in greater numbers: gender discrimination, sex-role socialization, and institutional inertia. All three of these explanations can be seen at work in the California congressional elections of 1992 and 1994. In assessing the validity of these three explanations for the candidates in this study, some caveats need to be made. The data presented in this chapter is based on perceptions of campaign managers that were often uncorroborated. Also, this analysis only focuses on experiences of candidates over two election cycles. Thus, we must be cautious in generalizing from the experiences of these candidates. Before making further comments on the accuracy of these explanations, Table 4.8 provides a summary of the experiences of male and female candidates in the areas of fund-raising, party support, and media coverage.

In turning to the first explanation, gender discrimination, it is clear that substantial vestiges of discrimination and exclusion remain. Some instances of discrimination can be uncovered in every aspect of the electoral process and that such discrimination still exists is an important discovery. Yet the general picture that emerges is one of an electoral process that does not overtly discriminate. Ultimately, the actual degree of discrimination is very difficult to measure. However, regardless of the actual degree of discrimination, female candidates were more likely than male candidates to perceive discrimination in fund-raising, party support, and media coverage. If women believe that the system is unfairly biased against them, this may have important consequences for the further participation of female candidates. Naff (1995), in a study of female government bureaucrats, has shown how the perception of discrimination in governmental agencies often causes women to leave before requesting a promotion. Similarly, if the election process is viewed as discriminatory, it may discourage more women from becoming involved. The perceptions of unfairness certainly make the system more difficult for female candidates and suggest that the various components of the electoral system have not done a good enough job at showing they are open to female candidates.

The second explanation for the slow progress of women into elected offices, sex-role socialization, also offers insight into the different experiences of female and male candidates. In this analysis, the effects of tradi-

Table 4.8   Summary of Different Experiences in the Electoral Process for Male and Female Candidates

Component of the Electoral Process	Differences	
	Female Candidates	*Male Candidates*
Fund-raising	More reliant on small contributors	Raised less money on average
	Women's PACs serve as important means of support	More reliant on candidate contributions
	Felt excluded from traditional fund-raising networks	
Party support	Perceived lower levels of party support	Expected less party support
	Were actively recruited to run for office in 1992	
	Noted some instances of party-based discrimination	
Media coverage	Received more media coverage	Believed women got too much coverage
	Perceived more media bias	
	Believed coverage often employed gender stereotypes	

tional socialization were most evident in the areas of fund-raising and media support. Women and men sought different sources of funding because the culture of political contributions is still lodged in the male-dominated business environment. Also, there was some evidence that female donors, who make up a substantial portion of the donor pool for female candidates, tend to give smaller contributions because of the way women have been socialized to conceive of politics. As a result, female candidates may be forced to work harder and be more resourceful in raising money because powerful corporate men are not comfortable contributing to women. Further, the election process is more challenging to women because the media are hesitant to grant women credibility. Women still have to contend with a press corps accustomed to gender stereotyping. Most traditional socialization patterns work against women in the electoral process because they tend to favor the stereotypical traits of male politicians and scrutinize more heavily the participation of women.

The third and final explanation, institutional inertia, is more difficult to evaluate. The evidence suggests that various components of the election process are becoming more tolerant toward the inclusion of women. Women are playing a broader role in party organizations, the media is slowly learning how to deal with women in a more objective manner, and the fund-raising success of female candidates seems to be on a par with male candidates. The number of women involved in politics is increasing incrementally across all levels of government. The California congressional elections in 1992 and 1994 clearly illustrate that institutional inertia is being slowly overcome. In 1992 the number of women in the California congressional delegation increased from three to seven. This substantial progress was made possible because sixteen of the fifty-two congressional races were open seat elections. Five of the women elected in 1992 were running for open seats. However, in 1994, there were only three open seats, two of which were won by women. The success of female candidates in open seat races may lead one to conclude that change is occurring, and that time will allow women to become full partners in the governing process.

The experiences of the candidates in the electoral process demonstrate that men and women face some different obstacles. Women and men often employ different strategies that help them be more successful in confronting the electoral process. These different strategies are often linked to how the political socialization process manifests itself in the institutions within the election. Adding to the differing experiences of men and women in the electoral process is the volatility of the political climate. The different environments in 1992 and 1994 reduced or exacerbated both the obstacles and advantages men and women faced in the electoral process. The 1992 elections appeared to break down some of the barriers women face in terms of fund-raising and media coverage. Yet many of the effects of political socialization still pose problems for female candidates. The electoral arena is currently very volatile in its treatment and acceptance of female candidates. Female candidates were coveted in 1992 and ignored in 1994. Women received favorable media coverage in some districts and biased and discriminatory coverage in other districts. In some districts women were embraced by the local party organizations and in others they were inexplicably dismissed. These experiences demonstrate that all three of the explanations are at work in limiting the number of successful female candidates. However, perhaps the most important conclusion here is that discrimination and traditional stereotyping still play a significant role in the experiences of female candidates.

Notes

1. Between 1917, which marked the arrival of the first woman to the House of Representatives, through 1970, over 40 percent of women serving in Congress were filling in the vacancy caused by the death of their husband (see Bullock and Heys 1972).

2. Margaret Chase preceded Kassebaum as the first Republican woman to win election to the Senate, but she first succeeded her husband in the House before seeking election in the Senate.

3. The findings in this chapter are based on the perceptions of the campaign managers. One possible explanation for gender differences in the experiences of male and female candidates could be the gender differences among the campaign managers. For instance, if female candidates were more likely to have women campaign managers, then the gender configuration of the managers might explain differences among the candidates. However, when comparing the gender of campaign managers across the candidates, there is almost no discrepancy. The percentage of women campaign managers for female challengers was 40%, for male challengers 34%, and for male incumbents 34%. Thus, we can be confident that the comparisons of the experiences of male and female candidates are not biased by the gendered perspectives of the campaign managers.

4. In postelection interviews, candidates were asked to identify the primary reasons for their victory or defeat. For winners and losers, district registration was the answer given most often.

5. Based on the FEC reports for congressional campaigns in 1992 and 1994, California candidates from both parties raised considerably more money than the national average. In 1992, California incumbents were on average $139,000 above the national average and challengers $100,000 above the national average. In 1994, the disparity was down a little: California incumbents were roughly $100,000 above the national average and challengers $60,000 above the national average.

6. To examine the personal wealth of male and female candidates would be useful, although this information is very difficult to acquire and no comprehensive examinations of candidate gender and personal wealth currently exists. For some data on gender and candidate wealth, see Brzinski and Nye (1993).

7. Other women's PACs making significant contributions in 1992 included the following: Hollywood Women's Political Committee ($543,671), National Organization for Women ($593,845), and the National Women's Political Caucus ($500,000). For further discussion of the role of women's PACs, see Nelson (1994) and Boles (1993).

8. For further analysis of the factors that have been at play in the recruitment of female candidates, see Rule (1990, 1981) and Welch (1978).

9. There are several other newspapers with substantial circulation in the Los Angeles area, such as the *Orange County Register* and the *Long Beach Press-Telegram*. However, even these papers do not have synchronicity with any congressional districts. Further, in the case of the

Register, which covers five congressional districts, there is only one potentially competitive congressional race.

10. Jacobson's *The Politics of Congressional Elections* (1992), perhaps the best analysis on House elections, only barely touches on the role of media coverage.

11. A complete collection of local newspapers' coverage was not possible because of the wide range of publications in some districts that are not archived or maintained. Some articles were collected for each race and little evidence of gender bias or stereotyping was perceptible in the samples examined.

The Candidates
Go to the Voters

I have never seen anything like this. Voters have been so enthusiastic for our candidate. I have run lots of House races, and I've never seen this kind of response to the candidate. The "year of the woman" [1992] is real, at least it is for the voters.

—*Campaign manager for an experienced female challenger running in northern California in 1992*

In 1994, the last thing I would want to be is a woman Democrat running for office. The Democrats have lost control of the policy agenda and there appears to be a backlash against women. I think with the "year of the woman" in 1992, many male voters saw the feminization of the Democratic party and they didn't like it.

—*Long-time political consultant working for a male challenger running in southern California in 1994*

The political environment over the 1992 and 1994 elections was very volatile for female candidates. In California, female candidates took part in campaigns for elective office in unprecedented numbers in 1992 and

143

1994. In both election years the two most prominent statewide races were contests between Republican men and Democratic women. More female candidates received their party's nomination to run for Congress in 1992 and 1994 than in the previous five elections combined. Prior to 1990, California voters had never been particularly receptive to female candidates. The state was ranked 23rd in the percentage of women serving in the state legislature and only three members of the forty-five seat congressional delegation were women. Only two women had ever won a statewide election prior to 1990: Republican Ivy Baker Priest, who served as the state treasurer from 1967 to 1975; and Democrat March Fong Eu, who served as the secretary of state from 1975 to 1994. When women won major nominations, beginning with Dianne Feinstein's bid for governor in 1990, California electoral politics took on a new face. Voters who had never been presented with women running for high elective office had to confront some of their own gender stereotypes when deciding how to vote.

This chapter turns to these voters and analyzes the role of candidate gender in voter decision making. After chronicling the experiences and behavior of the candidates through the electoral process, from the decision to run for office (Chapter 2) to their treatment by the media (Chapter 4), the final important step is assessing how the candidates were perceived by the voters. Many of the strategies employed by the candidates, such as those discussed in Chapters 2 and 3, were based on the candidates' conceptions of how voters employed traditional stereotyping of male and female candidates. For instance, male candidates were hesitant to attack women opponents because they feared the voters' reactions. Also, female candidates stressed their credentials and expertise on particular policy issues because they felt voters would be leery of women running for high elective office. As we turn to the voters, we find that traditional stereotypes about sex roles were an important component of the voting decision. In assessing the interaction of candidate gender and voting behavior, this chapter first analyzes the performance of the men and women House candidates in primary, general, and marginal elections. Examining the several types of elections demonstrates that the effect of candidate gender changes in different electoral circumstances. The chapter then examines the attitudes and motivations of voters across California, with particular emphasis on how voters took candidate gender into account. Unfortunately, voter opinion surveys are not available for the congressional districts; therefore statewide exit polls were used instead.

Candidate Gender and the Vote

In what way does candidate gender affect the voting decision? There are several possible responses voters may have in considering candidate gender. Individual voters might have an instant bias for or against a candidate based on gender—what we shall call *gender-response voting*. On the other end of the spectrum, voters may give absolutely no weight to candidate gender in their voting decision—*gender-neutral voting*. Finally, candidate gender may either consciously or unconsciously register in the voters' minds, interacting with the preconceived notions of gender roles that a voter might possess—*gender-socialized voting*.

Gender-response voting—This type of voting occurs when voters consciously and directly incorporate considerations of candidate gender into their voting decisions. Historically, gender-response voting has worked to the detriment of female candidates. Public opinion surveys over the years have shown a significant level of admitted bias by voters against female candidates. The central gender bias question asked by the National Election Studies (NES) survey since the early 1950s is, "If your party nominated a woman for president, would you vote for her if she were qualified for the job?" As late as the mid-1970s, almost 20 percent of both men and women said they would not be willing to vote for a female presidential candidate (Schreiber 1978; Ferree 1974). By 1993 the number had fallen to 9 percent. The most recent question regarding voter bias in congressional races was included in a 1984 Gallup poll, to which 6 percent of the population admitted a bias against voting for female congressional candidates (Darcy, Welch, and Clark 1994, 77). The percent of voters admitting bias against female candidates has been steadily declining. Although bias against female candidates has decreased considerably, asking someone if they are biased against female candidates is surely not the best way to uncover bias. Voter bias in the 1990s is more complex than ever before. Many voters may possess gender biases of which they are not aware. Further, many voters may employ gender stereotypes in voting and not even consider that bias.

In addition, gender bias in voting is no longer simply anti-woman. A number of polls conducted prior to the 1992 elections uncovered bias in favor of female candidates. A *U.S. News & World Report* survey taken in April of 1992 found that 61 percent of the electorate believed the country would be run better if more women held positions in government. A *Life* magazine poll

Table 5.1   Voters Acknowledging the Importance of Candidate Gender in Their Vote Selection

	Respondents Saying Candidate Gender Was Important in Their Vote Choice	Voted for	
		Woman	Man
1990 Pete Wilson vs. Dianne Feinstein (Governor)	3%	80%	20%
1992 Bruce Herschensohn vs. Barbara Boxer (U.S. Senate)	10	77	19
1992 John Seymour vs. Dianne Feinstein (U.S. Senate)	10	80	20
1994 Michael Huffington vs. Dianne Feinstein (U.S. Senate)	6	76	20
1994 Pete Wilson vs. Kathleen Brown (Governor)	4	92	5

SOURCE: Compiled from Voter Research and Surveys General Election Exit Poll: California Files, 1990, 1992, and 1994. (1990 $N = 3,313$; 1992 $N = 2,157$; 1994 $N = 1,017$).
NOTE: The exit poll question was worded as follows: "Were any of the items below VERY IMPORTANT in making your choices for SENATOR (or GOVERNOR)?" One of the eight possible responses was, "Sex of the candidate."

conducted in early 1992 found that roughly a third of the electorate believed women would do a better job of controlling the government than men, whereas the other two-thirds thought there would be no difference (see Chaney and Sinclair 1994, 127). A more recent academic survey of voters found that female voters are more likely to support female candidates and male voters are more likely to support male candidates (Rosenthal 1995, 604). In examining gender-response voting in the California elections, the exit polls from the 1990, 1992, and 1994 elections were used. Table 5.1 shows the degree to which voters admitted using gender as a consideration in how they cast their ballots in the major statewide races in California in 1990, 1992, and 1994.

Table 5.1 shows that in recent elections gender-response voting in California was employed by a small but significant portion of the electorate. These results also confirm some of the recent polls suggesting that women may have some advantages with voters because an overwhelming portion of the voters in California who said candidate gender was important to them voted for women. Based on these survey results, we can conclude that at least in larger races, up to 10 percent of the electorate acknowledges they are engaging in gender-response voting, and that in recent elections that may be working to the advantage of female candidates.

Gender-neutral voting—Another possible response to candidate gender is no response. *Gender-neutral voting* is defined as those instances in which voters do not in any way use gender considerations to make their vote choice. There is considerable evidence that candidate gender does not influence the outcome of an election. Studies have shown that male and female candidates perform equally well with voters (Darcy, Welch, and Clark 1994). Burrell (1994, 141) has concluded that candidate gender accounts for less than 1 percent of variation in the vote totals of men and women House candidates. In these analyses it certainly appears that most voters have neutral feelings toward the sex of the candidates or, at the very least, gender effects roughly balance each other out in final vote totals, with those voters biased against women canceled out by those voters biased in favor of women. The prevalence of gender-neutral voting is further supported by a number of experimental studies that have found no gender bias in how voters cast their ballots (see Leeper 1991; Kaid et al. 1984; Ekstrand and Eckert 1981).

Gender-socialized voting—The third possible response by voters to candidates is gender-socialized voting. This occurs when voters employ socialized and often subconscious stereotypes about women and men when appraising the candidates. These stereotypes may result in bias for or against female candidates but gender-socialized voting differs from gender-response voting because the use of gender in voter decision making is usually not overt or conscious. For instance, at the same time that admitted bias against female candidates was falling in the voter surveys, over 26 percent of respondents in the 1993 General Social Survey (GSS) still agreed with the statement that "most men are better suited emotionally for politics than are most women." Thus, although voters are saying that they are less biased, they are still demonstrating bias by adhering to this stereotype about women's suitability for politics. With over a quarter of the electorate clinging to this stereotype, we can be assured that traditional conceptions of sex roles persist and affect how voters assess candidates.

A number of studies have devised experiments to identify the stereotypes voters use and to discover any subconscious biases that voters may have. Sapiro (1981-82) published the first experimental study on voter perceptions about candidate gender and found voter stereotyping on some character and policy issues. Sapiro presented college students with a political speech by a candidate for public office. Half of the students were informed that the candidate was a man and the other half that the candidate was a woman. The female candidate in Sapiro's study was perceived to be better at improving the educational system, being honest, and dealing with the health care issue. Leeper (1991), in a similar study, presented to students a hypothetical election between a man and a woman. Leeper uncovered a number of different attitudes toward male and female candidates. First, he found that voters preferred "male" traits when selecting a candidate for executive-type offices. Also, Leeper asserts that in ambiguous electoral settings in which knowledge of the candidates is low, gender may emerge as a significant voting cue. Despite the different perceptions about male and female candidates revealed in these studies, when it came to making the vote choice, Leeper and Sapiro found that there was no bias against the female candidates. However, a recent experiment surveying students in Wyoming and California has turned up student bias against female candidates running for the House of Representatives (Fox and Smith 1996).

One of the clearest indicators of voter stereotyping occurs in the way voters associate candidate gender with regard to policy issues. Beginning with the Virginia Slims Poll in 1972, surveys show that voters perceive male and female politicians as having different areas of expertise. These differences fit neatly into the framework of sex-role stereotyping previously described in this study. A number of surveys in this area have shown that voters have more confidence in female politicians' abilities to address children's issues, health care, education, helping the poor, and consumer protection. Men are viewed as better suited to deal with foreign affairs, crime, economic development, and business interests. Following the Virginia Slims survey in 1972, the National Women's Political Caucus commissioned two surveys in 1984 and 1987. Both surveys found many of these same differences in how voters perceive candidate gender and issues. A more recent poll conducted by the Greenburg-Lake Analysis Group demonstrated that many of these differences in voter perceptions, although dwindling, were still present prior to the 1992 elections (Burrell 1994, 24-25).

Undoubtedly all three types of voting are at work in the electorate. However, we need to be leery of the studies that support the notion of gender-neutral voting. We have yet to devise an effective way of detecting the role of candidate gender in the decision-making process of voters. Certainly, the gender bias question used by the GSS and the NORC over the years, asking voters whether they would vote for a qualified woman for president, is a flawed measure of bias because it requires voters to admit that they discriminate (see Fox and Smith 1996). For the most part, the bias that exists today is much more subtle. Thus, what is important in considering the performance of the candidates in the California House elections is whether gender-response voting or gender-socialized voting played an important role

Table 5.2   Performance of California Congressional Candidates in Primary
and General Elections, by Gender and Type of Candidacy
(1992 and 1994 Combined)

	Women		Men	
	Won/Lost	*Win %*	*Won/Lost*	*Win %*
Primary election candidates				
Uncontested[a]	12	—	67	—
Incumbents[b]	4-0	100%	39-1	98%
Challengers running against incumbents	0-7	0	1-63	2
Challengers for incumbent-held seats[c]	10-5	67*	37-87	30
Challengers in open seat races	11-17	39*	16-110	14
General election candidates				
Uncontested	1	—	4	—
Incumbents	7-1	88	71-3	96
Challengers running against incumbents	0-17	0	3-62	5
Challengers in open seat races	7-5	58	11-13	46

a. Uncontested primaries combines both challengers and incumbents who ran unopposed.
b. Incumbents includes only those incumbents who were challenged in the primaries.
c. Challengers for incumbent-held seats were those candidates entering the opposing party's primary to run for an incumbent-held seat.
*$p < .05$; one-tailed t-test comparing winning percentage of male and female candidates in each category.

in the decisions of a significant number of voters. As this chapter shows, a substantial portion of the electorate engages in these types of voting. What emerges in this analysis is a portrait of voters who often rely on gender stereotypes in appraising male and female candidates. Although all voters do not engage in this style of voting behavior, it only takes a relatively small percentage of voters using either gender-response voting or gender-socialized voting to alter the outcome of an election.

Election Results

To begin assessing California voters' reactions to the new gender dynamics of the electoral system, we must first turn to the results of the elections. Were voters willing to send women to Congress? Table 5.2 compares the win/lose ratio and the winning percentage of female and male candidates in both the primary and the general elections in 1992 and 1994. All congressional candidates from California are included in Table 5.2, not just those interviewed for this study. The elections are categorized by the electoral opportunity of each candidate. The results are not broken down by year because there were no clear differences in the winning percentages across the two elections.

In 1992 and 1994 combined, sixty-six female candidates entered primaries and thirty-eight (58%) won their party's nomination. In comparison, 421 men entered primaries and only 161 (38%) emerged victorious. The incumbents, regardless of gender, performed well in the primaries; only one, Bob Lagomorsino of the 22nd district, was defeated. Lagomarsino was challenged by Michael Huffington, who spent more than $5 million in the race, a record level of spending for a House seat. Thus, his defeat occurred under highly unusual circumstances. However, in primaries with no incumbent running, women performed much better than their male counterparts. In the primaries in which a candidate was nominated to run against an incumbent, women were more than twice as successful as men in winning those nominations. Female challengers in primaries for open seat elections were almost three times as likely as men to win the nomination. The voters at the primary level were extremely receptive to female candidates.

In the general election, there were only minor differences in the overall success rates of female and male candidates. Male incumbents were a little more likely to win reelection than female incumbents, though this should not be overinterpreted because there were only nine female incumbents running in California in 1992 and 1994. Of the candidates challenging incumbents, not a single female challenger unseated an incumbent, whereas three male challengers were able to accomplish this feat. Even in the "year of the woman" election in 1992, no female candidate beat an incumbent in the general election. Women running for open seats performed slightly better than the male challengers, but this difference was not statistically significant. The women who won in general elections in 1992 and 1994 were all running in districts where their party affiliation made them solid favorites. Female candidates won two marginal races in 1992 but in both of these cases they were running against women. In the 36th district Jane Harman defeated Joan Milke-Flores, 48.4 percent to 42.2 percent, and in the 49th district Lynn Schenk defeated Judy Jarvis, 51.1 percent to 42.7 percent. With the exception of these races, all other female winners in 1992 were in safe districts.

Primary Voters

Female candidates had an extraordinary rate of success in the primary elections in California in 1992 and 1994. In races with both female and male

Table 5.3   Mean Variance From Expected Vote[a] in Contested Primaries[b] in 1992 and 1994

	1992		1994	
	Women (31)	Men (87)	Women (22)	Men (40)
Democratic candidates:				
Uncrowded primary	18.6%**	−11.9%	11.5%**	−7.8%
	(9)	(14)	(10)	(14)
Crowded primary	11.9**	−3.9	4.8	−1.5
	(15)	(46)	(3)	(9)
Republican candidates:				
Uncrowded primary	−11.1	8.4	−8.8*	7.7
	(3)	(4)	(7)	(8)
Crowded primary	16.9**	−2.9	6.0	−1.3
	(4)	(23)	(2)	(9)

a. Expected vote was calculated as the vote total divided by the number of candidates. For instance, in a primary with four candidates, the expected vote would be 25%. A positive percentage is the mean percentage above the expected vote and a negative percentage is the mean below the expected vote.
b. These are the primaries that had both men and women competing. The primaries were coded as follows: uncrowded, 2 to 4 candidates; crowded, 5 or more candidates.
*$p < .10$; **$p < .05$; one-tailed t-test compared the male and female candidates in the same year and in the same category.

candidates running, the women performed substantially better than the men. To compare the performance of female and male candidates, variance in "expected vote" is examined. Expected vote can be a more accurate measurement than a comparison of the raw averages of vote totals. Comparisons of raw vote totals, which are used in most analyses (Burrell 1994), can obscure the differences between candidates running in crowded and uncrowded primaries. Expected vote is the percentage of the vote each candidate would receive if they were all equal. The expected vote was determined by dividing 100 percent of the vote by the number of candidates in the primary. For instance, for five candidates, the expected vote for each candidate is 20 percent; for four candidates, 25 percent; for three candidates, 33 percent; and so forth. The figures in Table 5.3 show the mean variance from the "expected vote" in contested primaries in 1992 and 1994. A positive number indicates the percentage above the mean and negative number indicates the percentage below the mean in each category. The primaries in Table 5.3 were divided into two categories: crowded (more than four candidates) and uncrowded (two to four candidates). Primaries with a large number of candidates running have different dynamics from primaries with fewer candidates and should be considered separately. Greater knowledge of the candidates and a higher likelihood for candidate name recognition occurs in uncrowded primaries (Jacobsen 1992). Candidates running unopposed were dropped from the analysis in Table 5.3.

Female Democrats performed significantly better than male Democrats in both crowded and uncrowded primaries across both elections, although the difference in crowded primaries was not significant in 1994. The Democratic primary electorate in California provided the basis for women's success in 1992. The candidacies of female Republicans were not as uniformly success-ful. In both elections, Republican men performed better than Republican women in uncrowded primaries. Female Republicans in uncrowded prima-ries did not receive the same positive response as female Democrats. This is consistent with a finding that emerges throughout this chapter—the elector-ate demonstrates reluctance to support female Republican candidates.[1]

One of the most striking aspects of these primary results is the performance of women from both parties in crowded primaries. The women running in California in 1992 and 1994 had unprecedented success in gaining their party's nomination, particularly in large primary fields. Table 5.4 illustrates this success.

Female candidates won nine out of sixteen crowded primaries and finished second in six others. In 1992, the 36th congressional district in the South Bay area of Los Angeles was illustrative of women's success. On the Democratic side, seven candidates ran—three women and four men. The women finished first, second, and third. On the Republican side, two women ran in an eleven-candidate field and finished first and second. The two Republican women were Joan Milke-Flores, a Los Angeles City council-woman who had previously run for and lost a statewide election, and Maureen Reagan, the daughter of former President Ronald Reagan. These were high-profile women, which partially explains their rise to the top of the eleven-candidate field.

However, many of the female candidates who beat out large fields of men were not high-profile candidates. For instance, Judy Jarvis, running in the 1992 Republican primary in the 49th congressional district in San Diego, emerged victorious as the only woman in a field of ten. Jarvis, a politically inexperienced registered nurse, did not run an aggressive primary campaign

Table 5.4   Success of Female Candidates in Crowded Primaries

District	Party	Women	Men	Total	Finish of Women
		Number of Candidates			
1992					
6th	Democrat	2	7	9	1st, 5th
11th	Republican	1	5	6	2nd
14th	Democrat	1	7	8	1st
22nd	Democrat	1	4	5	1st
30th	Democrat	2	8	10	2nd, 6th
36th	Democrat	3	4	7	1st, 2nd, 3rd
36th	Republican	2	9	11	1st, 2nd
37th	Democrat	2	3	5	2nd, 3rd
43rd	Democrat	1	6	7	2nd
49th	Democrat	2	3	5	1st, 4th
49th	Republican	1	9	10	1st
51st	Democrat	1	4	5	1st
1994					
16th	Democrat	2	4	6	1st, 4th
41st	Republican	1	4	5	2nd
44th	Republican	1	5	6	2nd
46th	Democrat	1	5	6	3rd

SOURCE: Compiled from the *Congressional Quarterly Almanac,* 1992 and 1994.

yet she was the only candidate to receive over 20 percent of the vote. Similarly, Bea Herbert, running in the 1992 Democratic primary in the 51st district, also in the San Diego area, beat out four male candidates. She received more than one-third of the vote despite running a limited primary campaign. Male candidates who were running in crowded primaries were often angered by what they saw as female candidates' unfair advantage in primaries. One male primary loser in the Los Angeles area responded to his defeat by a female candidate:

Her winning is a joke. She did not do anything but put her name on the ballot. I printed up literature. . . . I was all over the district putting up signs and meeting with people . . . then on election day . . . [the female candidate] wins easily. People wanted to vote for a woman. I don't think she even spent enough on her campaign to file an FEC report. . . . She was by far the least-qualified and least-experienced member of the field.

Political consultants managing campaigns in 1992 also saw a potent advantage for women in primaries. As one of these consultants noted,

> You can look at some of the women who won this time around and see that the only reason for their victory was because they were women . . . Just look at the margin some of those women won by, and the only logical explanation is voters flipping the switch for a woman.

There are a number of possible explanations for the success of women in primary elections. Many of the female candidates who won were longtime politicians who had been working their way up the political career ladder. For instance, Anna Eshoo, who beat seven men in her primary in a northern California district in 1992, was a county supervisor and had just missed winning the same congressional nomination in 1988. Lynn Schenk, running in the 49th district in 1992, had been a political activist; working in both presidential and gubernatorial cabinets before entering her race, she defeated a field of three men and one woman. Many of the women winners were accomplished and qualified candidates who were the most experienced members of their field. Some female candidates had been waiting for an opportunity to run for Congress and, as mentioned in Chapter 1, the retirements and open seats in 1992 provided an opening.

Women's greater success can also be explained by the lower number of frivolous campaigns among female candidates. Female candidates were less likely than male candidates to enter a race knowing that it would be difficult or impossible to win. For instance, in 1992 there were forty-one male primary candidates who garnered less than five percent of the total vote, but in the same year, no female candidates received less than five percent of the vote. In 1994, ten men and only one woman received under five percent. Part of the explanation for higher vote totals for women in primaries was their unwillingness to engage in campaigns for which there was no prospect of succeeding. Women, even very qualified and able women, were much less overtly ambitious and appeared to be more judicious than men in deciding whether to get involved in an election. The male candidates in this study were much more likely "to give it a shot," as one candidate commented in discussing his decision to enter the race. Thus it appears that most of the women who entered a House race in California, regardless of their qualifications, weighed the decision carefully. The women in this study appeared to be much less cavalier in their electoral bids than a number of male candidates.

A final and compelling explanation for women's success in primaries is that gender may have been an important voting cue. Candidate name recognition in primary elections is generally low, and this was compounded in 1992 by the high number of crowded primaries. When a voter goes to the ballot to vote in a congressional election that has been lightly covered in the press, and is faced with ten names from the same party, gender may emerge as an important means of distinguishing between the candidates (see Leeper 1991). In crowded primaries most voters will not be able to make clear distinctions between the candidates. The larger vote totals for women in crowded primaries may indicate a potentially high level of gender-response voting, with some voters favoring women because of their sex. This explanation is further supported by a recent survey showing an advantage for female candidates among female voters. Rosenthal, in a study of Oklahoma City voters, found that over 40 percent of female voters, when presented with a choice between an equally qualified female and male candidate, preferred the woman (1995, 604). This phenomenon may be played out in primary elections where voters know little about the candidates and there are no big issue differences among the candidates. Voters in these instances, particularly female voters, may assume equal qualifications between the women and men on the ballot and choose the woman. This would give a great advantage to female Democratic candidates, because women currently compose 58 percent of the Democratic primary electorate (O'Brien 1995).

The behavior of primary voters bodes well for women's future prospects of moving into positions of high elective office. The political environment in a House primary appears to be beneficial for a female candidate. Lack of voter knowledge about the candidates and the often crowded fields in primary races help turn candidate gender into a voting cue, and this appears to have worked well for female primary candidates in California in 1992 and 1994. Therefore, what seems to be occurring in primary elections is a combination of gender response and gender-socialized voting. Voters identify the female candidate on the ballot—gender-response voting—then rely on stereotyping about how female candidates bring a fresh and honest approach to politics. Women become an easy selection for voters when little is known about any of the candidates (see Rosenthal 1995).

Table 5.5   Comparison of General Election Vote Totals in 1992 and 1994, by Gender, Party, and Incumbency

	Female Candidates		Male Candidates	
	1992	1994	1992	1994
All candidates	48.3%	45.1%	46.2%	49.2%
	(19)	(18)	(79)	(82)
Democratic candidates:				
Challengers	44.6	38.8	40.2	33.7
	(15)	(6)	(15)	(17)
Incumbents[a]	82.5	62.1	61.9	60.2
	(2)	(6)	(17)	(21)
Republican candidates:				
Challengers	42.5	34.3	35.8	38.3
	(2)	(6)	(32)	(24)
Incumbents	0	0	56.3	64.0
			(15)	(20)

NOTE: Entries are mean vote totals for each category of candidate.
a. One female incumbent in 1994 was running unopposed and was not included in the table.

General Election Voters

Although the female House candidates were widely successful in primaries, the results in general elections were mixed. Table 5.5 compares the average general election vote totals for female and male candidates. The candidates are categorized by gender, party, and challenger status and the results are broken down by election year.

Table 5.5 illustrates the change in electoral fortunes for the parties and female and male candidates between 1992 and 1994. The combined pool of female candidates dropped over three percentage points in their vote totals between the two elections, whereas male candidates gained three points over the same time period. The overall decline for women can be partially attributed to the disastrous showing for Democrats in California in 1994. Every category of Democratic candidate slipped substantially between the two elections, except that of male incumbents. Female Democratic challengers maintained almost a six-percentage-point edge over their male counterparts in both elections. This suggests that the advantage for Democratic women extended from the primary elections to the general elections. These results indicate that there is some degree of gender-response and gender-socialized voting favoring women throughout the election process. However, the big winners in 1994 were male Republican challengers and incumbents. The substantial gains by male Republican incumbents (on average, 8% over the 1992 totals) illustrate the Republican tidal wave that swept the state in 1994.

Despite the success of Republican candidates, female Republican challengers did not perform as well as their male counterparts. Although the small sample dictates caution in drawing conclusions, the poor performance by female Republican challengers in 1994 was not consistent with the gains of male Republican candidates across the state. The vote totals of female Democratic incumbents also dropped between the two elections but this can be explained by two female incumbents who were involved in extremely close elections in marginal districts. In 1994, male and female Democratic incumbents performed about equally well.

From these results it appears that Democratic women have a stronger base of support than Democratic men, but this is not the case on the Republican side. To assess the individual effect of gender, incumbency, party, and race type on vote totals in 1992 and 1994, regression equations were developed. Table 5.6 presents the results of these equations.

In 1992, women and Democrats performed significantly better than men and Republicans. By 1994, gender appeared to have almost no effect on the vote totals and Republicans gained the edge over Democrats. The vote advantage for incumbents and the effect of race type remained constant over the two election cycles.

Table 5.6 illustrates important changes in the electoral environment between the elections. Women had a significant advantage with voters in 1992 as gender-response and gender-socialized voting played an important role in propelling women forward. Voters viewed female candidates as fresh and new. However, by 1994 there was no significant gender effect in voting. As the following analysis demonstrates, women had certain disadvantages in 1994 that worked to mitigate the gender-response and gender-socialized voting that had favored them in 1992. What this suggests is that the electoral arena is more volatile for female candidates than for men. This has the possibility of presenting women with both electoral advantages and disadvantages, depending on the political environment in any given election.

Table 5.6   Regression Estimates of General Election Vote Totals for 1992 and 1994 Elections, by Gender, Party, Challenger Status, and Race Type

	1992	*1994*	*1992-1994 Combined*
Constant	52.24**	46.77**	49.10**
	(2.24)	(4.06)	(1.94)
Gender of candidate[a]	–5.86**	.07	–3.39*
	(2.61)	(2.47)	(1.81)
Challenger status[b]	27.46**	28.04**	27.71**
	(2.20)	(1.91)	(1.48)
Party affiliation[c]	–4.78**	3.41*	–.56
	(1.96)	(1.87)	(1.38)
Race type[d]	–11.47**	–14.29**	–11.91**
	(2.24)	(3.95)	(1.86)
Adjusted R^2	.65	.69	.65
N	(98)	(100)	(198)

a. Gender of candidate was coded 0 for female and 1 for male.
b. Challenger status was coded 0 for challenger and 1 for incumbent.
c. Party affiliation was coded 0 for Democrat and 1 for Republican.
d. Race type was coded 0 for open seat and 1 for incumbent-held seat.
Chi-square test, $*p < .10$; $**p < .05$; standard error in parentheses.

Marginal Contests

One area in which female candidates did not fare as well as male candidates was in marginal contests. There were a total of twenty-nine competitive races in this study, nineteen in 1992 and ten in 1994. *Competitive races* are defined as those in which the margin of victory was less than 10 percent or the winner received less than 55 percent of the total vote (these two standards are slightly different because there were a number of races where third-party candidates received between 5% and 10% of the vote).[2] Fifteen women and forty-three men ran for marginal seats in the general election. Four of the fifteen female candidates (27%) were victorious. Three of these female winners were running against other women, ensuring the election of a woman in these districts. In contrast, twenty-five out of forty-three male candidates (58%) won in marginal races.

To analyze more concisely the candidate performances in marginal races, regression equations were developed to test the effect of gender, party, challenger status, and race type in 1992 and 1994. Although the sample is small, some important differences become apparent. The results of these equations are presented in Table 5.7.

The gender variable is of borderline significance when we combine the two election totals. Male candidates, by a small margin, performed better than female candidates. This could be significant because there were three races in this study in which women lost to men by less than 5 percent. As expected, challenger status and race type have a significant effect on the outcomes in marginal contests. Also, Republicans performed better in close races in 1994 and in the combined totals of the two elections.

There were eight marginal races pitting a man against a woman in California in the 1992 and 1994 elections. The female candidate won only one of these races. The lone female winner was Republican Andrea Seastrand, running in the 22nd district in 1994. She beat Democrat Walter Capps by less than one percent of the vote, 49.3 percent to 48.5 percent. The small margin of victory is striking considering the district was won by Republican Michael Huffington by almost 18 percent two years earlier. Seastrand's small margin of victory is also conspicuous because Republican congressional candidates in California in 1994 on average gained three percentage points over their 1992 vote totals (Table 5.6). This adds a further piece of evidence to the thesis that female Republican candidates are not as well received as female Democrats by the electorate.

In three other marginal races in 1992, Patricia Malberg versus John Doolittle in the 4th district, Gloria Ochoa versus Michael Huffington in the 22nd district, and Anita Perez-Ferguson versus Elton Gallegly in the 23rd district, the Democratic party believed female candidates might be able to defeat Republican incumbents.[3] All of these candidates received monetary support from the Democratic Party and EMILY's List, both of which only support candidates with money when they are seen as viable contenders. In the end, the Malberg/Doolittle race was the only tight election, with Doolittle winning 49.8 percent to 45.7 percent. Perez-Ferguson and Ochoa were not close, losing by 13 and 18 percent, respectively. In a marginal contest to fill an open seat in the 11th district in 1992, Democrat Patricia Garamendi lost to Republican Richard Pombo by a narrow margin, 47.6 percent to 45.6 percent. Democrats had a 12-percent advantage in party registration in the district and were hopeful when the race began.[4]

The question of how male and female candidates perform in tight races deserves further attention. The women in this study had a harder time in close races. Certainly we cannot draw any broad generalizations from this small

Table 5.7   Regression Estimates of General Election Vote Totals for Marginal Races in 1992 and 1994, by Gender, Party, Challenger Status, and Race Type

	1992	1994	1992-1994 Combined
Constant	43.96**	45.01**	43.82**
	(1.58)	(2.02)	(1.41)
Gender of candidate[a]	2.25	1.30	2.03*
	(1.76)	(1.46)	(1.12)
Challenger status[b]	7.23**	7.25**	6.71**
	(1.73)	(1.30)	(1.06)
Party affiliation[c]	1.85	5.23**	3.05**
	(1.45)	(1.87)	(.95)
Race type[d]	−4.63**	−4.91**	−4.57**
	(1.59)	(3.95)	(1.16)
Adjusted R^2	.50	.69	.56
N	(36)	(22)	(58)

a. Gender of candidate was coded 0 for female and 1 for male.
b. Challenger status was coded 0 for challenger and 1 for incumbent.
c. Party affiliation was coded 0 for Democrat and 1 for Republican.
d. Race type was coded 0 for open seat and 1 for incumbent-held seat.
Chi-square test, $*p < .10$; $**p < .05$; standard error in parentheses.

sample of races. However, what is clear from this analysis of the results is that, unlike the votes cast in the primary, the votes cast in the general election did not appear to produce any female winners who would not have been elected in any other election year. There was not a single female candidate who won an election that she was not favored to win (this does not include women who were running against other women). Once female candidates had won their primaries, the configurations of party registration in the district and incumbency were clearly more important than candidate gender in determining the outcome. At the congressional level in the general elections, women, even in the "year of the woman," were not propelled forward to victory by pro-woman voting.

Voter Attitudes

Vote totals and winning percentages are instructive in assessing the performance of female and male candidates but they do not offer clear insight into the reasoning of the voters. For this study of voters in House elections, the ability to analyze voter attitudes is limited because voter surveys were not available for the congressional districts. Most of the campaigns conducted internal polls but almost uniformly refused to make these available.[5] Thus, to assess how voters responded to the congressional candidates, it was necessary to rely on statewide polls and the perceptions and descriptions revealed by the campaign managers in the interviews. Statewide polls will not allow precise measurement of voter dynamics in individual-level districts but they prove useful in assessing the mood of the electorate in California.[6] In addition, the presence of women running for statewide offices in 1992 and 1994 allows for some examination of voter attitudes toward female candidates.

A profile of California voters emerges based on the responses of the campaign managers and the statewide surveys. Ironically, the voters were described by the campaign managers as both angry and apathetic. The electorate often took little interest in the congressional races but when voters were engaged directly by the campaigns they demonstrated great anger toward the political system. The combination of anger and apathy resulted in what many managers thought was an extraordinarily volatile electorate. Voters also displayed striking differences in what issues they viewed as important in each of the two elections. Specifically in terms of candidate gender, some voters continued to view female and male candidates in terms of traditional sex-role stereotypes. Based on this composite of the California voter, the following analysis explores voter attitudes in four distinct areas: volatility and anger, apathy, policy priorities, and direct response to candidate gender.

Volatility and Anger

In 1992, California voters gave Democratic Senate candidate Dianne Feinstein a sixteen-point victory over moderate Republican John Seymour. They also sent the strongly partisan and left-leaning Barbara Boxer to the Senate, making California the first state to elect two female senators. Yet a short two years later, Dianne Feinstein was barely able to retain her Senate seat by holding off the Republican challenge from first-term multimillionaire Congressman Michael Huffington. Feinstein had to run in both 1992 and 1994; the 1992 election was held to complete the term left by Pete Wilson when he ran for governor as a U.S. senator in 1990. Feinstein's opponent, John Seymour, was appointed by Wilson. Pete Wilson, who was up for reelection as California's governor in 1994, defeated Kathleen Brown by almost fifteen points. Wilson won handily, despite the fact that two years prior to the election he had been plagued by some of the lowest approval ratings (28%) of any governor in the history of the state. Political professionals and campaign workers up and down the state were astounded by the volatility and tempestuousness of the electorate.

Voters were deeply concerned about the economic situation in the United States and California in 1992. The unemployment rate in California exceeded 10 percent and the state economy showed no signs of revival. In exit polls on election day, over 40 percent of California voters said that their financial situation was worse than it had been four years ago and only 21 percent said it was better. Over 85 percent of voters believed the condition of the national economy was "poor" or "not so good." In light of the situation in the country and in California, voters wanted to change government. Proposition 164, the term limits initiative, passed with almost two-thirds of the vote. Over 50 percent of the voters believed that any member of the House who had overdrafts at the House bank should lose their job for that reason alone. Ironically, 34 percent of those voters voted for Barbara Boxer in her campaign to move from the House to the Senate. Although Boxer was cleared of any wrongdoing by the Justice Department, she did have numerous overdrafts while serving in the House.

The electorate was fed up with Washington and espoused a high level of anti-incumbent sentiment. One of the most telling indicators was that almost 50 percent of the voters in exit polling agreed with the statement: "government would work better if all new people were elected this year." In interviews, the campaign managers for many of the incumbents running for reelection in 1992 (13 out of 17) spoke of the anti-incumbency fervor. The press secretary for one southern California incumbent discussed the political environment in 1992:

> People were upset with Congress and Bush. . . . All of the congressional scandals raised the desire for change to a fever pitch. . . . The voters still seemed to like us, so when we were out campaigning they would always tell us that it was the other members of Congress or Washington that were the problems.

An aide to another longtime member noted a similar sentiment:

> People were tired of feeling like the system was corrupt and that they could not trust us anymore. They wanted government to change its ways. We always talk

about how there is this big anti-incumbent sentiment, but it was really there this year [1992].

Another member of Congress felt the voters' wrath after it was revealed that he had bounced checks at the House bank. The campaign manager described the reaction by the voters in the district:

> When the scandal first broke we got lots of outraged phone calls and letters and our opponent tried to play it up to the hilt. The voters were fuming at first . . . but as we began to campaign . . . [the congressman] really tried to explain to voters what the overdrafts meant and why it happened. This diffused a lot of the anger towards us but people had had it with Congress.

These comments demonstrate the age-old political psychosis of voters who hold Washington in contempt but never seem to blame themselves for the people they send there. On election day in 1992 only one incumbent, Frank Riggs, a Republican running in California's 1st congressional district, was defeated. However, the highly charged atmosphere and anger toward incumbents may have played a part in the decisions of nine members of the California congressional delegation who chose to retire from the House.

In 1992 the California voters wanted change and they delivered it by sending two Democratic women to the Senate, a historical first, and by voting Democratic at the presidential level for the first time since 1964. This desire for change appeared to greatly help women and Democrats. Female candidates, as Chapter 3 suggested, believed they had a much easier time capitalizing on the change theme. The voters were receptive to female candidates; 77 percent of voters in California responded in an election day exit poll that it was "very" or "somewhat" important to elect more women to the U.S. Senate. The favorable attitude toward female candidates certainly helps explain their success in 1992 and indicates that gender-response and gender-socialized voting were helping to propel women forward (see Table 5.1). A substantial number of voters were inclined to vote for female candidates because they saw them as something new to politics.

By the 1994 election, voters in California had lost faith in the ability of Democrats to deliver change. They were angry with how the federal government was operating and with the failure of the Democrats to fulfill many of their promises. The voter anger leveled at Democrats hurt female candidates in California, most of whom were Democrats. The campaign managers for Democrats and even Republicans were caught off-guard by the tidal wave of anti-Democratic sentiment in 1994. The manager for a Democratic challenger who ran in both 1992 and 1994 assessed the Republican tidal wave:

> In 1992 we inched within striking distance and almost won the election in spite of a host of mistakes we made in the campaign. This year [1994] we ran a much better campaign and lost 10 percent of the vote over our 1992 total. . . . The day after the election we were cleaning up the office and we just kept staring at the numbers, we could not believe the results.

Another Democratic manager was also shocked by the 1994 election results:

> Our tracking [polls] had us within a few points right up until ten days out, then we fell back a little, I knew we were in trouble, but I could never have foreseen losing this district to our bumbling opponent by almost twenty points. Democrats all over this area were just wiped out. The voters were mad at the Democrats and they were visibly angry with Clinton.

Throughout the San Diego and Los Angeles areas, Democratic candidates lost substantial ground between the two elections.

The outcome in California's 43rd congressional district highlighted the dramatic partisan shift between 1992 and 1994. In 1992, the 43rd district race was the closest congressional race in the country, with Democrat Mark Takano losing to Republican Ken Calvert by just over five hundred votes out of more than 177,000 ballots cast. Takano actually declared himself the winner on election day only to have absentee ballots reverse the results several days after the election. In his two years in office, Calvert became embroiled in two damaging scandals. Police found him in his car with a prostitute and it was disclosed that he failed to pay property tax on a piece of property he owned.[7] Armed with these scandals and in light of his near win in 1992, Takano and the Democrats entered the 1994 race with the hope of taking a seat away from the Republicans. Gorman (1994), in an analysis of this race less than one month before the election, called this race a probable Democratic pick-up. In a startling result, Takano ended up losing the race by over 16 points.

In another district that featured the same candidates in both the 1992 and 1994 elections, the Democratic candidate again lost ground. Janet Gastil, running in the 52nd district, challenged incumbent Duncan Hunter in both elections. In 1992 Gastil finished respectably, losing by a margin of 53 percent to 41 percent. In the rematch in 1994, Gastil lost badly, 64 percent to 31 percent. One might argue that Takano and Gastil performed poorly in the rematches because there is evidence that losing candidates who run again often do poorly. Yet all of the Republican challengers who ran in both elections either maintained similar vote totals or increased their vote from the 1992 to the 1994 election. For example, Republican Robert Wick, running in the 15th district against longtime Democratic incumbent Norman Mineta, went from 32 percent in 1992 to 41 percent in 1994.

The exit polls illustrate the dramatic shift in the partisan ties of the electorate. Voters emerging from the polling booths were asked to state which party they belonged to regardless of how they had voted in the election. In 1992, 41 percent were Democrats and 36 percent Republicans. In the 1994 election, the two major parties each claimed 39 percent of the electorate. Although some of the change may be explained by the lower turnout of Democratic voters in 1994, there was a significant partisan shift in who chose to vote across the two elections. For instance, women and voters under thirty who had supported Democrats in 1992 had lower levels of turnout in 1994. For Republicans, the turnout rate of white evangelical Christians was up in 1994 (Wilcox 1995). This shift hurt female candidates in a number of ways. The majority of female candidates in California and across the country were Democrats. Thus, changes in the partisan leanings of the electorate will have disparate effects on female candidates until women have been fully integrated into both parties. Also, there is some evidence here and in other analyses that conservative voters are less likely to embrace female candidates. If the electorate becomes more conservative or Democratic constituencies become less likely to turn out, as in 1994, this may hurt female candidates from both parties. Finally, the gender-response voting that favored women in the 1992 primary and general elections was not apparent in 1994. Although the partisan political environment has more do to with the mood of the electorate than anything else, gender also appears to play an important role. There was tremendous voter excitement over women in 1992, followed by no excitement in 1994. What future electoral environments hold for female candidates is difficult to say, although the atmosphere in 1992 is not likely to be replayed in the near future.

Voter Apathy

Although the preceding discussion of a volatile and angry electorate seems to suggest an active and energetic electorate, this was not the case. The "year of the woman" in 1992 and the Republican tidal wave in 1994 were marked by what campaign managers viewed as high levels of voter apathy. Although anger and apathy may seem contradictory qualities, they often go hand-in-hand in the atmosphere of an election. Anger and disenchantment with the political system may actually be the principal cause of much voter apathy. Even managers who had candidates running in competitive districts with hard-fought campaigns reported that voters were apathetic. As one manager in a very tight race commented,

> We had one of the closest races in the country and there was absolutely no interest. We held meet-the-candidate forums at coffee shops and supporters' homes, but it seemed like we were always meeting the same small core of interested citizens. . . . The newspapers wouldn't even cover the race. . . . I thought the lack of interest was astounding. Here we had a tough campaign with two intelligent candidates with distinct messages and nobody gave a hoot.

A candidate running against an entrenched incumbent was dejected by the lack of interest in his race:

> Nothing motivates people. . . . Nobody really cared. You try to talk about important issues, but people are bored or uninterested. I really felt like nobody cared what I had to say. I entered the race trying to inform the voters and now feel like that is impossible.

One explanation for the apathy in congressional races was that voters in both elections had major statewide races to consider, in addition to some controversial ballot initiatives, and these diverted attention from the congressional races.

However, in 1992 the managers for women were much less likely to characterize the electorate as apathetic. Only one of sixteen female candidates running in 1992 complained of voter apathy and even her manager termed the voter response to his candidate as "favorable apathy." Compare this with the twenty out of forty-three managers for male candidates who mentioned apathy in describing the electorate. The excitement of female voters for female candidates in 1992 explains the disparity in the perceived levels of voter apathy between male and female candidates. As illustrated in Chapter 2 (see Table 2.3), female candidates were much more successful in attracting campaign volunteers and generally sensed a greater excitement about their candidacies. The excitement was partially tied to the voters' response to the confirmation hearings of Clarence Thomas. If we turn to the statewide races, it is evident that the fallout from the hearings helped female candidates. In 1992, when California voters were asked in exit polls whether Thomas should have been confirmed by the Senate, 41 percent said "no," 36 percent said "yes," and 21 percent were "not sure." Of the 41 percent who said "no," 77 percent voted for Dianne Feinstein and 71 percent voted for Barbara Boxer in the U.S. Senate races.

Female candidates and voters had a unifying theme in 1992; there was no such theme in California in 1994. The optimistic and enthusiastic desire for "change" that existed in 1992 helped female candidates. But in 1994 the campaign managers for women and men were equally likely to complain of voter apathy. Voters were no more responsive to the campaigns of women than to those of men. This is also supported by Table 2.3, which shows that women and men had almost identical numbers of volunteers working for them in 1994. As we see from many of these voter characteristics, at least over this two-election cycle, women's reception by the electorate is much less consistent than men's. The unevenness of the electoral environment certainly suggests that traditional stereotyping exists among voters. Women are seen as more viable under electoral circumstances which favor "women's issues" and "female traits." Voters still rely on gender stereotypes in particular political situations.

Policy Agendas of the Elections

One of the most important shifts in the attitudes of voters between 1992 and 1994 occurred over the issue agendas of the elections. Change in issue agendas has important ramifications for candidate gender if voters ascribe competency in handling issues based on gender stereotypes. This analysis has argued that the issue environments across the 1992 and 1994 elections played an important part in how voters received female and male candidates. Burrell (1994), writing about the success of female candidates in 1992, prophetically asserted that some of the expectations about women that worked well for them in 1992 might prove to be liabilities in future elections. Voter stereotyping over policy issues and prescribed gender expertise helped women in 1992 and worked against them in 1994.

To assess voters' issue concerns across the 1992 and 1994 elections, we must rely on the perceptions of the campaign managers for the California House candidates. The managers were asked to identify which policy issues were of greatest concern to the voters in their districts. Most of the managers based their answers on responses to their internal campaign polls. Early in

Table 5.8   Most Important Issues in the Congressional Districts in the 1992 and
1994 Elections Based on the Perceptions of Campaign Managers

		Issues Important to Voters[a]		
1992			*1994*	
Jobs/job creation	77%		Crime	91%
Health care	29		Immigration	64
Education	27		Jobs/job creation	30
Environment	27		Economic growth	27
Crime	25		Taxes	23
Economic growth	21		Health care	11
Abortion	18		Education	9
Immigration	16		Governmental reform	9
Transportation	11		Free trade	7
Agriculture/water	9		Gun control	5
Congressional reform	5		Welfare reform	5
Defense spending	4		Environment	5
Taxes	4		Agriculture	2
Budget deficit	2		Social security	2
Family values	2		Abortion	2
			Family Values	2

NOTE: Columns do not add up to 100% because the campaign managers listed between 1 and 4 issues that
were most important in their districts.
a. Fifty-six campaign managers answered this question in 1992 and 44 managers answered in 1994.

the campaign process, almost all campaigns with at least some level of
sophistication conduct a poll asking voters in an open-ended question to list
the issues that are most important to them. Campaigns use this information
to develop a campaign message and devise strategy. Because most of the
responses by the managers were drawn from polls, we can be fairly confident
of the accuracy of the district-level issue priorities. Table 5.8 is a compilation
of the three or four issues each campaign manager believed were the top
concerns of the voters in their districts in 1992 and 1994.

The differences in the issue priorities of the voters across the 1992 and
1994 elections are striking. In 1992, job creation was by far the most
important issue to the voters. Two of the next three issues were health care
and education, issues for which voters have demonstrated a preference for
female leadership. The fourth issue was the environment, and although the
gender politics literature does not uniformly classify this as a "woman's
issue," some surveys have shown that voters favor women's leadership for
this issue (Burrell 1994, 24-25). The issues for which some voters demon-

strate a preference for the expertise of male politicians—crime, economic growth, and immigration—were ranked fifth, sixth, and eighth, respectively. Abortion, a stereotypical "woman's issue," even outranked immigration as a concern for voters in 1992. Thus, the election agenda in 1992 emphasized issues for which voters have shown a preference for the expertise of women.

By 1994 the electoral environment had radically changed. Crime and immigration thoroughly dominated voters' agendas. Over 90 percent of campaign managers said that crime was a top issue in their district. Crime jumped from the fifth-most-important issue in 1992 to the top issue in 1994. The ascendance of the crime issue can be partially explained by the highly publicized kidnapping and murder of twelve-year-old Polly Klaas in 1993. Klaas, living in northern California, was taken from the bedroom of her home and was missing for many weeks. An extensive search followed her disappearance but she was found dead. Her killer, Richard Alton Harris, was a repeat offender out of prison on parole. This crime and the ensuing public outrage received national attention and led to an intense discussion and debate over tougher sentencing for repeat offenders. Governor Wilson responded by signing into law a "three strikes and you're out" measure. Fear of violent crime rose dramatically in California between 1992 and 1994 and was reflected in the issue concerns of the electorate.

The second most important issue for California voters in 1994 was immigration.[8] Proposition 187, the ballot initiative seeking to deny government services to illegal aliens, brought the immigration issue to the forefront. As California's economy remained stagnant, fear grew that the influx of illegal aliens might be draining state resources. These two issues, immigration and the economy, worked against Democratic and female candidates because voters believed Republican and male candidates would address them more effectively.

Although we cannot measure voter attitudes at the district level, we can look at how voters' issue priorities affected their votes at the statewide level. This is not an ideal means of testing the voter behavior faced by the House candidates in this study, but with the absence of systematic district-level surveys, it offers us the best opportunity available. In 1992 and 1994, exit polling in five statewide races examined how issues affected voter decision making. In 1992, polls targeted the two Senate races and the presidential race. Both Senate races featured Democratic women running against Republican men. To help gauge the acceptance of female Democratic candidates by California voters in 1992, we can compare their performance with that of

Democratic presidential candidate Bill Clinton. In 1994, the Senate race and the governor's race also pitted Democratic women against Republican men. As a comparison for the races in 1994, President Clinton's approval rating can then be compared to the performance of the Democratic female candidates. Although comparing the votes for the Democratic female candidates with Clinton's approval rating is an imperfect measure, it provides our only basis for comparison in the 1994 election. Also, unlike the case for many states, Clinton's popularity was not as big a drag on the Democratic candidates in California because his approval rating in that state was over 50 percent.

Table 5.9 identifies the relationship between voters' issue concerns and how they voted in these races. Unfortunately, the lists compiled in Table 5.9 are not drawn from open-ended questions. Exit polls provided voters with a list of issues and asked them to check off which one or two mattered most in how they cast their ballots.[9] Thus we cannot state conclusively that these were the most important policy issues for voters in these elections. Yet the exit poll does attempt to present the voters with the issues commonly believed to be most salient in the elections.[10] Many of the issues used in the exit poll correspond with the issues that campaign managers identified as important in their districts in Table 5.8. The entries in Table 5.9 show the percentage of voters who supported the Democratic candidate. The issues are divided by type of issue, using the same classifications used in Chapter 3—men's, women's, and general.

For both elections, 1992 and 1994, the effect of the policy issues on the voters' selections can be seen in partisan terms. Voters who were concerned with abortion, the economy/jobs, the environment, education, health care, and race relations supported Democratic candidates. Voters who were concerned with crime, immigration, taxes, welfare reform, the death penalty, foreign policy, and family values supported Republican candidates.

The important question, of course, is whether candidate gender has an important relationship with the issue agendas of voters. Table 5.9 reveals some subtle differences in the performance of female and male candidates running in the statewide elections. Beginning in 1992, we see that the issue agenda favored all of the Democratic candidates: Bill Clinton, Barbara Boxer, and Dianne Feinstein. However, on "men's issues," Clinton performed equally well or better than Feinstein with voters on all of the issues. Clinton decisively outperformed Boxer on each of the issues. For the category of "men's issues voters," which is composed of all of the voters who

Table 5.9   How Voters Cast Ballots for President, U.S. Senators, and Governor
Based on Issue Priorities (1992 and 1994)

1992:[a]	All Voters	Clinton (Bush)[b]	Feinstein (Seymour)	Boxer (Herschensohn)
Men's issues				
Budget deficit	26%	55%	52%	43%
Crime	25	50	46	37
Defense spending	17	54	53	46
Taxes	16	30	30	21
Foreign policy	7	16	17	11
"Men's issues" voters[c]	25	38	33	27
Women's issues				
Health care	20	75	67	61
Education	17	69	75	61
Race relations	16	72	72	65
Abortion	13	58	60	54
"Women's issues" voters	15	71	73	66
General issues				
Economy/jobs	45	63	61	54
Family values	8	27	29	18
Environment	7	77	72	72

1994:	All Voters	Clinton Approval	Feinstein (Huffington)	Brown (Wilson)
Men's issues				
Crime	28	33	33	24
Immigration	27	34	30	23
Welfare reform	10	32	31	23
Taxes	14	33	27	25
Death penalty	8	28	21	14
"Men's issues" voters	45	35	32	27
Women's issues				
Education	22	77	64	71
General issues				
Economy/jobs	30	54	54	51
Environment	6	69	60	69

SOURCE: Compiled from Voter Research and Surveys General Election Exit Poll: California Files, 1992 and 1994. Entries are the percentage supporting the Democratic candidate; the Republican opponent is in parentheses.
a. 1992, $N = 2,297$; 1994, $N = 1,017$.
b. In 1992, Clinton's vote total is the adjusted two-party vote. Based on the exit polls, the Perot voters were distributed equally among Bush and Clinton, thus this is a slightly misleading representation of the vote. In 1994 Clinton's approval rating is substituted for the vote.
c. "Men's issues" voters and "women's issues" voters were the voters who only mentioned that particular type of issue as important in their vote choice.

only identified "men's issues" as important in their vote choice, Clinton outperformed both of the female Senate candidates. This did not hurt the female Democrats too seriously in 1992 because only 25 percent of the voters were pure "men's issues voters."

For "women's issues," Boxer and Feinstein generally did not have any advantage over Clinton. This is evident with regard to "women's issues voters," which is the category composed of all the voters who only identified "women's issues" as important in their vote choice. Feinstein did marginally better than Clinton with "women's issues voters," although Clinton had the advantage over Boxer. Clinton's success with "women's issues" may be explained by his campaign's focus on education and health care. Ultimately there were no issues for which the female Senate candidates had a consistent advantage over Clinton. ᴍ 1992

Turning to the 1994 election, the change in the electoral environment was manifested in the number of "men's issues voters," which jumped 20 percentage points from 1992, to 45 percent in 1994. As in 1992, the voters who said "men's issues" were important to them were more favorable toward Clinton than toward the female Democratic candidates. Feinstein's portion of the vote was lower than Clinton's approval rating on every "men's" issue except crime. This seems to be an important difference because Clinton and Feinstein are both moderate Democrats who share similar positions on most of the "men's issues." For example, Feinstein supported Clinton's 1994 Crime Bill, both favor the death penalty, and both advocated a ban on assault weapons and on immigration Feinstein has taken an even harder line than President Clinton by trying to significantly increase the size of the border patrol. Kathleen Brown, in her race for the governorship, suffered an even greater disadvantage than Feinstein on the "men's issues." On the issues of crime, immigration, and the death penalty, Kathleen Brown lagged far behind her Democratic counterparts despite her tough rhetoric. In one exit poll question, voters were specifically asked which gubernatorial candidate "would be tough enough on crime?" Forty-five percent of voters said Wilson, whereas only 17 percent said Brown.[11] Thus, in both elections Clinton performed better than the female candidates on "men's issues."

The issue of crime is perennially one of the most important issues in California politics but it was not a top issue in 1992, which helped the female candidates. Male candidates, mostly Republican, in 1992 and 1994, attempted to exploit women's weakness on the issues of immigration and crime. This occurred not only in the statewide races but also in the House elections. One Republican political consultant working for a number of congressional campaigns in California in 1992 confided,

> The Republican Party is instructing their candidates who are running against women to hammer away on the issues of crime and immigration. The male candidates are stressing how tough they are on crime and how they will crack down on the illegal immigration problem. Their polling numbers show that voters do not think women can be tough on these issues.

Several other campaign officials for Republican House candidates were asked about this claim and denied that this was an orchestrated strategy. Also, Tables 3.4 and 3.5 show that Republican men running against women were no more likely to raise crime and immigration than Republican men running against men. However, Pete Wilson's campaign manager was quoted in a media interview stating that the crime and immigration issues work better for men (Berke 1994, B10). As issues such as crime and immigration were dominant in 1994, concerns over health care and abortion disappeared from the political landscape. In this study, the issue of health care was rarely raised by House candidates in 1994 except as a tool for attacking Democratic candidates over President Clinton's failed health care bill. The demise of health care reform as a viable campaign plank in 1994 can be seen in the outcome of Proposition 186, the ballot initiative to create a single-payer health care system in California. This initiative was crushed at the polls, garnering only 28 percent of the vote.

Although the degree of gender stereotype voting seen in Table 5.9 is quite small, the effect of gender stereotyping associated with policy issues could be greater in congressional elections. Because voters often have less information in these elections, they may rely more on stereotypes. In highly publicized statewide races, candidates are more likely to receive the attention from voters and the media that would allow them to combat some of the stereotypes. For instance, Dianne Feinstein, in her first race for governor in 1990, received a substantial boost from a widely run television ad that showed how she took control of the City of San Francisco in a time of crisis, after the assassination of Mayor George Moscone. The ad asserted that Feinstein's able political leadership was "forged in tragedy." In her 1994 Senate race, Feinstein ran at least one television ad showing how she authored legislation increasing the border patrol to crack down on illegal immigration. The commercial featured footage of border patrol agents apprehending immigrants as they came across the border. Feinstein was able to effectively use the paid media to present an image and a message designed to offset many of the gender stereotypes voters might possess about women. Breaking down harmful stereotypes may be more difficult in a congressional race because the races often do not get the coverage or have the advertising budgets of statewide races. Further, the issue stereotyping that emerged in the statewide polling data was corroborated by many of the campaign managers in congressional races. Chapter 3 showed how female candidates often felt they had credibility problems pertaining to many of the "male issues" listed in Tables 5.8 and 5.9. One manager who has worked for numerous congressional candidates in California commented,

> Women Democrats were in trouble this year [1994]. . . . The crime and immigration issues just do not work for women. It's all about selling toughness, those issues require toughness and that is still a problem for women. . . . The welfare issue also, the voters want to crack down on welfare recipients and they do not look to women for cracking down.

A campaign manager who had worked almost exclusively for female candidates in her career commented,

> The "women's issues" work for women. It is just obvious . . . who would you have more faith in when discussing child care, a businessman or a mother, a lawyer in a suit or a mother? . . . There are also issues that work against women . . . crime, the budget . . . and issues like that.

These comments, along with the analysis in Chapter 3, demonstrate that female candidates believed they had a harder time presenting themselves as competent and tough on these types of issues. Based on the experiences of the campaign managers and the voter attitudes appearing in Table 5.9, it would seem there is a segment of the voting public that continues to employ these stereotypes. The interplay between candidate gender and issues suggests that gender-socialized voting was taking place in California at the statewide level and in the congressional races. This could explain the overall drop in the average vote totals for female candidates between 1992 and 1994 (Table 5.5). However, we must be careful in drawing conclusions based on Table 5.9. The gender differences in how voters used issues is quite small and we are drawing conclusions based on only five electoral contests.

However, if traditional stereotypes persist in associating issue expertise with candidate gender, the electoral environment will remain an important predictor of female candidates' success in the election process. The electoral environment in 1992 helped female candidates both through the voters' desire for change and the issues that dominated the election. In 1994, the electoral environment erased any advantage female candidates may have had with gender-response voting because of issue-based gender-socialized voting. The playing field for candidates will not be entirely level or consistently fair until some of these stereotypes are discarded.

Voter Attitudes Toward Candidate Gender

The final aspect of voter attitudes to be addressed is the direct response of voters to female and male candidates. Did some voters admit to discriminating for or against female candidates in California House elections? The women running in 1992 felt a great deal of positive feedback from the voters on the campaign trail. The managers for women were much more likely to mention a positive reception by voters than were male candidates. Overall, when the managers for female candidates were asked if being women hurt them or helped them with voters, the majority, thirteen out of twenty-five (52%), said that they did not believe gender made a difference with voters in the concluding vote totals. Almost all of these managers did note that they experienced instances of bias for and against their candidate. Of the remaining twelve managers for female challengers, seven, all in 1992, believed that their gender helped them. Five women, three in 1994 and two in 1992, believed being a women hurt them with voters. The perceptions of those men who ran against women were a little different. Ten of the twenty-three (43%) managers for male candidates running against women thought that candidate gender was a neutral issue for the voters. The thirteen remaining managers all believed that their female opponent had at least a slight advantage with the voters. One seasoned campaign manager commented about the transformation in how women were received by the electorate in the 1990s:

> She was really well received. I think the voters' interests were piqued . . . [because she] was a woman. . . . This was a great change from the past when female candidates were met with instant skepticism. Now women are met with enthusiasm by a large chunk of the electorate.

Even the managers for male candidates were aware of the positive reception for female candidates. One manager for a male candidate who was running against a female candidate noted,

People were drawn to our opponent. She is a very nice person and she relates well and people seemed to feel so comfortable around her. We had a number of candidate forums and before anyone said anything, you could see the voters liked her and wanted to talk to her. . . . My candidate is a heck of a nice guy and very bright and personable but we were not greeted with open arms the way she was.

The manager for another male candidate was bitter about the difference in voter responses in 1992:

It seemed ridiculous, she got all of this undeserved media attention and that made her more exciting to the voters. I think she went on CNN and some other shows and then when she was out in the district everyone would excitedly say: "Oh I saw you last night." Then we would go out in the district and voters were like: "Who the hell are you?" The attention women got and the voter response was unfair to a lot of good male candidates.

Many of the women running in 1992 believed that being a woman helped them with voters, and to some extent Tables 5.3-5.5 support these perceptions. However, by the time of the 1994 elections there were very few comments or complaints by male candidates or their managers about women being received enthusiastically. The political environment had clearly changed.

Although female candidates received overall more positive attention and focus in 1992, they still had some mixed experiences with voters. The campaign managers and candidates in this study noted many examples of individual voter bias against female candidates. Almost every female candidate in this examination was able to report some specific instance of direct voter bias. As one female candidate commented,

I would guess it happened about two or three times while campaigning. It was always older women. They would come up to me and tell me that women should not be in politics. I remember this one older woman walking towards me shaking her head and she looked me in the eye and said that women needed to stay at home and that what I was doing was wrong . . . just wrong. The minute I knew where the conversation was going I quickly moved away.

Other managers reported similar incidents. One manager who was attending a speech given by her candidate was approached after the event by an older voter:

She had a heavy accent, maybe German or Polish, she immediately reminded me of someone from the old country. . . . She started pointing her finger at me, somehow she knew I worked for the campaign. I could not understand her that well but the gist of her remarks were that up behind the podium was no place for a woman. I started to argue with her, but then you realize that people who believe women should stay at home . . . are probably not worth debating.

These experiences were only a minor nuisance for the female candidates, although they do indicate that there might be some resistance toward female candidates from older voters. As mentioned previously, two female candidates in tight races believed their sex hurt them with older voters and possibly cost them the election.

Female candidates in 1992 were much more likely to encounter positive feedback from voters for being a woman. Many of the female candidates who ran in 1992 were the first ever to be nominated by a major party in their district, a historic event. Many voters who had never before had the opportunity to vote for a woman for Congress were supportive. One female candidate who waged an assertive campaign against a well-established incumbent recounted an experience with a voter:

I forget where I was, but I was not campaigning at the time. . . . A woman came up to me, she had recognized me and knew I was running for Congress. She took my hand and looked me in the eye and said we needed more strong women in politics and that she was voting for me and counting on me to do a good job in Washington. It was as if she were proud of me. . . . It was a special moment for me and was one of the few times in the campaign I felt good about the process.

Female voters were certainly more supportive of female candidates, but female voters were more supportive of all Democratic candidates so it is important to sort out gender and partisan effects. In returning to the statewide data for the Senate, gubernatorial, and presidential races in 1992 and 1994, we see that female and male voters, regardless of party affiliation, cast their ballots a little differently. The results are reported in Table 5.10, and again Clinton's approval rating is used as a comparison for the female Democratic candidates in 1994.

Although the third-party candidacy of Ross Perot makes the comparisons a little more difficult to interpret, the vote totals in 1992 show that female Democrats were more likely than their male counterparts to support the Democratic ticket, and in particular the female candidates. Male Democrats particularly shunned Barbara Boxer; over 30 percent of male Democrats did not support her in 1992. Among Republicans, women were less likely than men to vote for Bill Clinton in 1992, but they were more likely to cross over and vote for the female Democratic Senate candidates. Independent female voters also showed a preference for the female candidates. They provided Clinton with a solid margin of victory, a 15 percent edge over Perot, with Bush third, but came down much more heavily in favor of Feinstein over Seymour by 30 percent, and Boxer over Herschensohn by 38 percent. This is a particularly striking contrast with male Independents, who voted similarly to women Independents for Bill Clinton but were split on the female Senate candidates, favoring Feinstein by only 8 percent over Seymour, but favoring Herschensohn by 2 percent over Boxer.

Many of these patterns continued in the 1994 elections. Male and female Democrats gave Clinton almost identical approval ratings yet men were less likely to vote for the female Democratic candidates. The female Republicans were again more likely than their male counterparts to favor the female Democratic candidates, although fewer of them voted Democratic in 1994. One of the biggest shifts across the two elections was the movement of male Independent voters away from the female Democratic candidates. Male Independent voters gave Feinstein an 8 percent edge over Seymour in 1992 but went with Huffington over Feinstein by 4 percent in 1994. In the 1992 Senate race between Boxer and Herschensohn, the male Independents were evenly split, but in 1994 they gave Wilson a 25-percent margin of victory over Brown. The female Independents solidly supported the female Democratic candidates, although with lower margins than in 1992.

The results presented in Table 5.10 clearly indicate that female voters, regardless of party affiliation, were more likely to vote for the female candidates in the statewide elections. The differences between female and male voters in Table 5.10 have two probable explanations. First, female voters, regardless of party identification, tend to support the more liberal candidates. The gender gap in voting behavior appears to be growing and there is evidence that women as a group tend to be more liberal (Wilcox 1995; Conover 1988), although this would not explain their lower levels of support for President Clinton. The second explanation is that voters in California are engaging in gender-response and gender-socialized voting. This type of voting is the only clear explanation for why women prefer female candidates and men prefer male candidates. In California it appears that voters engaged in a considerable degree of stereotyping in terms of candidate gender and perceived issue competency. Ultimately, we can be assured that both of these types of voting are occurring and that in close elections these factors could be more than enough to alter the outcome of an

Table 5.10 How Voters Cast Ballots for President, U.S. Senators, and Governor Based on Party and Gender (1992 and 1994)

1992:[a]	All Voters	President			Short-Term Senate		Full-Term Senate	
		Clinton	Bush	Perot	Feinstein	Seymour	Boxer	Herschensohn
Democrats								
Women	22%	81%	7%	12%	86%	10%	81%	12%
Men	16	73	9	18	79	13	69	22
Republicans								
Women	17	13	68	20	26	67	18	73
Men	16	15	63	22	18	76	13	82
Independents								
Women	10	46	23	31	57	27	62	24
Men	11	42	24	34	46	38	42	44

1994:[b]	All Voters	Rating of Clinton		U.S. Senate		Governor	
		Approve	Disapprove	Feinstein	Huffington	Brown	Wilson
Democrats							
Women	22%	83%	17%	83%	11%	77%	22%
Men	17	84	16	79	17	74	24
Republicans							
Women	18	20	80	19	75	8	89
Men	21	16	84	11	86	5	92
Independents							
Women	8	51	49	46	30	50	38
Men	11	46	54	41	45	33	58

SOURCE: Compiled from Voter Research and Surveys General Election Exit Poll: California Files, 1992 and 1994.
NOTE: Entries are the percentage supporting the Democratic candidate.
a. 1992, $N = 2,297$.
b. 1994, $N = 1,017$.

election. For instance, Boxer won her Senate campaign in 1992 by less than 5 percent of the vote and Feinstein won her reelection campaign in 1994 by close to one percent of the vote. In these statewide races and in a number of the congressional races a shift of only a few percent can make the difference. Clearly the role of gender-response and gender-socialized voting can account for small shifts that could be crucial in an election.

Relating these findings from the statewide races to the voting behavior that transpired in the House elections is difficult. All of the statewide races received considerable media coverage and voter knowledge of the candidates was far greater for statewide races than for almost any of the House races. Thus, voters in House races can be assumed to be more likely to rely on gender stereotypes because they have less information with which to counteract gender as a voting cue (Leeper 1991). In House races, voters have less knowledge about the actual personal traits of the candidates and their issue positions and are thus forced to rely on preconceived notions about male and female candidates.

Conclusion

This chapter demonstrates that candidate gender may be an important factor in how voters choose candidates. Certainly the overwhelming majority of voters still employ party cues as the most important determinant of vote choice. However, voters have deeply ingrained attitudes about the roles of women and men in the political arena, though they may not be fully aware of their biases. Table 5.11 summarizes the differences in how voters treated female and male candidates in the California House elections.

Based on the differences depicted in Table 5.11, two conclusions may be drawn. First, this study has shown that the electoral environment may have an important effect on how female and male candidates are evaluated by the electorate. Many voters employed gender stereotypes to assess the particular capabilities of male and female candidates. The negative side for women is that the issues that are likely to dominate California politics in the coming years—affirmative action, immigration, crime, and the state budget—are all issues on which some of the voters prefer the leadership of men.

The second important conclusion is that gender bias in voting is now a two-way street. Although we have traditionally focused on biases against female candidates, it is now clear that there are number of instances in the electoral process in which gender bias and voter stereotyping work to female candidates' advantage. In some electoral environments, when particular issues are on the forefront of the political agenda, women are viewed more favorably than men by the electorate. However, we must remember that biases directed toward women and men have different qualities. Although there appears to some significant pro-woman bias in the electorate, there is also significant anti-woman bias. There is no corresponding anti-man bias in the electorate. No public opinion surveys have shown there is a group of

Table 5.11 Summary of Different Experiences With the Voters for Male and Female Candidates

Component of the Electoral Process	Differences	
	Female Candidates	Male Candidates
Primary elections	Experienced tremendous success, particularly in crowded primaries	Many more candidates
		Lower average vote totals
		More frivolous candidacies
General elections	Women Democratic challengers performed better than their male counterparts	Performed slightly better than women in marginal races
	Women Republican challengers did not perform as well as their male counterparts	
Voter attitudes	Felt less voter apathy in the 1992 elections	Were favored by "men's issues" voters
	Received higher levels of gender-response voting favoring their candidacies	Received higher levels of support from male voters
	Received higher levels of support from female voters	

voters who believe men should not be involved in politics. The traditional socialization of voters suggests only that women are less suited for politics. This ultimately makes the electoral arena more volatile and in some cases more difficult for female candidates. As the evidence in this chapter suggests, women face a much more unpredictable electorate than men. Some voters will always be against women, some voters will always be against them in particular political environments, some voters will favor them because they are women, and some voters will favor them because of the particular electoral environment. All of this inconsistency makes the election more challenging for female candidates. These are challenges men do not have to face. Women have a more demanding job developing campaign strategies because they must always be conscious of the political winds in ways male candidates need not.

Notes

1. This conclusion contradicts the analysis of Celinda Lake, who believes that female Republican candidates are particularly well-situated because female Democratic voters will often cross over and vote for a Republican woman. This did not appear to be the case in California but the samples were very small (see O'Brien 1995).

2. Determinations of marginality are quite arbitrary (see Jacobsen 1992); some set the number at 60 percent or 65 percent. I established my own arbitrary standard based on determinations of which races could have possibly gone the other way or whether the party organization supported the challenger. There is also a problem with determining marginality after the election results are in. In this study, some districts were marginal in 1992 and not in 1994. Thus, we need to be cautious in assessing the performance of the candidates in marginal contests.

3. In the Ochoa/Huffington race, there was no incumbent because Huffington defeated Lagomarsino in the primary. Yet when the Democrats began the race they believed they would be facing an incumbent in the general election.

4. Although Democrats have a numerical advantage, consultants for both sides noted that the district has a large percentage of Reagan Democrats. *California Journal,* previewing the race in 1992, called the district a toss-up.

5. Election winners, often the incumbents, generally refused to make their polling available to me because they said the results would be used in future elections. The internal polls often seemed to be shrouded in secrecy.

6. All of the public opinion percentages in this chapter are based on the Voter Research and Surveys, General Election Exit Polls, California Files, 1992 and 1994.

7. Both of these scandals were reported in the Riverside County newspaper, see Radovich (1994) and Robinson (1994).

8. The importance of immigration may be slightly overstated in Table 5.8 because the sample of campaign managers was weighted in favor of the southernmost districts in the state, where immigration is a larger concern. For instance, all five San Diego-area districts were included in the sample and the immigration issue has a higher profile in those areas. Nonetheless, immigration was certainly one of the top concerns across the state in 1994.

9. Another drawback in the format of the exit polls is that the issues posed to the voters were usually done so in conjunction with a particular election. For instance, in 1992, voters were asked who they voted for president, and then this was followed by the question: "Which 1 or 2 issues mattered most in deciding how to vote?" In compiling Table 5.9, these issue responses are not being used only for the presidential election but to analyze the Senate votes as well. Thus, the data and results need to be viewed with caution.

10. Voter Research and Surveys (VRS), the principal investigator for the network exit polls, chooses the issues they ask voters about based on other polls and analyses. The issues are chosen subjectively, based on what they believe to be the most important issues to the voters. This assessment is based on an interview with a (VRS) survey consultant, August, 1995.

11. Of the remaining voters, 24 percent said both candidates would be tough enough on crime and 13 percent said neither would be tough enough on crime.

6

Conclusion:
The Future of Candidate Gender
in Electoral Politics

The high level and high visibility of gender politics that existed in 1992 and 1994 will not be likely to figure as prominently in the 1996 elections in California. There are no major statewide races at stake. However, by 1998 Californians will again see women leading the Democratic ticket, as controversial Senator Barbara Boxer, who won narrowly in the 1992 election, will be up for reelection. Boxer's 1998 race, well out of the shadow of the "year of the woman" elections, will be an interesting testing ground for the further progress of women in California. Also, the likely reelection attempts by Senator Patty Murray of Washington and Senator Carol Moseley Braun in Illinois, women supposedly swept into office via the "year of the woman" elections, will be important barometers for determining women's clear acceptance in some of the nation's highest offices. The excitement over female candidates that existed in California and around the country in 1992 is not likely to occur again until there is a viable female presidential candidate or the country is presented with the second coming of Clarence Thomas. The ghosts of the Thomas/Hill confirmation hearings were preparing to reemerge with allegations of sexual misconduct leveled against Oregon Senator Bob

Packwood. However, Packwood's belated resignation appeared to quell the call for women activists to mobilize.

In the elections for congressional seats, the conditions that existed for women in 1992 and 1994 will most likely continue in 1996 and beyond. Female candidates again did extraordinarily well in the 1996 House primaries in California. All eight female incumbents were renominated and sixteen additional women received a major party nomination. A total of twenty-four women were nominated in California in 1996, setting a record and clearly exceeding the numbers in 1992 and 1994. In almost half of the congressional races, at least one of the candidates is a woman. However, with only two open seats in the fifty-two House contests in 1996, women are not likely to see much of an increase in their representation in the California House delegation. Also, the party breakdown of the candidacies in 1996 remains skewed toward the Democrats, with nineteen Democratic nominees and only five Republican nominees. Nonetheless, the increasing number of female nominees in California indicate that more and more women are making the decision to run for office. These trends suggest that 1992 may have made the process seem more accessible to women. Female candidates in California have remained an important force well after the "year of the woman" elections. The female House candidates nominated in 1996 will undoubtedly have mixed experiences in the electoral arena. The findings recounted in the preceding chapters show that the electoral arena is unpredictable for female candidates. Some female candidates are embraced when they enter an election and others face indifference and mild discrimination. This final chapter summarizes the central findings of this study. These findings are further augmented by concluding remarks and comments by the campaign managers. Finally, this chapter discusses future research directions for studying female candidates and the role of gender in the election process.

Summary of Findings

This study set out to substantiate and present evidence for a three-part thesis. First, that there are many small but important differences in the behavior and experiences of female and male candidates in the electoral process. The individual findings have been systematically recounted in the conclusion of each chapter, so there is no need to recount them here (see Tables 2.9, 3.7, 4.8, and 5.11). In chronicling the experiences of female and male candidates running for Congress, almost every aspect of the electoral process reveals different experiences and challenges for men and women. Women and men had different experiences with the media, the party structure, and the voters. Men and women also waged their campaigns differently, stressing different campaign messages, employing different campaigning styles, and relying on different strategies. As already noted, most of these gender differences were not overpowering, but they were subtle and pervasive. Many of them indicate a lack of fairness toward women in the electoral arena.

The second part of the thesis maintained that these differences were overwhelmingly the result of traditional sex-role socialization. The long-enduring perception in the history of the United States that women are not suited for politics still leaves behind vestiges of doubt about women's entrance into politics. Many stereotypes persist in American politics about female candidates. For instance, as discussed in Chapter 2, polls have shown that voters believe men are tougher, more aggressive, and better in a crisis. Women are perceived by the electorate as showing more honesty, compassion and commitment. However, the qualities ascribed to women are less uniformly beneficial to political candidacies, especially those for higher office. In this study, women were clearly concerned about how they presented themselves to voters and how voters would react to them.

The female candidates in this study also encountered several instances of gender stereotyping and bias from the institutions in the electoral arena: party organizations, campaign contributors, and media. Clearly, many actors in the electoral process in some way reflected the stereotypical gender socialization of American society. Examples of this socialization can manifest themselves in something as simple as the adjectives used to describe candidates in a news story to the blatant anti-woman bias of some individual voters to the direct discrimination of a local party organization.

The final portion of the thesis suggests that the continuing influence of traditional socialization makes the electoral process more challenging and less predictable for women. Women often have a difficult time working their way through the electoral process. Female candidates feel they face a more skeptical electorate (see Chapter 3). Some female candidates bring to an election a campaign style that is new and untested (see Chapter 2). Women in this study experienced many more direct disadvantages, ranging from outright discrimination to nuanced discrediting (see Chapter 4). A final factor that makes the electoral process more difficult for women is its volatility. For instance, in California, prior to the 1990 elections there was little excitement and support for female candidates as a group. In 1992 there was an outpouring of support and attention unlike ever before. However, by 1994, as Chapter 5 suggested, the political environment worked against women. Thus women are more likely to face a volatile electoral environment that ultimately forces them to strategize differently and consider the environment in ways male candidates generally need not.

In addition to this central thesis, two additional findings emerged throughout this investigation. The first concerns the perceptions of female and male candidates. In a number of instances male and female candidates viewed the electoral system differently. Managers for female candidates thought their candidates faced greater discrimination from voters, party organizations, and media, than did managers for male candidates. In discussing their experiences in these areas, campaign managers for female candidates were often likely to see challenges that the managers for male candidates did not. If women perceive the electoral process as unfair or discriminatory, the political system has not gone far enough in showing that it accepts female candidates (see also Blair and Stanley 1991). Further, if the system appears discriminatory, it may hinder women's willingness to enter electoral politics. In this instance, the perception of unfairness is every bit as harmful as actual unfairness. As long as the political system sends out the message that politics is a largely male world, the slow progress of women into positions of elective office is likely to continue.

The other important finding that emerged in this analysis is that the effect of female candidates in an election may be much broader than previously thought. Because of women's entrance into the political arena, many male politicians are now considering issues and strategy in ways that they never have before. On the positive side, this may mean that male politicians are now addressing "women's issues," whereas previously they have ignored them. The presence of female candidates who raise different agendas and concerns has caused some male politicians to reevaluate their own priorities (see Table 2.8). However, the possible negative side is that men facing female opponents for the first time are insincere in their attempts to appeal to women's concerns and are making no substantive policy changes as a result of women's presences. In some cases men are only using appeals to women as a manipulative tactic. Undoubtedly both phenomena are occurring, one hopes with greater emphasis on the former. If male candidates do alter their agenda, the nature of substantive political representation changes with the inclusion of female politicians.

Concluding Assessments of the Campaign Managers

At the conclusion of the interviews, a number of managers offered final assessments of the role of gender in the electoral process. Only at the conclusion of the interviews were the campaign managers asked extensively and directly about the role of candidate gender in their campaign (see Appendix C). For the most part, campaign managers were unaware that the focus of this study was the role of candidate gender in the election process. The true nature of the inquiry was concealed from the managers to avoid triggering a gender-sensitive response. Clear awareness of the purpose of the survey may have led some managers to either deny that candidate gender played any role in the election or to overemphasize the role of gender.

The majority of managers involved in races with female candidates stated that candidate gender was not a very important factor in deciding how to wage their campaigns. In response to a question about the overall role of candidate gender in the electoral process, several managers offered similar views:

> Yes, [candidate] gender has some impact on the voters . . . women probably got a boost this year [1992], but party affiliation always trumps gender with the voters. The importance of being a women ranks way behind party.

> Gender has an effect, but there are a lot of things that matter in an election—the issues, the quality of the candidate, the mood of the electorate—I think all of these things are probably more important than whether the candidate is a man or woman.

> I think the end result is minor. Sometimes it [running against a woman] might help you, other times it could hurt, but there are so many other things that matter more.

These comments are representative of the majority of campaign managers who had experience with female candidates. The managers acknowledged that candidate gender was a factor, but generally did not see it playing a decisive role in the outcome of their respective elections.

Although these assessments may seem to contradict many of the findings presented throughout this analysis, it is important to reemphasize that many of the differences found were more subtle than those that would have concerned the campaign managers. Further, we must consider that campaign managers and political professionals are trained to think in terms of winning and losing. Their assessments of the campaigns are preoccupied with what affects voters and in what directions. The campaign managers were often not concerned with, or even aware of, the broader theoretical issues discussed here (e.g., political representation or the perpetuation of traditional sex-role stereotyping) and thus ultimately overlooked many of the nuanced gender differences. Also, although most managers were forthcoming in the interviews, questions about the role of candidate gender were not always dealt with openly. The admission that they treated an opponent differently because of his or her sex would be controversial if it became known. Despite the hesitancy of the campaign managers in this area, two prominent trends came through in their remarks that help corroborate some of the conclusions that were drawn throughout this study. First, the managers for men and women had different perceptions about the fairness of the electoral arena. Second, managers for female candidates clearly felt that the electoral environment was more demanding for women.

Different Perceptions of
Male and Female Candidates

Although most managers downplayed the effect of candidate gender, there were some widely varying responses between the managers of female and male candidates over the fairness of the electoral process. Significantly, these responses broke down along gender lines. Several managers for male candidates running against women were emphatic that candidate gender played almost no role in their election. In sharp contrast to these assessments, the managers for the female candidates running against these male candidates saw gender as a major component of the election. Compare the responses in the following three election match-ups.

Open-seat race between a man and a woman in 1992:

> It made no difference whatsoever. Voters don't care whether you are a man or a woman, they care about what you have to say . . . we did not do anything differently because we faced a woman and it made no difference in this race. (Manager for the male challenger)

I think we may have lost the election because of it [being a female candidate] . . . it was much harder to appeal to certain voters. (Manager for the female challenger)

Race with a male challenger and female incumbent in 1994:

Everyone seems to make such a big deal about it [running against a female candidate], but I just did not see anything; maybe I am blind. I know in reality that it [candidate gender] mattered to some . . . but for the most part this race was fought over Proposition 187 [the statewide initiative on immigration]. (Manager for the male challenger)

The electoral system is more difficult for women. They have to keep proving themselves over and over again . . . [For instance] when people come to a congressional candidates forum not knowing who the candidates are, and then they see a women, they look at you with greater skepticism . . . any missteps that you make are noticed. Men don't have to deal with that kind of scrutiny. (Manager for the female incumbent)

Race with a female challenger and a male incumbent in 1994:

I don't think running against a woman made a bit of difference in this race. It just never came up. We ran the race the same way we always do. (Manager for the male incumbent)

I think . . . [being] a woman was a pretty important factor. It didn't change the outcome, I still would have lost if I were a man, but there were many more pitfalls for me during the campaign . . . things that are specific disadvantages for women and not men. (Female challenger)

These candidates and their campaign managers, running in the same election, saw the playing field and electoral environment considerably differently. This bolsters the previous conclusion that women often tend to see the electoral process as being less fair than men (see also Chapter 4). Men are more likely to view the system as a level playing field whereas women are more likely to see disadvantages. Other recent examinations have suggested that when women perceive the political process as unfair they are less likely to stay involved (Naff 1995). Thus, as long as there are disparities in the perceptions of female and male candidates and potential candidates regarding fairness, this will pose an impediment to the full inclusion of women into the electoral process.

"Women Have to be Better"

A second important point emerged in the final assessments of the managers for female candidates. A majority of the managers for female challengers (17 of 25) believed that women were held to higher standards throughout the campaign. This corresponds well with the third part of the central thesis: The electoral process is more demanding for women. Although this conclusion has been drawn throughout this analysis, it surfaced again in some of the final remarks of the managers. For instance, the manager for a female candidate running in northern California noted,

> Women just have to be near perfect. . . . They are watched more closely and any mistakes they make are immediately pounced on. Women have to be able to do everything well.

Another manager who had worked for many female candidates commented,

> Women politicians are held to a higher standard. This can work both ways though. If you do something well then you are a surprising success—if you fail that was partially expected anyway.

Another manager was emphatic in her response:

> Women have to be better, period. Better with the voters. Better with media. Better at fund-raising. . . .

The assessments that women are judged more strictly in the election process are consistent with the growing body of literature that suggests women in public life are evaluated on a more demanding scale (Jamieson 1995). Moncrief, Thompson, and Schuhmann (1991) have found that female state legislators often have substantially higher qualifications than their male counterparts. The implication of their finding is that female legislators must have superior qualifications to have the credibility to compete with men. Women in the public eye are often held to higher standards, which ultimately results in women having more difficulty succeeding. The treatment and performance of male candidates becomes the behavioral norm and female candidates are judged by that standard. However, in addition to conforming to the male standard, women must also adequately fulfill the extra expectations voters and others in the political process might have about female candidates (Burrell 1994). Thus, female candidates face a greater challenge presenting themselves to the public, a phenomenon that will not dissipate until the actors in the

political environment begin assessing female politicians on equitable terms
with men.

Researching the Role of Gender
in the Electoral Process

The 1992 election produced great academic interest on the subject of
gender dynamics in electoral politics. A number of recent book-length
works, cited throughout this analysis, have examined the effect of the 1992
elections (Carroll 1994; Cook, Thomas, and Wilcox 1994; Burrell 1994;
Witt, Paget, and Matthews 1994). Although this recent flurry of scholarly
activity has shed some light on current developments regarding the condition
of women in the electoral process, there are still many important questions
that require further investigation. Will women gain full acceptance into the
electoral arena? Will the set of "women's issues" and "interests" be fully
represented in the political process? Concerns over fundamental fairness and
the quality of both symbolic and substantive representation mandate that we
continue to monitor the progress of women seeking positions of high elective
office.

What does the future hold for female candidates in the electoral arena?
Predicting the rate of women's progress in acquiring top-level elected positions is highly speculative, although some have tried (Wolbrecht 1994;
Andersen and Thorson 1984). The more important question emerging from
this study is whether there will be substantial progress or change in the socialization patterns that played such a large role in the congressional campaigns in California. This is the fundamental question that we must address
as we continue to study the fluctuating fortunes of women in the electoral
arena.

In future explorations of the effect of female candidates on the electoral
process it is important to seek out innovative and in-depth approaches to the
subject. We have entered a period in which most overt discrimination against
women in the electoral process has disappeared. Yet the traditional political
socialization of male and female candidates and voters is still very much
present. In the course of this investigation, a number of areas have been
touched on that are primed for further investigation. In examining these
areas, researchers will be challenged to devise creative research approaches
to determine the full effect of traditional socialization on the political
process. For example, what remains very frustrating for students and scholars

interested in the success of female candidates and the need for greater female representation is that the disparities in the number of elected women do not seem to match the disparities in the individual components of the electoral process. A growing body of evidence, cited throughout this analysis, shows that women and men receive similar levels of voter, monetary, and party support. However, these findings may be misleading because of the methods employed by the political scientists who have chosen to examine these questions. For instance, most recent studies of candidate gender and fundraising show that women do as well or better than comparably situated men. However, Herrick (1996) found that female congressional candidates who were challengers in 1988 and 1992 did not do as well as the men they ran against. In an important and very clever reconfiguring of the campaign finance data, Herrick uses four resources to estimate the value of campaign spending—actual spending, party strength, party identification, and previous support. Herrick found an important disadvantage in the "value" of the money spent by female candidates in relation to the value of the money spent by male candidates. Many aspects of the electoral process covered in this investigation of California House candidates are ready for similar in-depth analysis. Following are a number of questions for further research.

Do men and women use different criteria in deciding whether or not to run for office?   The preponderance of evidence suggests that if women enter election campaigns they have a chance equal to or better than men to win (Burrell 1994; Darcy, Welch, and Clark 1994). Thus, an essential component for fully understanding why women remain so grossly underrepresented in Congress and elsewhere is understanding why more women are not running for office. Overall, this is a very difficult question to answer and a difficult subject to research. There are a lot of unrecorded psychological factors that go into the decision to run for office. Moreover, when a potential candidate decides not to run, the decision is undocumented and thus that individual is difficult to track down and survey. However, a study that could effectively measure gender differences in how one decides to run for office might go a long way in explaining the continued disparities between the number of men and women serving in elected positions.

What is the quality of media coverage in local level elections? Are "small town" newspapers or television stations likely sources of gender bias in reporting?   In Chapter 4 this study touched on the subject of gender differences in media coverage, but many important questions persist. Several of the female candidates in California believed there was bias in the local media. Poole (1993) also found considerable levels of bias in media coverage of local elections in Illinois. The cozy relationship between incumbents and the media can be more easily carried out with "small town" media sources. This may be one of the institutional roadblocks further limiting the access of women or any group historically excluded from the political process. Currently we have little understanding of the role media coverage plays in local and district-level elections.

What is the role of gender in campaign funding? Do male and female voters have different contributing patterns?   There are still many unanswered questions about the relationship between gender and campaign finances. The accessibility of fund-raising networks permits research on one of the clearest indicators of women's acceptance by and acclimation into the electoral process. For example, we are still not clear whether differences exist in the contribution patters of men and women. Also, the extent to which women have access to institutional money remains unclear. With money serving as the lifeblood of politics, it is important to develop a more complete understanding of how gender and campaign finances interact.

What is the role of geographic region and district-level demographics in determining the success of female candidates?   There are geographic areas throughout the United States in which women have been successful in electoral politics and areas where women have never been involved in politics as candidates. Early research showed that there were clear differences in the behavior and electability of women from different regions of the country (Hill 1981; Bullock and Heys 1972). A comparison of the districts and areas in which women have done well with those in which women have not done well may help explain what conditions must exist for female candidates to be successful.

How does the presence of women in the political process change the attitudes and norms of men in the political process?   This subject is one of the most underexplored aspects in the gender and politics literature. Almost all examinations of female political actors, especially female candidates, has focused on what women bring to the political process. This was the crucial first step and long overdue, but it is now time to broaden our investigation of the effect of gender on the political process. If women in the political process alter the behavior of men, then this must be investigated to determine how this affects legislative policy agendas, executive decision making, and election strategies. We must begin to assess the effect of women in the political process from a broader perspective to understand how the entire political system responds to female political actors.

How important is candidate gender in the voter's decision-making process? Polling data has found that a portion of the electorate, albeit a dwindling percentage, admits some degree of bias against female candidates. For the first time, in the 1992 elections, public opinion polls found an apparent preference of many voters for female candidates. What becomes clear is that voter bias concerning gender is more complex than we had considered. In measuring how voters weigh candidate gender, several factors must be considered, such as the electoral environment, the key issues in the election, the type of office being sought, the voter's level of political knowledge about the candidates, the geographic region, and the number of women on the ballot. Any of these factors may change how voters view the gender of the candidates when deciding how to vote. There are currently no comprehensive examinations of national survey data or large-scale experiments that have investigated the various ways gender might influence vote choice.

Conclusion

All of these questions attempt to go beyond noting the mere presence of gender differences between women and men by examining the broader effect of gender dynamics in the political process. Our analysis must extend beyond individual political actors to consider the effects of gender throughout our social and political institutions. Future studies of women and politics must continue to examine how the inclusion of women in the political process affects the process as a whole. Researchers must look for subtle and nuanced gender differences in the political process. Most of these differences are grounded in the traditional socialization processes that have produced a political system with different challenges for female and male candidates.

Appendix A

Sample of California Congressional Races

Reading Appendix A

Following is the sample of races studied for this project. The campaign manager for at least one of the candidates, and in most cases for both of the candidates, was interviewed (see Appendix B).

The "female candidate races" were chosen by selecting all races with female candidates. Ultimately six female candidates in five races were dropped from the sample. Five of the six candidates (Maxine Waters in 1992 and 1994, Nancy Pelosi in 1992 and 1994, and Lucille Roybal-Allard in 1994) were incumbents running for reelection in very "safe" districts who engaged in almost no public campaign. The sixth candidate was Elsa Cheung, who ran a token candidacy against Nancy Pelosi in 1994; she could not be reached for an interview.

The comparison group of "male candidate only races" was selected by matching the type of election (open, new [only in 1992], or incumbent-held) and the party registration in the district with the female candidate races. The female candidate races on the left were matched with the corresponding male candidate only races on the right. Where there is not a corresponding race opposite a race it means that there were no suitable comparisons. The matching is imperfect but the ultimate goal was to have two pools of races that were roughly equally competitive.

Among the candidate pairings, the Democrat is always on the left and the Republican on the right. Candidates in italics won the election.

The party registration columns have the Democratic percentage on the left and the Republican percentage on the right. The registration figures for 1992 were based on the figures released just prior to the 1992 June primary. The registration numbers for 1994 are based on the registration figures at the end of 1993 and do not reflect the changes that occurred after that.

In races with an incumbent running, the (I) indicates which candidate is the incumbent. The (#) indicates the congressional district in California.

Female Candidate Races			Male Candidate Only Races		
		Party Registration			Party Registration
Democrat/Republican	(D)	(R)	Democrat/Republican	(D)	(R)
Open Seat Races—1992					
Lucille Roybal-Allard (33)/Rob Guzman	65%	22%	*Xavier Becerra (30)*/Morry Waksberg	60%	25%
Anna Eshoo (14)/Tom Huening	47	37	Evan Anderson Braude (38)/*Steve Horn*	48	41
Gloria Ochoa (22)/*Michael Huffington*	40	44			
Molly McClanahan (39)/*Ed Royce*	39	50			
Lynn Woolsey (6)/Bill Filante	53	32			
Open Seat Races—1994					
Walter Capps (22)/*Andrea Seastrand*	41	42	Steve Clute (44)/*Sonny Bono*	43	46
Zoe Lofgren (16)/Lyle Smith	56	29			
New Seat Races—1992 (only)					
Patti Garamendi (11)/*Richard Pombo*	51	39	*Bob Filner (50)*/Tony Valencia	51	35
Jane Harman (36)/Joan Milke-Flores	42	45	Wendell Williams (10)/*Bill Baker*	42	45
Lynn Schenk (49)/Judy Jarvis	39	44	Mark Takano (43)/*Ken Calvert*	43	46
			James Gilmartin (25)/*Buck McKeon*	38	51
			Bob Baker (41)/*Jay Kim*	39	48
Incumbent Held Seats—1992					
Georgia Smith (44)/*Al McCandless* (I)	43	46	Doug Kahn (27)/*Carlos Moorhead* (I)	42	46
Patricia Malberg (4)/*John Doolittle* (I)	43	45	*Norman Minetta (15)* (I)/Robert Wick	46	40
Anita Ferguson (23)/*Elton Gallegly* (I)	42	44	Robert Banuelos (46)/*Robert Dornan* (I)	45	44
Deborah Volmer (21)/*Bill Thomas* (I)	42	47	Al Wachtel (28)/*David Dreier*(I)	41	48
Janet Gastil (52)/*Duncan Hunter* (I)	36	49	Don Rusk (40)/*Jerry Lewis* (I)	39	48
Patricia McCabe (45)/*Dana Rohrbacher* (I)	35	53	Michael Farber (48)/*Ron Packard* (I)	29	57
Bea Herbert (51)/*Duke Cunningham* (I)	30	53	John Anwiler (47)/*Christopher Cox* (I)	29	59
			Vic Fazio (3) (I)/H.L. Richardson	48	39
			George Miller (7) (I)/David Scholl	62	26
			Ron Dellums (9)/Bill Hunter	68	15
Incumbent Held Seats—1994					
Ronald Dellums (9) (I)/Deborah Wright	69	14	*Sam Farr (17)* (I)/Bill McCampbell	53	31
Tom Lantos (12) (I)/Deborah Wilder	56	28	*George Brown (42)* (I)/Rob Guzman	53	37
Lynn Woolsey (6) (I)/Michael Nugent	55	30	Randy Perry (11)/*Richard Pombo* (I)	51	38
Bob Filner (50) (I)/Mary Alice Acevedo	51	34	Peter Mathews (38)/*Steve Horn* (I)	50	38
Anna Eshoo (14) (I)/Ben Brink	48	35	Michael Farber (46)/*Robert Dornan* (I)	48	41
Mary Jacobs (2)/*Wally Herger* (I)	44	42	*Richard Lehman (19)* (I)/*George Radanovich*	47	42
Jane Harmon (36) (I)/Susan Brooks	43	43	Kevin Ready (23)/*Elton Gallegly* (I)	43	42
Ellen Schwartz (10)/*Bill Baker* (I)	43	44	Doug Kahn (27)/*Carlos Moorhead* (I)	43	44
Katie Hirning (4)/*John Doolittle* (I)	42	45	John Evans (21)/*Bill Thomas* (I)	42	46
Lynn Schenk (49) (I)/*Brian Bilbray*	39	43	Mark Takano (43)/*Ken Calvert* (I)	42	46
Janet Gastil (52)/*Duncan Hunter* (I)	39	46	R. O. Davis (39)/*Ed Royce* (I)	40	49
Rita Tamerius (51)/*Duke Cunningham* (I)	30	51	Brett Williamson (45)/*Dana Rohrbacher* (I)	35	51
			Anthony Beilenson (24) (I)/Rich Sybert	46	40
			James Gilmartin (25)/Howard McKeon (I)	39	49

Appendix B

Interview Roster

Arranging the Interviews

The procedures for arranging the interviews were different for 1992 and 1994. In 1992 I conducted pre- and postelection interviews. In 1994 I conducted only postelection interviews. For the 1992 interviews the following procedure was used. The first step in arranging the interviews was sending a letter to the campaign manager of each campaign to introduce them to the project and inform them that they would be contacted about the possibility of an interview. In campaigns where there was no manager, the correspondence was sent directly to the candidate. Ten days after the initial mailing, the managers were telephoned to ask if they would be willing to take part in an interview. Reaching the manager was often exceedingly difficult. Managers rarely returned phone calls and sometimes had to be called as many as twenty separate times before an interview could be arranged. A campaign manager has little incentive to take part in an academic survey during the course of a hectic campaign. The managers were much easier to contact after the election. Of the 64 campaign managers and candidates approached in 1992, 38 (59%) took part in a preelection interview and 57 (89%) took part in a postelection interview. In total, campaign officials or candidates were interviewed in at least one phase of the interview process for 61 of the 64 (95%) campaigns approached. Only three campaigns directly refused to take part in live interviews (Democratic incumbent George Miller of the 7th District, Republican challenger Bill Hunter of the 9th District, and Republican challenger Judy Jarvis of the 49th District).

In 1994 all interviews were conducted after the election and over the phone. Again, as in 1992, the campaign managers were sent an introductory letter prior to the election explaining the survey and asking if they would be willing to be interviewed after the election. In the final two weeks of the campaign each manager was called and asked to participate. Information was gathered about where the managers could be reached after the election.

Managers were contacted prior to the election because it would have been difficult to track them down after the election. Many managers were not from California and immediately dispersed across the country after the election. Of the 58 campaign managers and candidates approached in 1994, 48 (83%) took part in a postelection interview. Of the ten who were not interviewed, seven agreed to be interviewed after the election but could not be reached after the election. The other three campaigns directly refused to take part in live interviews (Democratic incumbent Tom Lantos of the 12th District, Republican challenger Andrea Seastrand of the 22nd District, and Republican challenger Rich Sybert of the 24th District).

Campaign literature was collected for 55 of the 64 (86%) campaigns in 1992, and 34 of the 58 (59%) campaigns in 1994. For the remaining 33 candidates, 8 said that they did not produce any campaign literature, and the other 25 never mailed the literature despite repeated reminders.

Reading Appendix B

In the following interview roster, candidates are categorized by sex and by year. The candidates are listed in numerical order by their congressional district.

Codes for Column Headings

1   Congressional district number followed by party affiliation (R = Republican, D = Democrat).
2   Whether a preelection interview was conducted (only applicable for 1992 interviews).
3   Whether a postelection interview was conducted.
4   The interviewee's position with the campaign (CM = Campaign Manager, ACM = Assistant Campaign Manager, PS = Press Secretary, CAN = Candidate).
5   Whether campaign literature was collected (a "no" might also mean that the campaign did not produce any literature).
6   Name of person interviewed.

	1	2	3	4	5	6
Female Candidates 1992						
Patricia Malberg	4D	yes	yes	CM	yes	Don Malberg
Lynn Woolsey	6D	yes	yes	CM	yes	Cynthia Wieland
Patti Garamendi	11D	yes	yes	CM	yes	Monica Mills
Anna Eshoo	14D	no	yes	—	yes	anonymous
Deborah Volmer	21D	no	yes	CM	yes	Glen Shilcrist
Gloria Ochoa	22D	yes	yes	CM	yes	Phil Peblican
Anita Ferguson	23D	yes	yes	CM	yes	Sam Rodriguez
Lucille Roybal Allard	33D	yes	yes	CM	yes	Maria Ochoa
Jane Harman	36D	no	yes	CM	yes	Roy Behr
Joan Milke-Flores	36R	yes	yes	CM	yes	Dora Kingsley
Molly McClanahan	39D	yes	yes	CM	yes	Diane Campbell
Georgia Smith	44D	yes	yes	—	yes	anonymous
Patricia McCabe	45D	no	yes	CM	yes	Janet Heartwell
Lynn Schenk	49D	yes	yes	CM	yes	Andrew Kennedy
Judy Jarvis	49R	no	no	—	no	—
Bea Herbert	51D	yes	yes	CAN	yes	Bea Herbert
Janet Gastil	52D	yes	yes	CM	yes	George Gastil
Female Candidates 1994						
Mary Jacobs	2D	—	yes	—	yes	anonymous
Katie Hirning	4D	—	yes	CM	no	Andy Hahn
Lynn Woolsey	6D	—	yes	CM	yes	Bryan Bloom
Deborah Wrigh	9R	—	yes	—	yes	anonymous
Ellen Schwartz	10D	—	yes	CM	no	Sharon Miller
Deborah Wilder	12R	—	yes	—	yes	anonymous
Anna Eshoo	14D	—	yes	CM	yes	Mary Hughes
Zoe Lofgren	16D	—	no	—	yes	—
Andrea Seastrand	22R	—	no	—	yes	—
Jane Harman	36D	—	yes	CM	yes	Judy Sitzer
Susan Brooks	36R	—	yes	CM	yes	John Perkins
Lynn Schenk	49D	—	yes	—	no	anonymous
Mary Alice Acevedo	50R	—	yes	CM	yes	anonymous
Rita Tamerius	51D	—	yes	CM	yes	Karen Tamerius
Janet Gastil	52D	—	yes	CM	yes	Ted Craig

(continued)

	1	*2*	*3*	*4*	*5*	*6*
Male Candidates 1992						
Vic Fazio	3D	yes	yes	CM	yes	Richard Harris
H. L. Richardson	3R	yes	yes	CM	yes	John Stoos
John Doolittle	4R	yes	yes	CM	yes	Richard Robinson
Bill Filante	6R	no	yes	CM	yes	anonymous
George Miller	7D	no	no	—	yes	—
David Scholl	7R	yes	no	CM	yes	—
Ron Dellums	9D	yes	yes	ACM	yes	Jennifer Freitas
Bill Hunter	9R	no	no	—	no	—
Wendell Williams	10D	yes	yes	—	yes	anonymous
Bill Baker	10R	yes	yes	CM	yes	Robin Swiggert
Richard Pombo	11R	no	yes	CM	yes	Wayne Johnson
Tom Huening	14R	yes	yes	CM	yes	Bob Marks
Norman Minetta	15D	no	yes	—	yes	anonymous
Robert Wick	15R	no	yes	CAN	yes	Robert Wick
Bill Thomas	21R	no	yes	CM	yes	Mark Abernathy
Michael Huffington	22R	no	yes	CM	yes	anonymous
Elton Gallegly	23R	no	yes	—	yes	anonymous
James Gilmartin	25D	yes	yes	CM	yes	Bob Funk
Buck McKeon	25R	yes	yes	CM	yes	Armando Azarloza
Doug Kahn	27D	yes	no	—	yes	anonymous
Carlos Moorhead	27R	yes	yes	—	yes	anonymous
Al Wachtel	28D	yes	yes	CM	yes	Tommy Randle
David Dreier	28R	no	yes	—	no	anonymous
Xavier Becerra	30D	yes	no	CM	yes	Elsa Marquez
Morry Waksberg	30R	no	no	—	no	—
Rob Guzman	33R	yes	yes	CM	yes	Mike Guzman
Evan Anderson-Braude	38D	yes	yes	CM	yes	Amy Pritchard
Steve Horn	38R	yes	yes	CM	yes	Steve Horn, Jr.
Ed Royce	39R	no	yes	—	yes	anonymous
Don Rusk	40D	yes	yes	CM	yes	Bryce Henderson
Jerry Lewis	40R	no	yes	—	yes	anonymous
Bob Baker	41D	no	yes	CAN	yes	Bob Baker
Jay Kim	41R	yes	yes	CM	yes	Sandra Garner
Mark Takano	43D	yes	yes	CM	yes	John Shallman
Ken Calvert	43R	yes	yes	CM	yes	Sue Miller
Al McCandless	44R	yes	yes	CM	yes	Alfred Ortiz
Dana Rohrbacher	45R	yes	yes	CM	yes	Gene Ferguson
Robert Banuelos	46D	no	yes	CAN	no	Robert Banuelos
Robert Dornan	46R	no	yes	—	no	anonymous
John Anwiler	47D	no	yes	CAN	no	John Anwiler
Christopher Cox	47R	no	yes	CM	yes	Marcella MacKenzie
John Farber	48D	yes	yes	—	yes	anonymous
Ron Packard	48R	no	yes	PS	no	anonymous
Bob Filner	50D	no	yes	CM	yes	David Ginsberg
Tony Valencia	50R	no	yes	CM	no	Uvaldo Martinez
Duke Cunningham	51R	yes	yes	CM	yes	Tex Burkett
Duncan Hunter	52R	yes	yes	CM	yes	Valerie Snesko

	1	2	3	4	5	6
Male Candidates 1994						
Wally Herger	2R	—	yes	CM	yes	Brad Zerby
John Doolittle	4R	—	yes	CM	yes	Mark Sasson
Michael Nugent	6R	—	yes	CM	no	Terese Clark
Ron Dellums	9D	—	no	—	no	—
Bill Baker	10R	—	yes	CM	yes	Jean Meredith
Randy Perry	11D	—	yes	CM	yes	Tony Corbo
Richard Pombo	11R	—	yes	CM	no	Wayne Johnson
Tom Lantos	12D	—	no	—	yes	—
Ben Brink	14R	—	yes	—	no	anonymous
Lyle Smith	16R	—	yes	CAN	yes	Lyle Smith
Sam Farr	17D	—	yes	CM	no	Jeff Jansen
Bill McCampbell	17R	—	yes	CM	no	—
Richard Lehman	19D	—	yes	CM	yes	Darry Sragou
George Radanovich	19R	—	yes	CM	yes	Tim Orman
John Evans	21D	—	yes	—	no	anonymous
Bill Thomas	21R	—	yes	—	no	anonymous
Walter Capps	22D	—	yes	—	yes	anonymous
Kevin Ready	23D	—	no	—	no	—
Elton Gallegly	23R	—	yes	—	yes	anonymous
Anthony Beilenson	24D	—	yes	—	no	anonymous
Rich Sybert	24R	—	no	—	no	—
James Gilmartin	25D	—	yes	CM	no	anonymous
Buck McKeon	25R	—	yes	CM	yes	Armando Azarloza
Doug Kahn	27D	—	yes	—	no	anonymous
Carlos Moorhead	27R	—	yes	CM	yes	anonymous
Peter Mathews	38D	—	no	—	no	—
Steve Horn	38R	—	yes	CM	yes	Steve Horn, Jr.
R.O. Davis	39D	—	yes	CM	no	—
Ed Royce	39R	—	yes	—	yes	anonymous
George Brown	42D	—	yes	CM	yes	Bobby Johnson
Rob Guzman	42R	—	no	—	no	—
Mark Takano	43D	—	yes	CM	yes	Hunter Cutting
Ken Calvert	43R	—	yes	—	yes	anonymous
Steve Clute	44D	—	yes	—	no	anonymous
Sonny Bono	44R	—	no	—	no	—
Brett Williamson	45D	—	yes	CM	yes	Bob Steens
Dana Rohrbacher	45R	—	yes	CM	yes	Rhonda Carmony
Michael Farber	46D	—	yes	CM	no	Diane Gould
Robert Dornan	46R	—	yes	CM	yes	Sally Dornan
Brian Bilbray	49R	—	yes	CM	yes	Marla Marshall
Bob Filner	50D	—	yes	CM	no	David Ginsberg
Duke Cunningham	51R	—	no	—	no	—
Duncan Hunter	52R	—	yes	CM	yes	Robert Hunter

Appendix C

Pre-Election Survey

Note About the Interviews

Following is a list of the questions that were asked of every campaign manager. The interviews were conducted in an open and free-flowing style. There were almost always follow-up questions to the managers' responses that are not listed below. Every effort was made to get the managers to explain their responses. Also, in elections where there were particular controversies or election issues, the campaign managers were asked about these. Thus, not all of the questions asked of the managers and mentioned in the text are listed here. The questions below are those that were asked uniformly of all the campaigns.

Introduce self and thank them for participation.

Before we proceed, let me ask you about confidentiality. Let me assure you that none of the results of my work will be published until long after the election. Would you like to remain completely anonymous, or would you mind if I cited you by name in this project, or would you prefer being cited as an official from the _____ campaign?
Confidentiality option _____.

Lastly, before we begin would you mind if I tape record the interview?

yes _____ no _____

Part I—Interview Facts
(When possible these were filled in prior to the interview)

Name of Candidate _____

Person Interviewed _____

Interviewee's Position with Campaign _____

Date of Interview _____

Age of Candidate _____   Party of Candidate _____

Which of the Following is the Candidate:
Challenger _____   Incumbent _____   Running for an Open Seat _____

Previous Occupation of the Candidate (if not an incumbent) _____

_____

District number _____   Name of the Opponent _____

Which of the Following is the Opponent:
Challenger _____   Incumbent _____   Running for an Open Seat _____

Previous Occupation of the Opponent (if not an incumbent) _____

_____

Part II—General Questions

1. To the best of your knowledge, what motivated your candidate to enter this race and pursue a seat in the U.S. House of Representatives? (not asked of incumbents)
2. What are the central themes being put forward in your campaign? (Central themes were defined as broad and general concepts—not specific issues.)
3. Of the themes you have just mentioned, can you order them in terms of priority? Also, how will you use or present each of the mentioned themes?

Theme	*How Used in Campaign*
#1 _____	_____
#2 _____	_____
#3 _____	_____
#4 _____	_____

4. Are there a few words you are attempting to associate with the candidate? If so, what are they? (or, Does the campaign have a slogan?)

5. What personal traits will you attempt to convey to the voters about your candidate?

6. Of the personal traits you have just mentioned, can you order them in terms of priority? Also, how will you use or present each of the mentioned personal traits?

Personal Trait	*How Used in Campaign*
#1 _____	_____
#2 _____	_____
#3 _____	_____
#4 _____	_____

7. What issues are most important to the voters in this district? (Please list the top four)

8. Among the list of the following issues, please answer two questions. One, is this issue part of your campaign message? (In other words, will the candidate intentionally raise the issue in any of the campaign activities?) Two, if it will be raised, how will it be used? (In other words, in what campaign materials will it be used and how will it be presented?)

Abortion?	yes _____	no _____	How is the issue used?
Defense Spending?	yes _____	no _____	How is the issue used?
Family Values?	yes _____	no _____	How is the issue used?
Gay Rights?	yes _____	no _____	How is the issue used?
Crime Issues?	yes _____	no _____	How is the issue used?
Immigration?	yes _____	no _____	How is the issue used?
Parental Leave?	yes _____	no _____	How is the issue used?
Tax Policy	yes _____	no _____	How is the issue used?
Job Creation?	yes _____	no _____	How is the issue used?
Government Regulation?	yes _____	no _____	How is the issue used?
Education?	yes _____	no _____	How is the issue used?
Health Care?	yes _____	no _____	How is the issue used?

Thomas/Hill Hearings (1992 only)? (Sexual harassment in 1994)

	yes _____	no _____	How was the issue used?
Children's Issues?	yes _____	no _____	How was the issue used?
Environment?	yes _____	no _____	How was the issue used?

NAFTA (1992 only)? (GATT in 1994)

	yes _____	no _____	How was the issue used?

Policy towards Haiti? (only asked in 1994)

	yes _____	no _____	How was the issue used?

9. Of all the issues, either mentioned already or not, could you list the four most important issues for the message of your campaign? Please do so in the order of importance. Also, how will you use or present each of the mentioned issues?

Issue	*How Used in Campaign*
#1 _____	_____
#2 _____	_____
#3 _____	_____
#4 _____	_____

10. Does your candidate have any specific policy proposals they plan to pursue when in office?

11. What techniques and methods of communicating with the voters are you using to get out the message of your candidate?

12. What method of communicating with the voters was the most important for your campaign?

13. Will you be discussing your opponent in the message of your campaign?

14. If you will be discussing your opponent, roughly what percentage of your public campaign message will focus on your opponent?

15. Which of your opponents' issue positions will be discussed in the campaign?

16. Which of your opponents' personal traits will be discussed in the campaign?

17. Are there any past events and activities in your opponents' life that you will discuss?

18. Will you be using radio or television advertising in the campaign? (Could be known from question 11.) If yes, could you please give a brief synopsis of the advertisements you used?

Radio	*Television*
yes _____ no _____	yes _____ no _____
Ad #1 _____	_____
_____	_____
_____	_____
Ad #2 _____	_____
_____	_____
_____	_____
Ad #3 _____	_____
_____	_____
_____	_____

19. What are the biggest obstacles you are facing during the course of the election process?

20. What are the biggest advantages you have had during the course of the election process?

21. Is fund-raising posing a major obstacle to your campaign? Please describe your fund-raising efforts.

22. From what sources is most of your money coming?

23. Have you experienced any gender bias from campaign contributors? (Asked only of women.)

24. Has party support posed a major obstacle to your campaign?

25. Were you recruited by your party to run for office?

26. Did you receive sufficient party support overall?

27. Did you receive adequate support from the: local party? state party? national party? Please describe your experiences with each level of party organization.

28. Did you feel there was party bias directed towards your candidate?

29. Did you feel there was party bias directed towards your candidate that was based on the gender of your candidate? (Asked only of women.)

30. Has media coverage posed a major obstacle to your campaign? Please describe your experiences with the media.

31. Overall, do you believe you were treated fairly by the media?

32. Do you believe there was media bias favoring or against your candidate?

33. Do you believe there was gender bias in the media coverage of your candidate? (Asked only of women.)

34. How has your candidate been received by the voters?

35. Do you feel you have had an advantage or disadvantage with the voters because you are a woman? (Asked only of women.)

36. Do you feel you have had an advantage or disadvantage with the voters because your opponent is a woman? (Asked only of men running against women.)

III. Questions Based on Type of Candidate

For Female Candidates Only:

37. Will you be stressing the candidate's gender as a reason for voting for the candidate? If so, how? If not, why not?

38. Do you believe that women campaign in ways different from that of men?

39. Overall, do you regard being a woman candidate an advantage or a disadvantage or neither? Why? Any evidence one way or the other?

40. Do you believe you have encountered any gender discrimination in your campaign? (If not already mentioned.)

41. Do you believe that the 1992 elections are different in terms of women candidates? Why, or why not? (Asked only in 1992.)

42. Do you feel 1994 is different for women candidates than 1992? If yes, how? (Asked only in 1994.)

43. In evaluating the entire electoral experience, do you believe men and women candidates behave differently? If so, how?

For Men Running Against Women:

37. Will you being changing your strategy in any way because you are running against a woman candidate? If yes, how?

38. Do you believe that women campaign in ways different from that of men?

39. How will you respond if your opponent uses her gender as a campaign issue?

40. How does your strategy differ this election from past elections? (Asked only of incumbents or challengers who had run before.)

41. Did you do anything differently in the campaign because your opponent is a woman?

42. Do you believe women candidates have an advantage, disadvantage, or neither in the electoral process? Why? Any evidence one way or the other?

43. Do you believe that the 1992 elections are different in terms of women candidates? Why, or why not? (Asked only in 1992.)

44. Do you feel 1994 is different for women candidates than 1992? If yes, how? (Asked only in 1994.)

45. In evaluating the entire electoral experience, do you believe men and women candidates behave differently while campaigning? If so, how?

For Men Running Against Men:

37. Do you believe that the 1992 elections are different in terms of women candidates? Why, or why not?

38. How does your strategy differ this election from past elections? (Asked only of incumbents or challengers who had run before.)

39. With all the attention that women candidates and women's issues are receiving this year, has this caused you to change your strategy in any way? (Asked only in 1992.)

Thank you very much for your time. Could you see that I receive any campaign literature? Also, would it be possible to speak with you again briefly following the campaign? How will I get ahold of you? Once again, thank you and good luck with the campaign.

Post-Election Survey

Note About the Post-Election Interviews

In 1992, when there had been a preelection interview, the postelection interview was conducted over the phone. If the postelection interview was the first interview conducted, then whenever possible the postelection interview was conducted in person and the questions from the pre- and post-election survey were combined. In 1994, there were only post-election interviews (all conducted over the phone) and the survey questions from both surveys were used.

I. Interview Facts
(When possible, filled out prior to the interview)

Candidate name _____

Person Spoke With _____

Date of Interview _____

Outcome of Election _____

Confidentiality/Taping Okay? _____

II. General Questions

1. What do you see as the primary reason for your defeat or victory? Could you list the reasons in order?
2. At the outset of the campaign, what were the central objectives of the campaign? What were your top priorities?
3. Did these objectives ever change throughout the campaign? If so, how?
4. How large a part of the campaign strategy involved attacking your opponent?
5. What was the most effective portion of your campaign message?
6. How would you assess the press coverage of the race? Was it biased? (Did the press treat your candidate differently because she was a woman? Asked only of female candidates.) Please describe coverage.
7. How would you characterize the amount of media coverage your campaign received? Which of the following would be most accurate?

_____ No Coverage (less than three news stories over the election)

_____ Little Coverage (news stories every two weeks)

_____ Moderate Coverage (weekly reporting)

_____ Extensive Coverage (daily reporting)

8. What media organizations covered your campaign? Local television? Local newspapers? National media?

9. How would you assess your overall success in fund-raising? Would more money have mattered in the outcome of your election? (Second part asked only of losing candidates.)

10. In the end, how would you assess the level of party support you received from: the local party, state party, and national party?

11. Among the list of the following issues please answer two questions. One, was this issue part of your campaign message? Two, if it was raised how was it used?

Abortion?	yes _____	no _____	How was the issue used?
Defense Spending?	yes _____	no _____	How was the issue used?
Family Values?	yes _____	no _____	How was the issue used?
Gay Rights?	yes _____	no _____	How was the issue used?
Crime Issues?	yes _____	no _____	How was the issue used?
Immigration?	yes _____	no _____	How was the issue used?
Parental Leave?	yes _____	no _____	How was the issue used?
Tax Policy?	yes _____	no _____	How was the issue used?
Job Creation?	yes _____	no _____	How was the issue used?
Government Regulation?	yes _____	no _____	How was the issue used?
Education?	yes _____	no _____	How was the issue used?
Health Care?	yes _____	no _____	How was the issue used?

Thomas/Hill Hearings (1992 only)? (Sexual harassment in 1994)

	yes _____	no _____	How was the issue used?
Children's Issues?	yes _____	no _____	How was the issue used?
Environment?	yes _____	no _____	How was the issue used?

NAFTA (1992 only)? (GATT in 1994)

	yes _____	no _____	How was the issue used?

Policy towards Haiti? (only asked in 1994)

	yes _____	no _____	How was the issue used?

12. Of all the issues, either mentioned above or not mentioned, could you please list the four most important issues for the message of your campaign?

13. If not already mentioned, how many TV and radio ads did you run, and could you give me a synopsis of them? (Or if you have copies could you please provide them?)

14. Regarding your campaign organization:

   a) How many paid staff were working for the campaign?

   b) How many active volunteers were working for the campaign? (Active volunteers were defined as people who put in a minimum of ten hours on the campaign.)

   c) Did you have political consultants working for the campaign? If so, what types? How many?

   d) Did you have campaign offices open to the public? If so, how many?

   e) Did your campaign target specific groups of voters? If so, which groups of voters did you target and how were they targeted?

III. Questions Based on Type of Candidate
(Interview ends at this point for men running against men)

For Female Candidates Only:

15. What role did you feel being a woman had on the outcome of the election?

16. How did being a woman affect your campaign strategy?

17. Did you feel the voters reacted differently toward you because your candidate was a woman?

18. In evaluating the entire electoral experience, what characteristics of the campaign process are different for women candidates?

For Men Running Against Women:

15. What role did you feel running against a woman had in the outcome of the election?

16. How did running against a woman affect your campaign strategy?

17. Did you feel the voters reacted differently toward you because your opponent was a woman?

18. In evaluating the entire electoral experience, what characteristics of the campaign process are different when you are running against a woman?

Thank you for your time. Good luck in the future.

References

Abrams Beck, Susan. 1991. Rethinking municipal governance: Gender distinctions on local councils. In *Gender and policy-making,* edited by Debra Dodson. Eagleton Institute of Politics, Rutgers, NJ: Center for the American Woman and Politics.

Agranoff, Robert, ed. 1980. *The new style in election campaigns.* Boston: Holbrook.

Alexander, Deborah, and Kristi Anderson. 1993. Gender as a factor in the attribution of leadership traits. *Political Research Quarterly* 46: 527-46.

Amundsen, Kirsten. 1971. *The silenced majority: Women and American democracy.* Englewood Cliffs, NJ: Prentice Hall.

Andersen, Kristi, and Elizabeth A. Cook. 1985. Women, work, and political attitudes. *American Journal of Political Science* 30: 237-55.

Andersen, Kristi, and Stuart J. Thorson. 1984. Congressional turnover and the election of women. *Western Political Quarterly* 37: 143-56.

Arnold, R. Douglas. 1990. *The logic of congressional action.* New Haven: Yale University Press.

Astin, Helen S., and Carole Leland. 1991. *Women of influence, women of vision: A cross-generational study of leadership and social change.* San Francisco: Jossey-Bass.

Atkins, Chester. 1973. *Getting elected.* Boston: Houghton Mifflin.

Bachrach, Peter. 1967. *The theory of democratic elitism: A critique.* Boston: Little, Brown.

Baer, Denise L. 1993. Political parties: The missing variable in women and politics research. *Political Research Quarterly* 46: 547-76.

Baxter, Sandra, and Marjorie Lansing. 1980. *Women and politics: The invisible majority.* Ann Arbor: University of Michigan Press.

Belenky, Mary Field, Blythe McVicker Clinchy, Nancy Rule Goldberger, and Jill Mattuck Tarule. 1986. *Women's ways of knowing.* New York: Basic Books.

Bennett, Linda L. M., and Stephen E. Bennett. 1996. Changing views about gender equality in politics: Gradual change and lingering doubts. In *Women in politics: Outsiders or insiders?* 2nd ed., edited by Lois Lovelace Duke. Englewood Cliffs, NJ: Prentice Hall.

213

Benze, James G., and Eugene R. DeClercq. 1985. Content of television political spot ads for female candidates. *Journalism Quarterly* 62: 278-88.

Berch, Neil. 1994. The "Year of the Woman" in historical context. Paper presented at the annual meeting of the American Political Science Association, New York, Sept. 1-4.

Berke, Richard. 1994. In '94, "Vote for Woman" does not play so well. *New York Times* 3 October, A1, B10.

Berkman, Michael B., and Robert E. O'Connor. 1993. Do women state legislators matter: Female legislators and state abortion policy. *American Politics Quarterly* 21: 102-24.

Bernstein, Robert A. 1986. Why are there so few women in the House? *Western Political Quarterly* 39: 155-64.

Beschloss, Michael R. 1995. The end of an era? *Newsweek,* 9 January, 45.

Biersack, Robert, and Paul S. Herrnson. 1994. Political parties and the Year of the Woman. In *The year of the woman,* edited by Elizabeth Adell Cook, Sue Thomas, and Clyde Wilcox. Boulder, CO: Westview.

Blair, Diane D., and Jeanie R. Stanley. 1991. Personal relationships and legislative power: Male and female perceptions. *Legislative Studies Quarterly* 16: 495-507.

Bledsoe, Timothy, and Mary Herring. 1990. Victims of circumstances: Women in pursuit of political office. *American Political Science Review* 84: 213-23.

Boles, Janet. 1991. Advancing the women's agenda within local legislatures: The role of female elected officials. In *Gender and policy-making,* edited by Debra Dodson. Eagleton Institute of Politics, Rutgers, NJ: Center for the American Woman and Politics.

———. 1993. The year of the woman. In *America's choice: The election of 1992,* edited by William Crotty. Guilford, CT: Dushkin.

Boneparth, Ellen. 1977. Women in campaigns. *American Political Quarterly* 5: 289-300.

Brest, Paul. 1976. In defense of the antidiscrimination principle. *Harvard Law Review* 90: 1-52.

Brzinski, Joanne Bay, and Bernadette Nye. 1993. Recruitment of women candidates in the 1992 Congressional election. Paper presented at the annual meeting of the American Political Science Association, Washington, DC, Sept. 2-5.

Bullock, Charles S., III, and Patricia Lee Findley Heys. 1972. Recruitment of women for Congress: A research note. *Western Political Quarterly* 25: 416-23.

Burrell, Barbara. 1985. Women's and men's campaigns for the U.S. House of Representatives, 1972-1982: A finance gap? *American Political Quarterly* 13: 251-72.

———. 1992. Women candidates in open-seat primaries for the U.S. House: 1968-1990. *Legislative Studies Quarterly* 17: 493-508.

———. 1994. *A woman's place is in the House.* Ann Arbor: University of Michigan Press.

Burt-Way, Barbara J., and Rita Mae Kelly. 1991. Gender and sustaining political ambition: A study of Arizona elected officials. *Western Political Quarterly* 44: 11-23.

Carpini, Michael X. Delli, and Ester R. Fuchs. 1993. The year of the woman? Candidates, voters, and the 1992 elections. *Political Science Quarterly* 108: 29-36.

Carroll, Susan J. 1984. Woman candidates and support for feminist concerns: The closet feminist syndrome. *Western Political Quarterly* 37: 307-23.

———. 1985. Political elites and sex differences in political ambition: A reconsideration. *Journal of Politics* 47: 1231-43.

———. 1994. *Women as candidates in American politics,* 2nd ed. Bloomington: Indiana University Press.

CAWP Fact Sheet. 1992. Women in elective office 1992. New Brunswick, NJ: Center for the American Woman and Politics.

Chaney, Carole, and Barbara Sinclair. 1994. Women and the 1992 House elections. In *The year of the woman,* edited by Elizabeth Adell Cook, Sue Thomas, and Clyde Wilcox. Boulder, CO: Westview.

Clarke, Harold D., and Allan Kornberg. 1979. Women Party Officials. *Journal of Politics* 41: 442-77.

Congressional quarterly almanac 1992. 1993. Washington, DC: Congressional Quarterly.

Congressional quarterly almanac 1994. 1995. Washington, DC: Congressional Quarterly.

Conover, Pamela Johnston. 1988. Feminists and the gender gap. *Journal of Politics* 50: 985-1010.

Conover, Pamela Johnston, and Virginia Gray. 1983. *Feminism and the new right: Conflict over the American family.* New York: Praeger.

Cook, Elizabeth Adell, Sue Thomas, and Clyde Wilcox, eds. 1994. *The year of the woman: Myths and realities.* Boulder, CO: Westview.

Cook, F., T. Tyler, E. Goetz, M. Gordon, D. Protess, D. Leff, and H. Molotch. 1983. Media and agenda setting: Effects on the public, interest group leaders, policy makers, and policy. *Public Opinion Quarterly* 47: 16-35.

Costantini, Edmond. 1990. Political women and political ambitions. Closing the gender gap. *American Journal of Political Science* 34: 741-70.

Costantini, Edmond, and Kenneth Craik. 1972. Women as politicians: The social background, personality, and political careers of female party leaders. *Journal of Social Issues* 28: 217-36.

Cotter, Cornelius P., James L. Gibson, John F. Bibby, and Robert J. Huckshorn. 1984. *Party organizations in American politics.* New York: Praeger.

Crier & Co. 1992. The year of the women? (transcript). Atlanta: Cable News Network, Inc. 15 July.

Darcy, R., Susan Welch, and Janet Clark. 1994. *Women, elections, and representation.* Lincoln: University of Nebraska Press.

Davidson, Roger H,. and Walter J. Oleszek. 1994. *Congress and its members.* Washington, DC: CQ Press.

Davis, James A. and Smith, Tom W. 1993. *General Social Surveys, 1992-1993.* [machine-readable data file]. NORC ed. Chicago: National Opinion Research Center, producer, 1993. Storrs, CT: The Roper Center for Public Opinion Research, University of Connecticut, distributor.

Deber, Raisa B. 1982. The fault, dear Brutus: Women as Congressional candidates in Pennsylvania. *Journal of Politics* 44: 463-79.

De Boer, Connie. 1977. The polls: Women at work. *Public Opinion Quarterly* 41: 268-77.

Diamond, Irene. 1977. *Sex roles in the state House.* New Haven: Yale University Press.

Dodson, Debra, ed. 1991. *Gender and policymaking.* Eagleton Institute of Politics, Rutgers, NJ: Center for the American Woman and Politics.

Dodson, Debra, and Susan J. Carroll. 1991. *Reshaping the agenda: Women in state legislatures.* Eagleton Institute of Politics, Rutgers, NJ: Center for the American Woman and Politics.

Edelman, Murray. 1964. *The symbolic uses of politics.* Urbana: University of Illinois Press.

Ekstrand, Laurie E., and William A. Eckert. The impact of candidate's sex on voter choice. *Western Political Quarterly* 1981: 78-87.

Ely, John Hart. 1980. *Democracy and distrust.* Cambridge: Harvard University Press.

Fenno, Richard F., Jr. 1978. *Home style: House members in their districts.* Boston: Little, Brown.

Ferree, Myra Marx. 1974. A woman for president? Changing responses: 1958-1972. *Public Opinion Quarterly* 38: 390-99.

Fiorina, Morris P. 1981. *Retrospective voting in American national elections.* New Haven, CT: Yale University Press.

———. 1989. *Congress: Keystone of the Washington establishment,* 2nd ed. New Haven, CT: Yale University Press.

Fiss, Owen M. 1976. Groups and the Equal Protection Clause. *Philosophy and Public Affairs* 5: 107-56.

Fowler, Linda L., and Robert McClure. 1989. *Political ambition.* New Haven, CT: Yale University Press.

Fox, Richard, and Eric R.A.N. Smith. 1996. The role of gender stereotyping in voter decision-making. Paper presented at the annual meeting of the Western Political Science Association, San Francisco, March 13-16.

Gertzog, Irwin N. 1980. The matrimonial connection: The nomination of Congressmen's widows for the House of Representatives. *Journal of Politics* 42: 820-31.

Gertzog, Irwin N., and Michele Simard. 1991. Women and "hopeless" Congressional candidacies: Nomination frequency, 1916-1978. *American Politics Quarterly* 9: 449-66.

Gilligan, Carol. 1982. *In a different voice: Psychological theory and women's development.* Cambridge: Harvard University Press.

Gilligan, Carol, Janie V. Ward, Jill McLean Taylor, and Betty Bardige, eds. 1988. *Mapping the moral domain: A contribution of women's thinking to psychological theory and education.* Cambridge: Harvard University Press.

Gilligan, Carol, Nona P. Lyons, and Trudy J. Hanmer, eds. 1990. *Making connections: The relational worlds of adolescent girls at Emma Willard School.* Cambridge: Harvard University Press.

Githens, Marianne, and Jewel L. Prestage, eds. 1977. *A portrait of marginality.* New York: David McKay.

Gorman, Tom. 1994. Candidates' private lives become issue in 43rd district. *Los Angeles Times* 11 October, A3, A21.

Greenberg, Stanley. 1994. The revolt against politics. Washington, DC: Democratic Leadership Council, 17 November.

Hansen, Susan B. 1994. Lynn Yeakel versus Arlen Specter in Pennsylvania: Why she lost. In *The year of the woman,* edited by Elizabeth Adell Cook, Sue Thomas, and Clyde Wilcox. Boulder, CO: Westview.

Havens, Catharine M., and Lynne M. Healy. 1991. Cabinet-level appointees in Connecticut: Women making a difference. In *Gender and policymaking,* edited by Debra Dodson. Eagleton Institute of Politics, Rutgers, NJ: Center for the American Woman and Politics.

Herrick, Rebekah. 1996. Is there a gender gap in the value of campaign resources? *American Politics Quarterly* 24: 68-80.

Herrnson, Paul S. 1988. *Party campaigning in the 1980s.* Cambridge: Harvard University Press.

Hershey, Marjorie Randon. 1984. *Running for office.* Chatham, NJ: Chatham House.

Hill, David B. 1981. Political culture and female political representation. *Journal of Politics* 43: 159-68.

Holbrook, Thomas M. 1996. *Do campaigns matter?* Thousand Oaks, CA: Sage.

Huddy, Leonie, and Nayda Terkildsen. 1993a. Gender stereotypes and the perception of male and female candidates. *American Journal of Political Science* 37: 119-47.

———, and ———. 1993b. The consequences of gender stereotypes for women candidates at different levels and types of office. *Political Research Quarterly* 46: 503-25.

Jacobson, Gary C. 1992. *The politics of Congressional elections,* 3rd ed. New York: Harper-Collins.

———. 1993. Congress: Unusual year, unusual elections. In *The elections of 1992,* edited by Michael Nelson (pp. 153-82). Washington, DC: CQ Press.

Jamieson, Kathleen Hall. 1995. *Beyond the double bind.* New York: Oxford University Press.

Jelen, Ted. 1994. Carol Moseley-Braun: The insider as insurgent. In *The year of the woman,* edited by Elizabeth Adell Cook, Sue Thomas, and Clyde Wilcox. Boulder, CO: Westview.

Jennings, M. Kent. 1990. Women in party politics. In *Women, politics, and change,* edited by Louise A. Tilly and Patricia Gurin. New York: Russell Sage Foundation.

Jennings, M. Kent, and Richard G. Niemi. 1971. The division of political labor between mothers and fathers. *American Political Science Review* 65: 69-82.

Jennings, M. Kent, and Norman Thomas. 1966. Men and women in party elites: Social roles and political resources. *Midwest Journal of Political Science* 12: 469-92.

Jones, Del. 1995. Companies won't derail diversity. *USA Today* 15 May, B1, B3.

Kahn, K F. 1992. Does being male help: An investigation of gender and media effects in U.S. Senate races. *Journal of Politics* 54: 497-517.

———. 1993. Gender differences in campaign messages: The political advertisements of men and women candidates for U.S. Senate. *Political Research Quarterly* 46: 481-502.

Kahn, K.F., and E. N. Goldenberg. 1991. Women candidates in the news: An examination of gender differences in U.S. Senate campaign coverage. *Public Opinion Quarterly* 55: 180-99.

Kaid, Lynda Lee, Sandra L. Myers, Val Pipps, and Jan Hunter. 1984. Sex role perceptions and televised political advertising: Comparing male and female candidates. *Women and Politics* 4: 41-53.

Kathlene, Lyn. 1989. Uncovering the political impacts of gender: An exploratory study. *Western Political Quarterly* 42: 397-421.

———. 1995. Alternative views of crime: Legislative policy-making in gendered terms. *Journal of Politics* 57: 696-723.

Kayden, Xandra, and Eddie Mahe, Jr. 1985. *The party goes on.* New York: Basic Books.

Kendrigan, Mary Lou. 1984. *Political equality in a Democratic society: Women in the U.S.* Westport, CT: Greenwood.

Kern, Montague. 1989. *30-second politics: Political advertising in the Eighties.* New York: Praeger.

Kincaid, Diane D. 1978. Over his dead body: A positive perspective on widows in the U.S. Congress. *Western Political Quarterly* 31: 96-104.

Kingdon, John W. 1989. *Congressmen's voting decisions.* New York: Harper and Row.

Kirkpatrick, Jeane. 1974. *Political woman.* New York: Basic Books.

Lamson, Peggy. 1968. *Few are chosen.* Boston: Houghton Mifflin.

Lane, Robert E. 1959. *Political life.* New York: Free Press.

Lawrence, Charles R. 1987. The id, the ego, and equal protection: Reckoning with unconscious racism. *Stanford Law Review* 39: 317-55.

Lee, Marcia Manning. 1976. Why few women hold public office: Democracy and sexual roles. *Political Science Quarterly* 91: 297-314.

Leeper, Mark. 1991. The impact of prejudice on female candidates: An experimental look at voter inference. *American Politics Quarterly* 19: 248-61.

Lodge, Milton, Kathleen M. McGraw, and Patrick Stroh. 1989. An impression-driven model of candidate evaluation. *American Political Science Review* 83: 399-419.

Los Angeles Times. 1992. Bush vs. Clinton: The "year of the woman"—and of families. 5 October, B7.

Luttbeg, Norman R., and Michael M. Gant. 1995. *American electoral behavior 1952-1992,* 2nd ed. Itasca, IL: F.E. Peacock.

MacKinnon, Catharine. 1989. *Toward a feminist theory of the state.* Cambridge: Harvard University Press.

———. 1993. *Only words.* Cambridge: Harvard University Press.

Mandel, Ruth B. 1981. *In the running: The new woman candidate.* New York: Ticknor and Fields.

Mandel, Ruth B., Kathy Kleeman, and Lucy Baruch. 1995. No year of the woman, then or now. *Extensions: A Journal of the Carl Albert Congressional Research and Studies Center* Spring: 7-10.

Matthews, Glenna. 1995. Women candidates in the 1990s: Behind the numbers. *Extensions: A Journal of the Carl Albert Congressional Research and Studies Center* Spring: 3-6.

Mayhew, David R. 1974. *Congress: The electoral connection.* New Haven, CT: Yale University Press.

———. 1986. *Placing parties in American politics.* Princeton: Princeton University Press.

McCormick, Katheryne, and Lucy Baruch. 1994. Women show strength as campaign fundraisers. *CAWP News & Notes* 10: 16-8.

McGlen, Nancy E., and Karen O'Connor. 1995. *Women, politics, and American society.* Englewood Cliffs, NJ: Prentice Hall.

Mezey, Susan Gluck. 1978. Does sex make a difference? A case study of women in politics. *Western Political Quarterly* 31: 492-501.

Miller, Warren E., Donald R. Kinder, Steven J. Rosenstone, and the National Election Studies. 1992. *American national election study, 1990: Post-election survey,* 2nd ed. Ann Arbor, MI: Inter-University Consortium for Political and Social Research.

Moncrief, Gary, Joel Thompson, and Robert Schuhmann. 1991. Gender, race and the state legislature: A research note on the double disadvantage hypothesis. *Social Science Journal* 28: 481-87.

Morris, Celia. 1992. *Storming the statehouse: Running for governor with Ann Richards and Dianne Feinstein.* New York: Charles Scribner's Sons.

Mott, Jonathan D. 1995. Getting ahead by holding ground. *Extensions: A Journal of the Carl Albert Congressional Research and Studies Center* Spring: 11-4.

Naff, Katherine C. 1995. Subjective vs. objective discrimination in government: Adding to the picture of barriers to the advancement of women. *Political Research Quarterly* 48: 535-58.

Nelson, Candice J. 1994. Women's PACs in the year of the woman. In *The year of the woman,* edited by Elizabeth Adell Cook, Sue Thomas, and Clyde Wilcox (pp. 181-96). Boulder, CO: Westview.

Nelson, Michael, ed. 1993. *The elections of 1992.* Washington, DC: CQ Press.

Niemi, Richard, and Herbert Weisberg, eds. 1993. *Controversies in voting behavior,* 3rd ed. Washington, DC: CQ Press.

Norris, Pippa. 1994. The impact of the electoral system on election of women to national legislatures. In *Different roles, different voices,* edited by Marianne Githens, Pippa Norris, and Joni Lovenduski. New York: HarperCollins.

O'Brien, Sue. 1995. Voting *la difference. The Denver Post* 15 October, E1.

Okin, Susan Moller. 1989. *Justice, gender and the family.* New York: Basic Books.

Page, Benjamin. 1978. *Choices and echoes in presidential elections.* Chicago: University of Chicago Press.

Parker, Glenn R. 1986. *Homeward bound: Explaining changes in Congressional behavior.* Pittsburgh, PA: University of Pittsburgh Press.

Pateman, Carole. 1989. *The disorder of women: Democracy, feminism and political theory.* Stanford: Stanford University Press.

Perry, Michael J. 1979. Modern equal protection: A conceptualization and appraisal. *Columbia Law Review* 79: 1023-32.

Pomper, Gerald. 1989. *The election of 1988: Reports and interpretations.* Chatham, NJ: Chatham House.

———. 1993. *The election of 1992: Reports and interpretations.* Chatham, NJ: Chatham House.

Poole, Barbara. 1993. Should women identify themselves as feminists when running for political office? Paper presented at the annual meeting of the American Political Science Association, Washington, DC, Sept. 2-5.

Quirk, Paul J., and Jon K. Dalager. 1993. The election: A "new democrat" and a new kind of presidential election. In *The elections of 1992,* edited by Michael Nelson (pp. 57-88). Washington, DC: CQ Press.

Radovich, Joan. 1994. Tax delinquent on Calvert lot. *The Press Telegram,* August 30, B3.

Reingold, Beth. 1992. Concepts of representation among female and male state legislators. *Legislative Studies Quarterly* 17: 509-37.

Renner, Tari. 1993. Lynn Yeakel versus Arlen Specter: The year of the woman in Pennsylvania. Paper presented at annual meeting of the American Political Science Association, Washington, DC, Sept. 2-5.

Richards, Ann W. 1987. Fund-raising for women candidates: All the equality you can afford. *The Journal of State Government* 60: 216-18.

Riesman, David. 1956. Orbits of tolerance, interviews, and elites. *Public Opinion Quarterly* 20: 49-73.

Robinson, Jack. 1994. Two years have brought Calvert crises, lessons. *The Press Telegram* 3 November, B1.

Rosenthal, Cindy Simon. 1995. The role of gender in descriptive representation. *Political Research Quarterly* 48: 599-612.

Rule, Wilma. 1981. Why women don't run: The critical contextual factors in women's legislative recruitment. *Western Political Quarterly* 34: 60-77.

———. 1990. Why more women are state legislators: A research note. *Western Political Quarterly* 43: 437-48.

Sabato, Larry. 1988. *The party's just begun: Shaping political parties for America's future.* Glenview, IL: Scott, Foresman.

Saint-Germain, Michelle A. 1989. Does their difference make a difference? The impact of women on public policy in the Arizona legislature. *Social Science Quarterly* 70: 956-68.

Sapiro, Virginia. 1981. Research frontier essay: When are interests interesting? The problem of political representation of women. *American Political Science Review* 75: 701-16.

———. 1981-82. If Senator Baker were a woman: An experimental study of candidate images. *Political Psychology* 3: 61-83.

———. 1982. Private costs of public commitments or public costs of private commitments? Family roles versus political ambition. *American Journal of Political Science* 26: 265-79.

Schreiber, E. M. 1978. Education and change of American opinions on a woman for president. *Public Opinion Quarterly* 42: 171-82.

Schumaker, Paul, and Nancy Elizabeth Burns. 1988. Gender cleavages and the resolution of local policy issues. *American Journal of Political Science* 32: 1070-95.

Shapiro, Robert Y., and Harpreet Mahajan. 1986. Gender differences in policy preferences: A summary of trends from the 1960s to the 1980s. *Public Opinion Quarterly* 50: 42-61.

Sherry, Suzanna. 1986. Civic virtue and the feminine voice in Constitutional adjudication. *Virginia Law Review* 72: 580-91.

Siltanen, Janet, and Michelle Stanworth, eds. 1984. *Women and the public sphere.* London: Hutchinson.

Simon, Rita J., and Jean M. Landis. 1989. Women's and men's attitudes about a woman's place and role. *Public Opinion Quarterly* 53: 265-76.

Staton/Hughes Research Group. 1992. To be continued: A study of Democratic women's races for the House of Representatives in 1992. Prepared for EMILY's List. San Francisco: Staton/Hughes.

Stokes, Donald E., and Warren E. Miller. 1962. Party government and the saliency of Congress. *Public Opinion Quarterly* 26: 531-46.

Studlar, Donley T., and Susan Welch. 1991. Does district magnitude matter? Women candidates in London local elections. *Western Political Quarterly* 44: 457-66.

Thomas, Sue. 1991. The impact of women on state legislative policies. *Journal of Politics* 53: 958-76.

————. 1994. *How women legislate.* New York: Oxford University Press.

Tolleson Rinehart, Sue. 1991. Do women leaders make a difference? Substance, style and perceptions. In *Gender and policy-making,* edited by Debra Dodson. Eagleton Institute of Politics, Rutgers, NJ: Center for the American Woman and Politics.

————. 1992. *Gender consciousness and politics.* New York: Routledge.

————. 1994. The California Senate races: A case study in the gendered paradoxes of politics. In *The year of the woman,* edited by Elizabeth Adell Cook, Sue Thomas, and Clyde Wilcox (pp. 25-48). Boulder, CO: Westview.

Tolleson Rinehart, Sue, and Jeanie Stanley. 1994. *Claytie and the lady: Ann Richards, gender, and politics in Texas.* Austin: University of Texas Press.

Trent, Judith S., and Robert V. Friedenberg. 1995. *Political campaign communication,* 3rd edition. New York: Praeger.

Uhlaner, Carole Jean, and Kay Lehman Schlozman. 1986. Candidate gender and Congressional campaign receipts. *Journal of Politics* 48: 30-50.

Verba, Sidney, and Norman Nie. 1972. *Participation in America.* New York: Harper and Row.

Voter Research and Surveys. 1991. General election exit polls, 1990, California files, 2d release. [Computer file and codebook]. New York: Voter Research and Surveys; distributor, Ann Arbor, MI: Inter-University Consortium for Political and Social Research.

Voter Research and Surveys. 1993. General election exit polls, 1992, California files, 2d release. [Computer file and codebook]. New York: Voter Research and Surveys; distributor, Ann Arbor, MI: Inter-University Consortium for Political and Social Research.

Voter Research and Surveys. 1995. General election exit polls, 1994, California files, 2d release. [Computer file and codebook]. New York: Voter Research and Surveys; distributor, Ann Arbor, MI: Inter-University Consortium for Political and Social Research.

Welch, Susan. 1978. Recruitment of women to public office: A discriminant analysis. *Western Political Quarterly* 31(1), 373-80.

Welch, Susan, and Timothy Bledsoe. 1988. *Urban reform and its consequences.* Chicago: University of Chicago Press.

Welch, Susan, and Donley T. Studlar. 1990. Multi-member districts and the representation of women: Evidence from Britain and the United States. *Journal of Politics* 52: 391-409.

Wilcox, Clyde. 1994. Why was 1992 the "year of the woman?" Explaining women's gains in 1992. In *The year of the woman,* edited by Elizabeth Adell Cook, Sue Thomas, and Clyde Wilcox (pp. 1-24). Boulder, CO: Westview.

————. 1995. *The latest American revolution?* New York: St. Martin's.

Wilcox, Clyde, Clifford Brown, Jr., and Lynda Powell. 1993. Sex and the political contributor: The gender gap among Presidential contributors. *Political Research Quarterly* 46: 355-76.

Williams, Leonard. 1994. Political advertising in the year of the woman: Did X mark the spot? In *The year of the woman,* edited by Elizabeth Adell Cook, Sue Thomas, and Clyde Wilcox (pp. 197-216). Boulder, CO: Westview.

Witt, Linda, Karen M. Paget, and Glenna Matthews. 1994. *Running as a woman.* New York: Free Press.

Wolbrecht, Christina. 1994. Institutionalization and female representation in the U.S. House of Representatives: A dynamic model. Paper presented at the annual meeting of the American Political Science Association, New York, Sept. 1-4.

Woods, Harriet. 1992. Are women becoming too nasty? *Los Angeles Times,* 14 September, B5.

Index

About the Author

Richard Logan Fox received a B.A. in Government from Claremont McKenna College in 1989. He then received an M.A. and Ph.D. in Political Science from the University of California, Santa Barbara, completing his Ph.D. in 1994. He is currently an assistant professor in the Political Science Department at Union College in Schenectady, New York. He has also taught in the Political Science Department at the University of Wyoming. He is working on a project exploring the role of candidate gender in voter decision making. His primary teaching and research interests lie in electoral politics, congressional politics, and gender politics.